Mastering Julia

Develop your analytical and programming skills further in Julia to solve complex data processing problems

Malcolm Sherrington

[PACKT] open source ✷

PUBLISHING   community experience distilled

BIRMINGHAM - MUMBAI

Mastering Julia

First published: July 2015

Production reference: 1160715

Published by Packt Publishing Ltd.
Livery Place
35 Livery Street
Birmingham B3 2PB, UK.

ISBN 978-1-78355-331-0

www.packtpub.com

Credits

Author
Malcolm Sherrington

Reviewers
Gururaghav Gopal
Zhuo QL
Dan Wlasiuk

Commissioning Editor
Kunal Parikh

Acquisition Editors
Meeta Rajani
Greg Wild

Content Development Editor
Rohit Kumar Singh

Technical Editor
Tanmayee Patil

Copy Editors
Mario Cecere
Tani Kothari
Kausambhi Majumdar

Project Coordinator
Mary Alex

Proofreader
Safis Editing

Indexer
Tejal Soni

Graphics
Abhinash Sahu

Production Coordinator
Manu Joseph

Cover Work
Manu Joseph

About the Author

Malcolm Sherrington has been working in computing for over 35 years. He holds degrees in mathematics, chemistry, and engineering and has given lectures at two different universities in the UK as well as worked in the aerospace and healthcare industries. Currently, he is running his own company in the finance sector, with specific interests in High Performance Computing and applications of GPUs and parallelism.

Always hands-on, Malcolm started programming scientific problems in Fortran and C, progressing through Ada and Common Lisp, and recently became involved with data processing and analytics in Perl, Python, and R.

Malcolm is the organizer of the London Julia User Group. In addition, he is a co-organizer of the UK High Performance Computing and the financial engineers and Quant London meetup groups.

I would like to dedicate this book to the memory of my late wife, Hazel Sherrington, without whose encouragement and support, my involvement in Julia would not have started but who is no longer here to see the culmination of her vision.

Also, I wish to give special thanks to Barbara Doré and James Weymes for their substantive help and material assistance in the preparation of this book.

About the Reviewers

Gururaghav Gopal is presently working as a risk management consultant in a start-up. Previously, he worked at Paterson Securities as an quant developer/trader consultant .He has also worked as a data science consultant and was associated with an e-commerce organization. He has been teaching graduate and post-graduate students of VIT University, Vellore, in the areas of pattern recognition, machine learning, and big data. He has been associated with several research organizations, namely IFMR and NAL, as a research associate. He has also reviewed *Learning Data Mining with R, Packt Publishing* and has been a reviewer for a few journals and conferences.

He did his bachelor's degree in electrical and electronics engineering with a master's degree in computer science and engineering. He later did his course work from IFMR in financial engineering and risk management, and since then, he has been associated with the financial industry. He has won many awards and has a few international publications to his credit.

He is interested in programming, teaching, and doing consulting work. During his free time, he listens to music.

He can be contacted for professional consulting through LinkedIn at `in.linkedin.com/in/gururaghavg`.

Zhuo QL (a.k.a KDr2 online) is a free developer from China who has about 10 years' experience in Linux, C, C++, Java, Python, and Perl development. He loves to participate in and contribute to the open source community (which, of course, includes the Julia community). He maintains a personal website at `http://kdr2.com`; you can find out more about him there.

Dan Wlasiuk is the author of various Julia packages including TimeSeries and Quandl, and he is also the founder of the JuliaQuant GitHub organization of quantitative finance related packages.

www.PacktPub.com

Support files, eBooks, discount offers, and more

For support files and downloads related to your book, please visit www.PacktPub.com.

Did you know that Packt offers eBook versions of every book published, with PDF and ePub files available? You can upgrade to the eBook version at www.PacktPub.com and as a print book customer, you are entitled to a discount on the eBook copy. Get in touch with us at service@packtpub.com for more details.

At www.PacktPub.com, you can also read a collection of free technical articles, sign up for a range of free newsletters and receive exclusive discounts and offers on Packt books and eBooks.

https://www2.packtpub.com/books/subscription/packtlib

Do you need instant solutions to your IT questions? PacktLib is Packt's online digital book library. Here, you can search, access, and read Packt's entire library of books.

Why subscribe?

- Fully searchable across every book published by Packt
- Copy and paste, print, and bookmark content
- On demand and accessible via a web browser

Free access for Packt account holders

If you have an account with Packt at www.PacktPub.com, you can use this to access PacktLib today and view 9 entirely free books. Simply use your login credentials for immediate access.

Table of Contents

Preface   ix

Chapter 1: The Julia Environment   1

Introduction   1
  Philosophy   2
  Role in data science and big data   3
  Comparison with other languages   4
  Features   5
Getting started   6
  Julia sources   7
  Building from source   8
    Installing on CentOS   8
    Mac OS X and Windows   11
  Exploring the source stack   12
  Juno   13
  IJulia   14
A quick look at some Julia   15
  Julia via the console   16
  Installing some packages   20
    A bit of graphics creating more realistic graphics with Winston   22
  My benchmarks   24
Package management   24
  Listing, adding, and removing   24
  Choosing and exploring packages   26
    Statistics and mathematics   27
    Data visualization   27
    Web and networking   28
    Database and specialist packages   29
  How to uninstall Julia   29
  Adding an unregistered package   30

What makes Julia special   **30**
Parallel processing   30
Multiple dispatch   31
Homoiconic macros   31
Interlanguage cooperation   31
Summary   **32**
Chapter 2: Developing in Julia   **33**
Integers, bits, bytes, and bools   **33**
Integers   34
Logical and arithmetic operators   36
Booleans   36
Arrays   **37**
Operations on matrices   39
Elemental operations   40
A simple Markov chain – cat and mouse   41
Char and strings   **42**
Characters   42
Strings   42
Unicode support   44
Regular expressions   44
Byte array literals   45
Version literals   46
An example   46
Real, complex, and rational numbers   **48**
Reals   48
Operators and built-in functions   49
Special values   49
BigFloats   49
Rationals   50
Complex numbers   50
Juliasets   51
Composite types   **54**
More about matrices   **55**
Vectorized and devectorized code   55
Multidimensional arrays   56
Broadcasting   58
Sparse matrices   59
Data arrays and data frames   **60**
Dictionaries, sets, and others   **61**
Dictionaries   61
Sets   63

Other data structures 64
Summary 65
Chapter 3: Types and Dispatch 67
Functions 67
First-class objects 68
Passing arguments 71
Default and optional arguments 72
Variable argument list 74
Named parameters 76
Scope 76
The Queen's problem 79
Julia's type system 81
A look at the rational type 81
A vehicle datatype 84
Typealias and unions 92
Enumerations (revisited) 94
Multiple dispatch 95
Parametric types 97
Conversion and promotion 99
Conversion 99
Promotion 100
A fixed vector module 101
Summary 103
Chapter 4: Interoperability 105
Interfacing with other programming environments 105
Calling C and Fortran 106
Mapping C types 108
Calling a Fortran routine 109
Calling curl to retrieve a web page 110
Python 111
Some others to watch 113
The Julia API 114
Calling API from C 114
Metaprogramming 116
Symbols 117
Macros 118
Testing 121
Error handling 123
The enum macro 124
Tasks 126
Parallel operations 128

Distributed arrays	130
A simple MapReduce	132
Executing commands	**132**
Running commands	134
Working with the filesystem	136
Redirection and pipes	137
Perl one-liners	139
Summary	**141**
Chapter 5: Working with Data	**143**
Basic I/O	**143**
Terminal I/O	143
Disk files	145
Text processing	148
Binary files	150
Structured datasets	**152**
CSV and DLM files	153
HDF5	157
XML files	160
DataFrames and RDatasets	**163**
The DataFrames package	163
DataFrames	164
RDatasets	167
Subsetting, sorting, and joining data	168
Statistics	**172**
Simple statistics	173
Samples and estimations	175
Pandas	175
Selected topics	**177**
Time series	177
Distributions	180
Kernel density	181
Hypothesis testing	183
GLM	185
Summary	**188**
Chapter 6: Scientific Programming	**189**
Linear algebra	**190**
Simultaneous equations	190
Decompositions	192
Eigenvalues and eigenvectors	193

Special matrices   196
    A symmetric eigenproblem   196
Signal processing   **197**
    Frequency analysis   197
    Filtering and smoothing   198
    Digital signal filters   200
    Image processing   202
Differential equations   **203**
    The solution of ordinary differential equations   204
    Non-linear ordinary differential equations   206
    Partial differential equations   209
Optimization problems   **211**
    JuMP   212
    Optim   214
    NLopt   217
        Using with the MathProgBase interface   220
Stochastic problems   **220**
    Stochastic simulations   221
        SimJulia   221
        Bank teller example   222
    Bayesian methods and Markov processes   225
        Monte Carlo Markov Chains   226
        MCMC frameworks   226
Summary   **230**
Chapter 7: Graphics   **231**
Basic graphics in Julia   **232**
    Text plotting   232
    Cairo   234
    Winston   236
Data visualization   **240**
    Gadfly   240
    Compose   244
Graphic engines   **247**
    PyPlot   247
    Gaston   250
    PGF plots   253
Using the Web   **255**
    Bokeh   255
    Plotly   256

Raster graphics   **259**
  Cairo (revisited)   260
  Winston (revisited)   261
  Images and ImageView   262
Summary   **265**

Chapter 8: Databases   **267**
A basic view of databases   **267**
  The red pill or the blue pill?   268
  Interfacing to databases   269
  Other considerations   270
Relational databases   **271**
  Building and loading   272
  Native interfaces   275
  ODBC   278
  Other interfacing techniques   283
  DBI   283
    SQLite   283
    MySQL   283
    PostgreSQL   285
  PyCall   286
  JDBC   288
NoSQL datastores   **290**
  Key-value systems   291
  Document datastores   294
RESTful interfacing   **296**
  JSON   297
  Web-based databases   299
  Graphic systems   302
Summary   **304**

Chapter 9: Networking   **305**
Sockets and servers   **305**
  Well-known ports   305
  UDP and TCP sockets in Julia   306
  A "Looking-Glass World" echo server   307
  Named pipes   311
Working with the Web   **311**
  A TCP web service   312
  The JuliaWeb group   313
  The "quotes" server   316
  WebSockets   318

Messaging — **321**
  E-mail — 321
  Twitter — 323
  SMS and esendex — 325
Cloud services — **327**
  Introducing Amazon Web Services — 328
  The AWS.jl package — 329
  The Google Cloud — 333
Summary — **337**

Chapter 10: Working with Julia — **339**
Under the hood — **339**
  Femtolisp — 340
  The Julia API — 341
  Code generation — 343
Performance tips — **346**
  Best practice — 346
  Profiling — 348
  Lint — 350
  Debugging — 352
Developing a package — **355**
  Anatomy — 355
  Taxonomy — 358
  Using Git — 360
  Publishing — 361
Community groups — **362**
  Classifications — 363
  JuliaAstro — 364
    Cosmology models — 364
    The Flexible Image Transport System — 366
  JuliaGPU — 370
What's missing? — **374**
Summary — **375**

Index — **377**

Preface

Julia is a relatively young programming language. The initial design work on the Julia project began at MIT in August 2009, and by February 2012, it became open source. It is largely the work of three developers Stefan Karpinski, Jeff Bezanson, and Viral Shah. These three, together with Alan Edelman, still remain actively committed to Julia and MIT currently hosts a variety of courses in Julia, many of which are available over the Internet.

Initially, Julia was envisaged by the designers as a scientific language sufficiently rapid to make the necessity of modeling in an interactive language and subsequently having to redevelop in a compiled language, such as C or Fortran. At that time the major scientific languages were propriety ones such as MATLAB and Mathematica, and were relatively slow. There were clones of these languages in the open source domain, such as GNU Octave and Scilab, but these were even slower. When it launched, the community saw Julia as a replacement for MATLAB, but this is not exactly case. Although the syntax of Julia is similar to MATLAB, so much so that anyone competent in MATLAB can easily learn Julia, it was not designed as a clone. It is a more feature-rich language with many significant differences that will be discussed in depth later.

The period since 2009 has seen the rise of two new computing disciplines: big data/cloud computing, and data science. Big data processing on Hadoop is conventionally seen as the realm of Java programming, since Hadoop runs on the Java virtual machine. It is, of course, possible to process big data by using programming languages other than those that are Java-based and utilize the streaming-jar paradigm and Julia can be used in a way similar to C++, C#, and Python.

The emergence of data science heralded the use of programming languages that were simple for analysts with some programming skills but who were not principally programmers. The two languages that stepped up to fill the breach have been R and Python. Both of these are relatively old with their origins back in the 1990s. However, the popularity of these two has seen a rapid growth, ironically from around the time when Julia was introduced to the world. Even so, with such estimated and staid opposition, Julia has excited the scientific programming community and continues to make inroads in this space.

The aim of this book is to cover all aspects of Julia that make it appealing to the data scientist. The language is evolving quickly. Binary distributions are available for Linux, Mac OS X, and Linux, but these will lag behind the current sources. So, to do some serious work with Julia, it is important to understand how to obtain and build a running system from source. In addition, there are interactive development environments available for Julia and the book will discuss both the Jupyter and Juno IDEs.

What this book covers

Chapter 1, The Julia Environment, deals with the steps needed to get a working distribution of Julia up and running. It is important to be able to acquire the latest sources and build the system from scratch, as well as find and install appropriate packages and also to remove them when necessary.

Chapter 2, Developing in Julia, is a quick overview of some of Julia's basic syntax. Julia is a new language, but it is not unfamiliar to readers with a background in MATLAB, R, or Python, so the aim of the chapter is to briefly bring readers up to speed, using examples, with Julia and to point them to online sources. Also, it is important to be aware of the differences between working via the console in contrast to the JuliaStudio IDE.

Chapter3, Types and Dispatch, looks at the Julia type system and shows how this exposes powerful techniques to the developer by means of its de facto functional dispatch system.

Chapter4, Interoperability, covers the methods by which Julia can interact with the operating system and other programming languages. These methods are largely native to Julia and the chapter concludes with an introduction to parallelism that is discussed further in *Chapter 9, Networking*.

Chapter 5, Working with Data, begins the journey the data scientist would take from data source to analytics results. Most projects begin with data, which has to be read, cleaned up, and sampled. The chapter starts here and goes on to describe simple statistics and analytics.

Chapter 6, Scientific Programming, is seen as a principle reason to program in Julia. Its strength is the speed of execution combined with the ease of developing in a scripting language that makes it particularly useful in tackling compute-bound processes. The chapter looks at various techniques used in approaching mathematical and scientific problems.

Chapter 7, Graphics, in Julia is often compared unfavorably to other alternate languages such as MATLAB and R. While earlier versions of the language had limited graphics options, this is certainly not the case now and this chapter describes a wide variety of sophisticated approaches both to display to screen and save to disk files.

Chapter 8, Databases, deals with interaction with databases in Julia. Data to be analyzed may be stored in a database or it may be necessary to save the results in a database after analysis. Various approaches are considered for SQL and NoSQL datastores. These are not built in to the language, rather rely totally on contributed packages, and so may be enhanced in the near future.

Chapter 9, Networking, covers aspects of working with distributed data sources. Big data and cloud systems are becoming more prevalent in data science and the chapter covers network programming at the socket level and interfacing via the Web. Also, it includes a discussion on running Julia on Amazon Web Services and the Google compute server.

Chapter 10, Working with Julia, aims to provide information and encouragement to go on and contribute as a Julia developer. This may be as a sole author contributing to an existing package or as a member of the Julia groups.

What you need for this book

Developing in Julia can be done under any of the familiar computing operating systems: Linux, OS X, and Windows. To explore the language in depth, the reader may wish to acquire the latest versions and to build from source under Linux. However, to work with the language using a binary distribution on any of the three platforms, the installation is very straightforward and convenient. In addition, Julia now comes pre-packaged with the Juno IDE, which just requires expansion from a compressed (zipped) archive.

Some of the examples in the later chapters on database support, networking, and cloud services will require additional installation and resources, and how to acquire these is discussed at the relevant point.

Who this book is for

This is not an introduction to programming, so it is assumed that the reader is familiar with the concepts of at least one programming language. For those familiar with scripting languages such as Python, R, and MATLAB, the task is not a difficult one, as well as for people using similar-style languages such as C, Java, and C#.

However, for the data scientist, possibly with a background in analytics methods using spreadsheets, such as Excel, or statistical packages, such as SPSS and Stata, most parts of the text should prove rewarding.

Conventions

In this book, you will find a number of text styles that distinguish between different kinds of information. Here are some examples of these styles and an explanation of their meaning.

Code words in text, database table names, folder names, filenames, file extensions, pathnames, dummy URLs, user input, and Twitter handles are shown as follows: "The `test` folder has some code that illustrates how to write test scripts and use the `Base.Test` system."

A block of code is set as follows:

```
function isAdmin2(_mc::Dict{ASCIIString,UserCreds}, _
name::ASCIIString)
    check_admin::Bool = false;
    try
        check_admin = _mc[_name].admin
    catch
        check_admin = false
    finally
        return check_admin
    end
end
```

Any command-line input or output is written as follows:

```
julia> include("asian.jl")
julia> run_asian()
```

New terms and **important words** are shown in bold. Words that you see on the screen, for example, in menus or dialog boxes, appear in the text like this: "However, there are others that may occur, such as in case of redirection and error, one being the infamous **404, Page not found**."

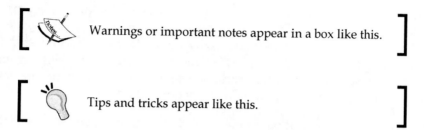

> Warnings or important notes appear in a box like this.

> Tips and tricks appear like this.

Reader feedback

Feedback from our readers is always welcome. Let us know what you think about this book — what you liked or disliked. Reader feedback is important for us as it helps us develop titles that you will really get the most out of.

To send us general feedback, simply e-mail feedback@packtpub.com, and mention the book's title in the subject of your message.

If there is a topic that you have expertise in and you are interested in either writing or contributing to a book, see our author guide at www.packtpub.com/authors.

Customer support

Now that you are the proud owner of a Packt book, we have a number of things to help you to get the most from your purchase.

Downloading the example code

You can download the example code files from your account at http://www.packtpub.com for all the Packt Publishing books you have purchased. If you purchased this book elsewhere, you can visit http://www.packtpub.com/support and register to have the files e-mailed directly to you.

Errata

Although we have taken every care to ensure the accuracy of our content, mistakes do happen. If you find a mistake in one of our books—maybe a mistake in the text or the code—we would be grateful if you could report this to us. By doing so, you can save other readers from frustration and help us improve subsequent versions of this book. If you find any errata, please report them by visiting `http://www.packtpub.com/submit-errata`, selecting your book, clicking on the **Errata Submission Form** link, and entering the details of your errata. Once your errata are verified, your submission will be accepted and the errata will be uploaded to our website or added to any list of existing errata under the Errata section of that title.

To view the previously submitted errata, go to `https://www.packtpub.com/books/content/support` and enter the name of the book in the search field. The required information will appear under the **Errata** section.

Piracy

Piracy of copyrighted material on the Internet is an ongoing problem across all media. At Packt, we take the protection of our copyright and licenses very seriously. If you come across any illegal copies of our works in any form on the Internet, please provide us with the location address or website name immediately so that we can pursue a remedy.

Please contact us at `copyright@packtpub.com` with a link to the suspected pirated material.

We appreciate your help in protecting our authors and our ability to bring you valuable content.

Questions

If you have a problem with any aspect of this book, you can contact us at `questions@packtpub.com`, and we will do our best to address the problem.

1
The Julia Environment

In this chapter, we explore all you need to get started on Julia, to build it from source or to get prebuilt binaries. Julia can also be downloaded bundled with the Juno IDE. It can be run using IPython, and this is available on the Internet via the `https://juliabox.org/` website. Julia is a high-level, high-performance dynamic programming language for technical computing. It runs on Linux, OS X, and Windows. We will look at building it from source on CentOS Linux, as well as downloading as a prebuilt binary distribution. We will normally be using v0.3.x, which is the stable version at the time of writing but the current development version is v0.4.x and nightly builds can be downloaded from the Julia website.

Introduction

Julia was first released to the world in February 2012 after a couple of years of development at the Massachusetts Institute of Technology (MIT).

All the principal developers—Jeff Bezanson, Stefan Karpinski, Viral Shah, and Alan Edelman—still maintain active roles in the language and are responsible for the core, but also have authored and contributed to many of the packages.

The language is open source, so all is available to view. There is a small amount of C/C++ code plus some Lisp and Scheme, but much of core is (very well) written in Julia itself and may be perused at your leisure. If you wish to write exemplary Julia code, this is a good place to go in order to seek inspiration. Towards the end of this chapter, we will have a quick run-down of the Julia source tree as part of exploring the Julia environment.

Julia is often compared with programming languages such as Python, R, and MATLAB. It is important to realize that Python and R have been around since the mid-1990s and MATLAB since 1984. Since MATLAB is proprietary (® MathWorks), there are a few clones, particularly GNU Octave, which again dates from the same era as Python and R. Just how far the language has come is a tribute to the original developers and the many enthusiastic ones who have followed on. Julia uses GitHub as both for a repository for its source and for the registered packages. While it is useful to have Git installed on your computer, normal interaction is largely hidden from the user since Julia incorporates a working version of Git, wrapped up in a package manager (Pkg), which can be called from the console While Julia has no simple built-in graphics, there are several different graphics packages and I will be devoting a chapter later particularly to these.

Philosophy

Julia was designed with scientific computing in mind. The developers all tell us that they came with a wide array of programming skills—Lisp, Python, Ruby, R, and MATLAB. Some like myself even claim to originate as Perl hackers. However, all need a *fast* compiled language in their armory such as C or Fortran as the current languages listed previously are pitifully slow.

So, to quote the development team:

> *"We want a language that's open source, with a liberal license. We want the speed of C with the dynamism of Ruby. We want a language that's homoiconic, with true macros like Lisp, but with obvious, familiar mathematical notation like Matlab. We want something as usable for general programming as Python, as easy for statistics as R, as natural for string processing as Perl, as powerful for linear algebra as Matlab, as good at gluing programs together as the shell. Something that is dirt simple to learn, yet keeps the most serious hackers happy. We want it interactive and we want it compiled.*
>
> *(Did we mention it should be as fast as C?)"*
>
> `http://julialang.org/blog/2012/02/why-we-created-julia`

With the introduction of the **Low-Level Virtual Machine (LLVM)** compilation, it has become possible to achieve this goal and to design a language from the outset, which makes the two-language approach largely redundant.

Julia was designed as a language similar to other scripting languages and so should be easy to learn for anyone familiar to Python, R, and MATLAB. It is syntactically closest to MATLAB, but it is important to note that it is not a drop-in clone. There are many important differences, which we will look at later.

It is important not to be too overwhelmed by considering Julia as a challenger to Python and R. In fact, we will illustrate instances where the languages are used to complement each other. Certainly, Julia was not conceived as such, and there are certain things that Julia does which makes it ideal for use in the scientific community.

Role in data science and big data

Julia was initially designed with scientific computing in mind. Although the term "data science" was coined as early as the 1970s, it was only given prominence in 2001, in an article by William S. Cleveland, *Data Science: An Action Plan for Expanding the Technical Areas of the Field of Statistics*. Almost in parallel with the development of Julia has been the growth in data science and the demand for data science practitioners.

What is data science?

The following might be one definition:

Data science is the study of the generalizable extraction of knowledge from data. It incorporates varying elements and builds on techniques and theories from many fields, including signal processing, mathematics, probability models, machine learning, statistical learning, computer programming, data engineering, pattern recognition, learning, visualization, uncertainty modeling, data warehousing, and high-performance computing with the goal of extracting meaning from data and creating data products.

If this sounds familiar, then it should be. These were the precise goals laid out at the onset of the design of Julia. To fill the void, most data scientists have turned to Python and to a lesser extent, to R. One principal cause in the growth of the popularity of Python and R can be traced directly to the interest in data science.

So, what we set out to achieve in this book is to show you as a budding data scientist, why you should consider using Julia, and if convinced, then how to do it.

Along with data science, the other "new kids on the block" are big data and the cloud. Big data was originally the realm of Java largely because of the uptake of the Hadoop/HDFS framework, which, being written in Java, made it convenient to program MapReduce algorithms in it or any language, which runs on the JVM. This leads to an obscene amount of bloated boilerplate coding.

However, here, with the introduction of YARN and Hadoop stream processing, the paradigm of processing big data is opened up to a wider variety of approaches. Python is beginning to be considered an alternative to Java, but upon inspection, Julia makes an excellent candidate in this category too.

Comparison with other languages

Julia has the reputation for speed. The home page of the main Julia website, as of July 2014, includes references to benchmarks. The following table shows benchmark times relative to C (smaller is better, C performance = 1.0):

	Fortran	Julia	Python	R	MATLAB	Octave	Mathe matica	Java Script	Go
fib	0.26	0.91	30.37	411.31	1992.0	3211.81	64.46	2.18	1.0
mandel	0.86	0.85	14.19	106.97	64.58	316.95	6.07	3.49	2.36
pi_sum	0.80	1.00	16.33	15.42	1.29	237.41	1.32	0.84	1.41
rand_mat_stat	0.64	1.66	13.52	10.84	6.61	14.98	4.52	3.28	8.12
rand_mat_mul	0.96	1.01	3.41	3.98	1.10	3.41	1.16	14.60	8.51

Benchmarks can be notoriously misleading; indeed, to paraphrase the common saying: *there are lies, damned lies, and benchmarks.*

The Julia site does its best to lay down the parameters for these tests by providing details of the workstation used — processor type, CPU clock speed, amount of RAM, and so on — and the operating system deployed. For each test, the version of the software is provided plus any external packages or libraries; for example, for the rand_mat test, Python uses NumPy, and C, Fortran, and Julia use OpenBLAS.

Julia provides a website for checking its performance: http://speed.julialang.org.

The source code for all the tests is available on GitHub. This is not just the Julia code but also that used in C, MATLAB, Python, and so on. Indeed, extra language examples are being added, and you will find benchmarks to try in Scala and Lua too:

https://Github.com/JuliaLang/julia/tree/master/test/perf/micro.

This table is useful in another respect too, as it lists all the major comparative languages of Julia. No real surprises here, except perhaps the range of execution times.

- **Python**: This has become the de facto data science language, and the range of modules available is overwhelming. Both version 2 and version 3 are in common usage; the latter is NOT a superset of the former and is around 10% slower. In general, Julia is an order of magnitude faster than Python, so often when the established Python code is compiled or rewritten in C.

- **R**: Started life as an open source version of the commercial S+ statistics package (® TIBCO Software Inc.), but has largely superseded it for use in statistics projects and has a large set of contributed packages. It is single-threaded, which accounts for the disappointing execution times and parallelization is not straightforward. R has very good graphics and data visualization packages.

- **MATLAB/Octave**: MATLAB is a commercial product (® MathWorks) for matrix operations, hence, the reasonable times for the last two benchmarks, but others are very long. GNU Octave is a free MATLAB clone. It has been designed for compatibility rather than efficiency, which accounts for the execution times being even longer.

- **Mathematica**: Another commercial product (® Wolfram Research) for general-purpose mathematical problems. There is no obvious clone although the Sage framework is open source and uses Python as its computation engine, so its timings are similar to Python.

- **JavaScript and Go**: These are linked together since they both use the Google V8 engine. V8 compiles to native machine code before executing it; hence, the excellent performance timings but both languages are more targeted at web-based applications.

So, Julia would seem to be an ideal language for tackling data science problems. It's important to recognize that many of the built-in functions in R and Python are not implemented natively but are written in C. Julia performs roughly as well as C, so Julia won't do any better than R or Python if most of the work you do in R or Python calls built-in functions without performing any explicit iteration or recursion.

However, when you start doing custom work, Julia will come into its own. It is the perfect language for advanced users of R or Python, who are trying to build advanced tools inside of these languages. The alternative to Julia is typically resorting to C; R offers this through **Rcpp**, and Python offers it through **Cython**.

There is a possibility of more cooperation between Julia with R and/or Python than competition, although this is not the common view.

Features

The Julia programming language is free and open source (MIT licensed), and the source is available on GitHub.

To the veteran programmer, it has looks and feels similar to MATLAB. Blocks created by the `for`, `while`, and `if` statements are all terminated by `end` rather than by `endfor`, `endwhile`, and `endif` or by using the familiar { } style syntax. However, it is not a MATLAB clone, and sources written for MATLAB will not run on Julia.

The following are some of Julia's features:

- Designed for parallelism and distributed computation (multicore and cluster)
- C functions called directly (no wrappers or special APIs needed)
- Powerful shell-like capabilities for managing other processes
- Lisp-like macros and other meta-programming facilities
- User-defined types are as fast and compact as built-ins
- LLVM-based, **just-in-time (JIT)** compiler that allows Julia to approach and often match the performance of C/C++
- An extensive mathematical function library (written in Julia)
- Integrated mature, best-of-breed C and Fortran libraries for linear algebra, random number generation, **Fast Fourier Transform (FFT)**, and string processing

Julia's core is implemented in C and C++, and its parser in Scheme; the LLVM compiler framework is used for the JIT generation of machine code.

The standard library is written in Julia itself by using Node.js's `libuv` library for efficient, cross-platform I/O.

Julia has a rich language of types for constructing and describing objects that can also optionally be used to make type declarations. It has the ability to define function behavior across many combinations of argument types via a multiple dispatch, which is the key cornerstone of language design.

Julia can utilize code in other programming languages by directly calling routines written in C or Fortran and stored in shared libraries or DLLs. This is a feature of the language syntax and will be discussed in detail later.

In addition, it is possible to interact with Python via **PyCall** and this is used in the implementation of the **IJulia** programming environment.

Getting started

Starting to program in Julia is very easy. The first place to look at is the main Julia language website: `http://julialang.org`. This is not blotted with graphics, just the Julia logo, some useful major links to other parts of the site, and a quick sampler on the home page.

The Julia documentation is comprehensive of the docs link: `http://docs.julialang.org`. There are further links to the Julia manual, the standard library, and the package system, all of which we will be discussing later. Moreover, the documentation can be downloaded as a PDF file, a zipped file of HTML pages, or an ePub file.

Julia sources

At present, we will be looking at the download link. This provides links to 32-bit and 64-bit distros for Windows, Mac OS X, CentOS, and Ubuntu; both the stable release and the nightly development snapshot. So, a majority of the users getting started require nothing more than a download and a standard installation procedure.

For Windows, this is by running the downloaded `.exe` file, which will extract Julia into a folder. Inside this folder is a batch file `julia.bat`, which can be used to start the Julia console.

For Mac OS X, the users need to click on the downloaded `.dmg` file to run the disk image and drag the *app* icon into the `Applications` folder. On Mac OS X, you will be prompted to continue as the source has been downloaded from the Internet and so is not considered secure.

Similarly, uninstallation is a simple process. In Windows, delete the `julia` folder, and in Mac OS X, delete `Julia.app`. To do a "clean" uninstall, it is also necessary to tidy up a few hidden files/folders, and we will consider this after talking about the package system.

For Ubuntu (Linux), it's a little bit more involved as you need to add a reference to **Personal Package Archive (PPA)** to your system. You will have to have the root privilege for this to execute the following commands:

```
sudo apt-get add-repository ppa:staticfloat/juliareleases
sudo add-apt-repository ppa:staticfloat/julia-deps
sudo apt-get update
sudo apt-get install julia
```

Downloading the example code

You can download the example code files from your account at `http://www.packtpub.com` for all the Packt Publishing books that you have purchased. If you purchased this book elsewhere, you can visit `http://www.packtpub.com/support` and register to have the files e-mailed directly to you.

The releases are provided by Elliot Saba, and there is a separate PPA for the nightly snapshots: `ppa:staticfloat/julianightlies`.

It is only necessary to add PPA once, so for updates, all you need to do is execute the following command:

```
sudo apt-get update
```

Building from source

Ubuntu is part of the Debian family of Linux distributions, others being Debian itself, **Linux Mint Debian Edition (LMDE)**, and Knoppix. All can install DEB packages and use the previous `apt-get` command.

The other major Linux family is based on the Red Hat distribution: Red Hat Enterprise, CentOS, Fedora, Scientific Linux, and so on. These use a different package management mechanism based on RPM files. There are also distros based on SUSE, Mandriva, and Slackware.

For a comprehensive list, look at the Wikipedia page: `http://en.wikipedia.org/wiki/List_of_Linux_distributions`.

The link is again available from the `julialang.org` downloads page. Julia uses GitHub as a repository for its source distribution as well as for various Julia packages. We will look at installing on CentOS, which is the community edition of Red Hat and is widely used.

Installing on CentOS

CentOS can be downloaded as an ISO image from `http://www.centos.org` and written to a DVD. It can be installed as a replacement for an existing Windows system or to run alongside Windows as a dual-booted configuration.

CentOS does not come with the `git` command as a standard; upon installation, the first task will be to install it. For this and other installation processes, we use the `yum` command (**Yellowdog Updater and Modified (YUM)**).

You will need the `root`/`superuser` privileges, so typically, you would type `su -`:

```
su -
(type root password)
yum update
yum install git
```

Yum will fetch the Git sources for a Red Hat repository, list what needs to be installed, and prompt you to press Y/N to continue.

Once you have installed Git, we will need to grab the Julia sources from GitHub by using the following command:

```
git clone git://Github.com/JuliaLang/julia.git
```

(It is also possible to use `https://` instead of `git://`, if behind a firewall).

```
git clone git://Github.com/JuliaLang/julia.git
Cloning into 'julia'...
remote: Counting objects: 97173, done.
remote: Compressing objects: 100% (24020/2
```

This will produce a subfolder at the current location called `julia` with all the sources and documentation.

To build, Julia requires development tools that are not normally present in a standard CentOS distribution, particularly GCC, g++, and gfortran.

These can be installed as follows:

```
sudo yum install gcc
sudo yum install gcc-c++
sudo yum install gcc-gfortran
```

Or, more conveniently, via a group install bundle:

```
sudo yum groupinstall 'Development tools'
```

Other tools (which are usually present) such as GNU Make, Perl, and patch are needed, but `groupinstall` should take care of these too if not present. We did find that an installation on Fedora 19 failed because the M4 processor was not found, but again, `yum install m4` was all that was required and the process could be resumed from where it failed.

So, to proceed with the build, we change into the cloned `julia` folder and issue the `make` command. Note that for seasoned Linux open source builders, there is no need for a configuration step. All the prerequisites are assumed to be in place (or else the make fails), and the executable is created in the `julia` folder, so there is no `make install` step.

The build process can take considerable time and produces a number of warnings on individual source files but when it has finished, it produces a file called `julia` in the build folder. This is a symbolic link to the actual executable in the `usr/bin` folder.

So, typically, if all the tools are in place, the process may look like this:

```
[malcolm@localhost] cd ~
[malcolm@localhost] mkdir Build
[malcolm@localhost] cd Build
 [malcolm@localhost Build] git clone git://github.com/JuliaLang/julia.git
[malcolm@localhost julia] cd julia
[malcolm@localhost julia] make


After the build:
[malcolm@localhost julia] ls -l julia
lrwxrwxrwx 1 malcolm malcolm 39 Jun 10 09:11 julia -> /home/malcolm/
Build/julia/usr/bin/julia
```

If you have (or create) a `bin` folder just under the `home` folder, it is worth recreating the link there as it will be automatically appended to the path.

```
[malcolm@localhost] cd ~/bin
[malcolm@localhost bin] ln -s /home/malcolm/Build/julia/usr/bin/julia
julia
```

To test out the installation (assuming `julia` is on your path), use the following command:

```
[malcolm@localhost] julia -q
```

The `-q` switch on the `julia` command represses the print of the Julia banner.

```
julia> println("I've just installed Julia")
I've just installed Julia
```

The `julia>` prompt indicates the normal command mode. It is worth noting that there are a couple of other modes, which can be used at the console help (?) and shell (;).

For example:

```
julia>?print
?print
Base.print(x)
    Write (to the default output stream) a canonical (un-decorated)
    text representation of a value if there is one, otherwise call
    "show". The representation used by "print" includes minimal
    formatting and tries to avoid Julia-specific details.

 julia> ;ls
```

```
;ls
asian-ascplot.jl  asian-winplot.jl  asian.jl  asian.m  asian.o  asian.r
run-asian.jl  time-asian.jl
```

We will be looking at an example of Julia code in the next section, but if you want to be a little more adventurous, try typing in the following at the `julia>` prompt:

```
sumsq(x,y) = x^2 + y^2;
N=1000000; x = 0;
for i = 1:N
  if sumsq(rand(), rand()) < 1.0
    x += 1;
  end
end
@printf "Estimate of PI for %d trials is %8.5f\n" N 4.0*(x / N);
```

1. This is a simple estimate of PI by generating pairs of random numbers distributed uniformly over a unit square [`0.0:1.0, 0.0:1.0`]. If the sum of the squares of the pairs of numbers is less than `1.0`, then the point defined by the two numbers lies within the unit circle. The ratio of the sum of all such points to the total number of pairs will be in the region of one quarter PI.

2. The line `sumsq(x,y) = x^2 + y^2` is an example of an inline function definition. Of course, multiline definitions are possible and more common but the use of one-liners is very convenient. It is possible to define anonymous functions too, as we will see later.

3. Although Julia is strictly typed, a variables type is inferred from the assignment unless explicitly defined.

4. Constructs such as `for` loops and `if` statements are terminated with `end`, and there are no curly brackets {} or matching `endfor` or `endif`. Printing to the standard output can be done using the `println` call, which is a function and needs the brackets. `@printf` is an example of a macro that mimics the C-like `printf` function allowing us to format outputted values.

Mac OS X and Windows

It is possible to download the stable build and the nightly release on Mac OS X, Windows, and Ubuntu. So, building Julia from source is less important than under distributions that do not provide a distro. However, since Julia is open source, it is possible to get detailed instructions from the Julia language website `https://Github.com/JuliaLang/julia/blob/master/README.md`.

On Mac OS X, you need to use a 64-bit gfortran compiler to build Julia. This can be downloaded from HPC - Mac OS X on SourceForge http://hpc.sourceforge.net. In order to work correctly, HPC gfortran requires HPC GCC to be installed as well. From OS X 10.7, Clang is now used by default to build Julia, and Xcode version 5 or later should be used. The minimum version of Clang needed to build Julia is v3.1.

Building under Windows is tricky and will not be covered here. It uses the **Minimalist GNU for Windows (MinGW)** distribution, and there are many caveats. If you wish to try it out, there is a comprehensive guide on the Julia site.

Exploring the source stack

Let's look at the top-level folders in the source tree that we get from GitHub:

Folder	Contents
Base	Contains the Julia sources that make up the core
contrib	A miscellaneous set of scripts, configuration files, and so on
deps	Dependencies and patches
doc	The reStructuredText files to build the technical documentation
etc	The juliarc file
examples	A selection of examples of Julia coding
src	The C/C++, Lisp, and Scheme files to build the Julia kernel
test	A comprehensive test suite
ui	The source for the console REPL

To gain some insight into Julia coding, the best folders to look at are base, examples, and test.

1. The base folder contains a great portion of the standard library and the coding style exemplary.
2. The test folder has some code that illustrates how to write test scripts and use the Base.Test system.
3. The examples folder gives Julia's take on some well-known old computing chestnuts such as *Queens Problem, Wordcounts,* and *Game of Life.*

If you have created Julia from source, you will have all the folders available in the Git/build folder; the build process creates a new folder tree in the folder starting with usr and the executable is in the usr/bin folder.

Installing on a Mac under OS X creates Julia in `/Applications/Julia-[version].app`, where `version` is the build number being installed. The executables required are in a subfolder of `Contents/Resources/julia/bin`. To find the Julia sources, look into the `share` folder and go down one level in to the `julia` subfolder.

So, the complete path will be similar to `/Applications/julia-0.2.1.app/Contents/Resources/julia/share/julia`. This has the Julia files but not the C/C++ and Scheme files and so on; for these, you will need to checkout a source tree from GitHub.

For Windows, the situation is similar to that of Mac OS X. The installation file creates a folder called `julia-[build-number]` where `build-number` is typically an alpha string such as `e44b593905`. Immediately under it are the `bin` and `share` folders (among others), and the `share` folder contains a subfolder named `julia` with the Julia scripts in it.

Juno

Juno is an IDE, which is bundled, for stable distributions on the Julia website. There are different versions for most popular operating systems.

It requires unzipping into a subfolder and putting the Juno executable on the run-search path, so it is one of the easiest ways to get started on a variety of platforms. It uses Light Table, so unlike IJulia (explained in the following section), it does not need a helper task (viz. Python) to be present.

The driver is the `Jewel.jl` package, which is a collection of IDE-related code and is responsible for communication with Light Table. The IDE has a built-in workspace and navigator. Opening a folder in the workspace will display all the files via the navigator.

Juno handles things such as the following:

- Extensible autocomplete
- Pulling code blocks out of files at a given cursor position
- Finding relevant documentation or method definitions at the cursor
- Detecting the module to which a file belongs
- Evaluation of code blocks with the correct file, line, and module data

Juno's basic job is to transform expressions into values, which it does on pressing *Ctrl* + *Enter*, (*Cmd* + *Enter* on Mac OS X) inside a block. The code block is evaluated as a whole, rather than line by line, and the final result returned.

By default, the result is "collapsed." It is necessary to click on the bold text to toggle the content of the result. Graphs, from Winston and Gadfly, say, are displayed in line within Juno, not as a separate window.

IJulia

IJulia is a backend interface to the Julia language, which uses the IPython interactive environment. It is now part of Jupyter, a project to port the agnostic parts of IPython for use with other programming languages.

This combination allows you to interact with the Julia language by using IPython's powerful graphical notebook, which combines code, formatted text, math support, and multimedia in a single document.

You need version 1.0 or later of IPython. Note that IPython 1.0 was released in August 2013, so the version of Python required is 2.7 and the version pre-packaged with `operating-system` distribution may be too old to run it. If so, you may have to install IPython manually.

On Mac OS X and Windows systems, the easiest way is to use the Anaconda Python installer. After installing Anaconda, use the `conda` command to install IPython:

```
conda update conda conda update ipython
```

On Ubuntu, we use the `apt-get` command and it's a good idea to install `matplotlib` (for graphics) plus a cocktail of other useful modules.

```
sudo apt-get install python-matplotlib python-scipy python-pandas python-sympy python-nose
```

IPython is available on Fedora (v18+) but not yet on CentOS (v6.5) although this should be resolved with CentOS 7. Installation is via `yum` as follows:

```
sudo yum install python-matplotlib scipy python-pandas sympy python-nose
```

The IPython notebook interface runs in your web browser and provides a rich multimedia environment. Furthermore, it is possible to produce some graphic output via Python's `matplotlib` by using a Julia to Python interface. This requires installation of the IJulia package.

Start IJulia from the command line by typing `ipython notebook --profile julia`, which opens a window in your browser.

This can be used as a console interface to Julia; using the `PyPlot` package is also a convenient way to plot some curves.

The following screenshot displays a damped sinusoid of the form `x*exp(-0.1x)*cos(2.0x)`:

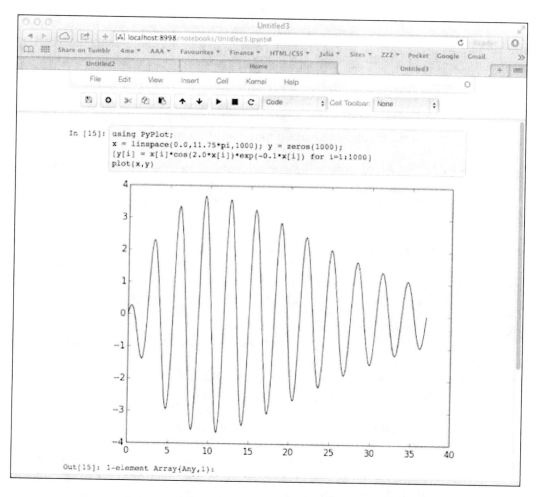

A quick look at some Julia

To get flavor, look at an example that uses random numbers to price an Asian derivative on the options market.

A share option is the right to purchase a specific stock at a nominated price sometime in the future. The person granting the option is called the grantor and the person who has the benefit of the option is the beneficiary. At the time the option matures, the beneficiary may choose to exercise the option if it is in his/her interest and the grantor is then obliged to complete the contract.

In order to set up the contract, the beneficiary must pay an agreed fee to the grantor. The beneficiary's liability is therefore limited by this fee, while the grantor's liability is unlimited. The following question arises: How can we arrive at a price that is fair to both the grantor and the beneficiary? The price will be dependent on a number of factors such as the price that the beneficiary wishes to pay, the time to exercise the option, the rate of inflation, and the volatility of the stock.

Options characteristically exist in one of two forms: call options and put options.

Call options, which give the beneficiary the right to require the grantor to sell the stock to him/her at the agreed price upon exercise, and put options, which give the beneficiary the right to require the grantor to buy the stock at the agreed price on exercise. The problem of the determination of option price was largely solved in the 1970s by Fisher Black and Myron Scholes by producing a formula for the price after treating the stock movement as random (Brownian) and making a number of simplifying assumptions.

We are going to look at the example of an Asian option, which is one for which there can be no formula. This is a type of option (sometimes termed an average value option) where the payoff is determined by the average underlying price over some preset period of time up to exercise rather than just the final price at that time.

So, to solve this type of problem, we must simulate the possible paths (often called random walks) for the stock by generating these paths using random numbers. We have seen a simple use of random numbers earlier while estimating the value of Pi. Our problem is that the accuracy of the result typically depends on the square of the number of trials, so obtaining an extra significant figure needs a hundred times more work. For our example, we are going to do 100000 simulations, each 100 steps representing a daily movement over a period of around 3 months. For each simulation, we determine at the end whether based on the average price of the stock, there would be a positive increase for a call option or a negative one for a put option. In which case, we are "in the money" and would exercise the option. By averaging all the cases where there is a gain, we can arrive at a fair price.

The code that we need to do this is relatively short and needs no special features other than simple coding.

Julia via the console

We can create a file called `asian.jl` by using the following code:

```
function run_asian(N = 100000, PutCall = 'C';)
# European Asian option.
# Uses geometric or arithmetic average.
```

```
# Euler and Milstein discretization for Black-Scholes.
# Option features.
  println("Setting option parameters");
  S0  = 100;        # Spot price
  K   = 100;        # Strike price
  r   = 0.05;       # Risk free rate
  q   = 0.0;        # Dividend yield
  v   = 0.2;        # Volatility
  tma = 0.25;       # Time to maturity


  Averaging = 'A';  # 'A'rithmetic or 'G'eometric
  OptType = (PutCall == 'C' ? "CALL" : "PUT");
  println("Option type is $OptType");
# Simulation settings.
  println("Setting simulation parameters");
  T = 100;          # Number of time steps
  dt = tma/T;       # Time increment


# Initialize the terminal stock price matrices
# for the Euler and Milstein discretization schemes.
S = zeros(Float64,N,T);
  for n=1:N
    S[n,1] = S0;
  end


# Simulate the stock price under the Euler and Milstein schemes.
# Take average of terminal stock price.
  println("Looping $N times.");
  A = zeros(Float64,N);
  for n=1:N
    for t=2:T
      dW = (randn(1)[1])*sqrt(dt);
      z0 = (r - q - 0.5*v*v)*S[n,t-1]*dt;
      z1 = v*S[n,t-1]*dW;
      z2 = 0.5*v*v*S[n,t-1]*dW*dW;
      S[n,t] = S[n,t-1] + z0 + z1 + z2;
```

```
      end
    if cmp(Averaging,'A') == 0
      A[n]  = mean(S[n,:]);
    elseif cmp(Averaging,'G') == 0
      A[n]  = exp(mean(log(S[n,:])));
    end
  end


# Define the payoff
  P = zeros(Float64,N);
  if cmp(PutCall,'C') == 0
    for n = 1:N
      P[n]  = max(A[n] - K, 0);
    end
  elseif cmp(PutCall,'P') == 0
    for n = 1:N
      P[n]  = max(K - A[n], 0);
    end
  end
# Calculate the price of the Asian option
AsianPrice = exp(-r*tma)*mean(P);
@printf "Price: %10.4f\n" AsianPrice;
end
```

We have wrapped the main body of the code in a function run_asian(N, PutCall) .... end statement. The reason for this is to be able to time the execution of the task in Julia, thereby eliminating the startup times associated with the Julia runtime when using the console.

The stochastic behavior of the stock is modeled by the randn function; randn(N) provides an array of N elements, normally distributed with zero mean and unit variance.

All the work is done in the inner loop; the z-variables are just written to decompose the calculation.

To store the averages for each track, use the zeros function to allocate and initialise the array.

The option would only be exercised if the average value of the stock is above the "agreed" prices. This is called the payoff and is stored for each run in the array P.

It is possible to use arithmetic or geometric averaging. The code sets this as arithmetic, but it could be parameterized.

The final price is set by applying the mean function to the P array. This is an example of vectorized coding.

So, to run this simulation, start the Julia console and load the script as follows:

```
julia> include("asian.jl")
julia> run_asian()
```

To get an estimate of the time taken to execute this command, we can use the `tic()`/ `toc()` function or the `@elapsed` macro:

```
include("asian.jl")
tic(); run_asian(1000000, 'C'); toc();
Option Price: 1.6788 elapsed: time 1.277005471 seconds
```

If we are not interested in the execution times, there are a couple of ways in which we can proceed.

The first is just to append to the code a single line calling the function as follows:

```
run_asian(1000000, 'C')
```

Then, we can run the Asian option from the command prompt by simply typing the following: `julia asian.jl`.

This is pretty inflexible since we would like to pass different values of the number of trials N and to determine the price for either a call option or a put option.

Julia provides an ARG array when a script is started from the command line to hold the passed arguments. So, we add the following code at the end of `asian.jl`:

```
nArgs = length(ARGS)
if nArgs >= 2
    run_asian(ARGS[1], ARGS[2])
elseif nArgs == 1
    run_asian(ARGS[1])
else
    run_asian()
end
```

Julia variables are case-sensitive, so we must use ARGS (uppercase) to pass the arguments.

Because we have specified the default values in the function definition, this will run from the command line or if loaded into the console.

Arguments to Julia are passed as strings but will be converted automatically although we are not doing any checking on what is passed for the number of trials (*N*) or the PutCall option.

Installing some packages

We will discuss the package system in the next section, but to get going, let's look at a simple example that produces a plot by using the ASCIIPlots package. This is not dependent on any other package and works at the console prompt.

You can find it at http://docs.julialang.org and choose the "Available Packages" link. Then, click on **ASCIIPlots**, which will take you to the GitHub repository.

It is always a good idea when looking at a package to read the markdown file: README.md for examples and guidance.

Let's use the same parameters as before. We will be doing a single walk so there is no need for an outer loop or for accumulating the price estimates and averaging them to produce an option price.

By compacting the inner loop, we can write this as follows:

```
using ASCIIPlots;


S0   = 100;        # Spot price

K    = 102;        # Strike price

r    = 0.05;       # Risk free rate

q    = 0.0;        # Dividend yield

v    = 0.2;        # Volatility

tma = 0.25;        # Time to maturity

T = 100;           # Number of time steps

dt = tma/T;        # Time increment

S = zeros(Float64,T);

S[1] = S0;
```

```
dW = randn(T)*sqrt(dt)

[ S[t] = S[t-1] * (1 + (r - q - 0.5*v*v)*dt + v*dW[t] +
0.5*v*v*dW[t]*dW[t]) for t=2:T ]

x = linspace(1,T);

scatterplot(x,S,sym='*');
```

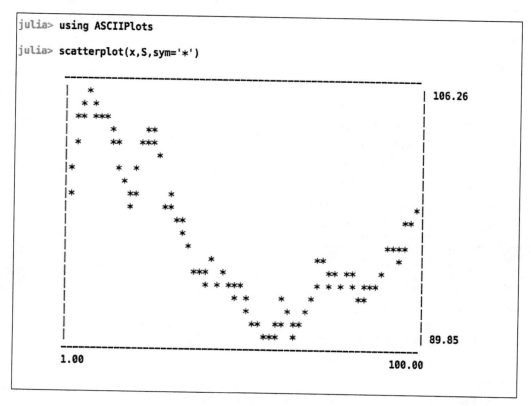

Note that when adding a package the statement using its name as an `ASCIIPlots` string, whereas when using the package, it does not.

A bit of graphics creating more realistic graphics with Winston

To produce a more realistic plot, we turn to another package called `Winston`.

Add this by typing `Pkg.add("Winston")`, which also adds a number of other "required" packages. By condensing the earlier code (for a single pass), it reduces the earlier code to the following:

```julia
using Winston;


S0   = 100;        # Spot price

K    = 102;        # Strike price

r    = 0.05;       # Risk free rate

q    = 0.0;        # Dividend yield

v    = 0.2;        # Volatility

tma = 0.25;        # Time to maturity

T = 100;           # Number of time steps

dt = tma/T;        # Time increment

S = zeros(Float64,T)

S[1] = S0;

dW = randn(T)*sqrt(dt);

[ S[t] = S[t-1] * (1 + (r - q - 0.5*v*v)*dt + v*dW[t] +
0.5*v*v*dW[t]*dW[t]) for t=2:T ]


x = linspace(1, T, length(T));

p = FramedPlot(title = "Random Walk, drift 5%, volatility 2%")

add(p, Curve(x,S,color="red"))

display(p)
```

1. Plot one track, so only compute vector s of T elements.

2. Compute stochastic variance dW in a single vectorized statement.

3. Compute track s by using "list comprehension."

4. Create array x by using linespace to define a linear absicca for the plot.

5. Use the Winston package to produce the display, which only requires three statements: to define the plot space, add a curve to it, and display the plot as shown in the following figure:

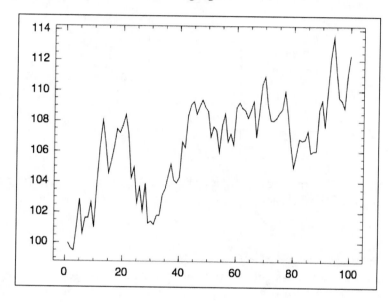

My benchmarks

We compared the Asian option code above with similar implementations in the "usual" data science languages discussed earlier.

The point of these benchmarks is to compare the performance of specific algorithms for each language implementation. The code used is available to download.

Language	Timing (c = 1)	Asian option
C	1.0	1.681
Julia	1.41	1.680
Python (v3)	32.67	1.671
R	154.3	1.646
Octave	789.3	1.632

The runs were executed on a Samsung RV711 laptop with an i5 processor and 4GB RAM running CentOS 6.5 (Final).

Package management

We have noted that Julia uses Git as a repository for itself and for its package and that the installation has a built-in package manager, so there is no need to interface directly to GitHub. This repository is located in the Git folder of the installed system.

As a full discussion of the package system is given on the Julia website, we will only cover some of the main commands to use.

Listing, adding, and removing

After installing Julia, the user can create a new repository by using the `Pkg.init()` command. This clones the metadata from a "well-known" repository and creates a local folder called `.julia`:

```
julia> Pkg.init()
INFO: Initializing package repository C:\Users\Malcolm
INFO: Cloning METADATA from git://Github.com/JuliaLang
```

The latest versions of all installed packages can be updated with the
`Pkg.update()` command.

Notice that if the repository does not exist, the first use of a package command
such as `Pkg.update()` or `Pkg.add()` will call `Pkg.init()` to create it:

```
julia> Pkg.update()

Pkg.update()

INFO: Updating METADATA...

INFO: Computing changes...

INFO: No packages to install, update or remove.
```

We previously discussed how to install the `ASCIIPlots` package by using the
`Pkg.add("ASCIIPlots")` command. The `Pkg.status()` command can be used
to show the current packages installed and `Pkg.rm()` to remove them:

```
julia> Pkg.status()

Pkg.status()

Required packages:

- ASCIIPlots 0.0.2


julia> Pkg.rm("ASCIIPlots")

Pkg.rm("ASCIIPlots")

INFO: Removing ASCIIPlots INFO: REQUIRE updated.
```

After adding `ASCIIPlots`, we added the `Winston` graphics package. Most
packages have a set of others on which they depend and the list can be found
in the `REQUIRE` file.

For instance, `Winston` requires the `Cairo`, `Color`, `IniFile`, and `Tk` packages.
Some of these packages also have dependencies, so `Pkg.add()` will recursively
resolve, clone, and install all of these. The `Cairo` package is interesting since it
requires **Homebrew** on Mac OS X and **WinRPM** on Windows.

WinRPM further needs `URLParse`, `HTTPClient`, `LibExpat`, and `ZLib`. So, if we
use `Pkg.status()` again on a Windows installation, we get the following:

```
julia> Pkg.status()

Required packages:

 - ASCIIPlots            0.0.2

 - Winston               0.11.0

Additional packages:
```

- `BinDeps`   0.2.14
- `Cairo`   0.2.13
- `Color 0.2.10`
- `HTTPClient`   0.1.0
- `IniFile 0.2.2`
- `LibCURL`   0.1.3
- `LibExpat0.0.4`
- `Tk`   0.2.12
- `URIParser 0.0.2`
- `URLParse 0.0.0`
- `WinRPM`   0.0.13
- `Zlib`   0.1.5

All the packages installed as dependencies are listed as additional packages. Removing the `Winston` package will also remove all the additional packages. When adding complex packages, you may wish to add some of the dependent ones first. So, with Winston, you can add both `Cairo` and `Tk`, which will then show the required rather than the additional packages.

Choosing and exploring packages

For such a young language, Julia has a rich and rapidly developing set of packages covering all aspects of use to the data scientist and the mathematical analyst. Registered packages are available on GitHub, and the list of these packages can be referenced via http://docs.julialang.org/.

Because the core language is still under review from release to release, some features are deprecated, others changed, and the others dropped, so it is possible that specific packages may be at variance with the release of Julia you are using, even if it is designated as the current "stable" one. Furthermore, it may be that a package may not work under different operating systems. In general, use under the Linux operating system fares the best and under Windows fares the worst.

How then should we select a package? The best indicators are the version number; packages designated v0.0.0 should always be viewed with some suspicion. Furthermore, the date of the last update is useful here. The docs website also lists the individual contributors to each individual package with the principal author listed first. Ones with multiple developers are clearly of interest to a variety of contributors and tend to be better discussed and maintained. There is strength here in numbers. The winner in this respect seems to be (as of July 2014) the `DataFrames` package, which is up to version 0.3.15 and has attracted the attention of 33 separate authors.

Even with an old relatively untouched package, there is nothing to stop you checking out the code and modifying or building on it. Any enhancements or modifications can be applied and the code returned; that's how open source grows. Furthermore, the principal author is likely to be delighted that someone else is finding the package useful and taking an interest in the work.

It is not possible to create a specific taxonomy of Julia packages but certain groupings emerge, which build on the backs of the earlier ones. We will be meeting many of these later in this book, but before that, it may be useful to quickly list a few.

Statistics and mathematics

Statistics is seen rightly as the realm of R and mathematics of MATLAB and Mathematica, while Python impresses in both. The base Julia system provides much of the functionality available in NumPy, while additional packages add that of SciPy and Pandas.

Statistics is well provided in Julia on GitHub by both the `https://Github.com/ JuliaStats` group and a Google group called `https://groups.google.com/ forum/#!forum/julia-stats`.

Much of the basic statistics is provided by `Stats.jl` and `StatsBase.jl`. There are various means of working with R-style data frames and loading some of the datasets available to R. The distributions package covers the probability distributions and the associated functions. Moreover, there is support for time series, cluster analysis, hypothesis testing, MCMC methods, and more.

Mathematical operations such as random number generators and exotic functions are largely in the core (unlike Python), but packages exist for elemental calculus operations, ODE solvers, Monte-Carlo methods, mathematical programming, and optimization. There is a GitHub page for the `https://Github.com/JuliaOpt/` group, which lists the packages under the umbrella of optimization.

Data visualization

Graphics support in Julia has sometimes been given less than favorable press in comparison with other languages such as Python, R, and MATLAB. It is a stated aim of the developers to incorporate some degree of graphics support in the core, but at present, this is largely the realm of package developers.

While it was true that v0.1.x offered very limited and flaky graphics, v0.2.x vastly improved the situation and this continues with v0.3.x.

Firstly, there is a module in the core called `Base.Graphics`, which acts as an abstract layer to packages such as `Cairo` and `Tk/Gtk`, which serve to implement much of the required functionality.

Layered on top of these are a couple of packages, namely `Winston` (which we have introduced already) and Gadfly. Normally, as a user, you will probably work with one or the other of these.

Winston is a 2D graphics package that provides methods for curve plotting and creating histograms and scatter diagrams. Axis labels and display titles can be added, and the resulting display can be saved to files as well as shown on the screen.

Gadfly is a system for plotting and visualization equivalent to the `ggplot2` module in R. It can be used to render the graphics output to PNG, PostScript, PDF, and SVG files. Gadfly works best with the following C libraries installed: `cairo`, `pango`, and `fontconfig`. The PNG, PS, and PDF backends all require `cairo`, but without it, it is still possible to create displays to SVG and Javascript/D3.

There are a couple of different approaches, which are worthy of note: Gaston and PyPlot.

Gaston is an interface to the **gnuplot** program on Linux. You need to check whether gnuplot is available, and if not, it must be installed in the usual way via `yum` or `apt-get`. For this, you need to install XQuartz, which must be started separately before using Gaston.

Gaston can do whatever gnuplot is capable of. There is a very comprehensive script available in the package by running `Gaston.demo()`.

We have discussed Pyplot briefly before when looking at IJulia. The package uses Julia's `PyCall` package to call the `Matplotlib` Python module directly and can display plots in any Julia graphical backend, including as we have seen, inline graphics in IJulia.

Web and networking

Distributed computing is well represented in Julia. TCP/IP sockets are implemented in the core. Additionally, there is support for Curl, SMTP and for WebSockets. HTTP protocols and parsing are provided for with a number of packages, such as HTTP, HttpParser, HttpServer, JSON, and Mustache.

Working in the cloud at present, there are a couple of packages. One is AWS, which addresses the use of **Amazon Simple Storage System (S3)** and **Elastic Compute Cloud (EC2)**. The other is HDFS, which provides a wrapper over **libhdfs** and a Julia MapReduce functionality.

Database and specialist packages

The database is supported mainly through the use of the ODBC package. On Windows, ODBC is the standard, while Linux and Mac OS X require the installation of unixODBC or iODBC. There is currently no native support for the main SQL databases such as Oracle, MySQL, and PostgreSQL.

The package SQLite provides an interface to that database and there is a Mongo package, which implements bindings to the NoSQL database MongoDB. Other NoSQL databases such as CouchDB and Neo4j exposed a RESTful API, so some of the HTTP packages coupled with JSON can be used to interact with these.

A couple of specialist Julia groups are JuliaQuant and JuliaGPU.

JuliaQuant encompasses a variety of packages for quantitative financial modeling. This is an area that has been heavily supported by developers in R, MATLAB, and Python, and the Quant group is addressing the same problems in Julia.

JuliaGPU is a set of packages supporting OpenCL and CUDA interfacing to GPU cards for high-speed parallel processing.

Both of these are very much works in progress, and interest and support in the development of the packages would be welcome.

How to uninstall Julia

Removing Julia is very simple; there is no explicit uninstallation process. It consists of deleting the source tree, which was created by the build process or from the DMG file on Mac OS X or the EXE file on Windows. Everything runs within this tree, so there are no files installed to any `system` folders.

In addition, we need to attend to the `package` folder. Recall that under Linux and Mac OS X this is a hidden folder called `.julia` in the user's home folder. In Windows, it is located in the user's profile typically in `C:\Users\[my-user-name]`. Removing this folder will erase all the packages that were previously installed.

There is another hidden file called `.julia_history` that should be deleted; it keeps an historical track of the commands listed.

Adding an unregistered package

The official repository for the registered packages in Julia is here:

`https://Github.com/JuliaLang/METADATA.jl.`

Any packages here will be listed using the package manager or in Julia Studio.

However, it is possible to use an unregistered package by using `Pkg.clone(url)`, where the `url` is a Git URL from which the package can be cloned. The package should have the `src` and `test` folders and may have several others. If it contains a `REQUIRE` file at the top of the source tree, that file can be used to determine any dependent registered packages; these packages will be automatically installed.

If you are developing a package, it is possible to place the source in the `.julia` folder alongside packages added with `Pkg.add()` or `Pkg.clone()`. Eventually, you will wish to use GitHub in a more formal way; we will deal with that later when considering package implementation.

What makes Julia special

Julia, as a programming language, has made rapid progress since its launch in 2012, which is a testimony to the soundness and quality of its design and coding. It is true that Julia is fast, but speed alone is not sufficient to guarantee a progression to a main stream language rather than a cult language.

Indeed, the last few years have witnessed the decline of Perl (largely self-inflicted) and a rapid rise in the popularity of R and Python. This we have attributed to a new breed of analysts and researchers who are moving into the fields of data science and big data and who are looking for tool kits that fulfill their requirements.

To occupy this space, Julia needs to offer some features that others find hard to achieve. Some such features are listed as follows:

Parallel processing

As a language aimed at the scientific community, it is natural that Julia should provide facilities for executing code in parallel. In running tasks on multiple processors, Julia takes a different approach to the popular **message passing interface (MPI)**. In Julia, communication is one-sided and appears to the programmer more as a function call than the traditional message send and receive paradigm typified by **pyMPI** on Python and **Rmpi** on R.

Julia provides two in-built primitives: remote references and remote calls. A remote reference is an object that can be used from any processor to refer to an object stored on a particular processor. A remote call is a request by one processor to call a certain function or certain arguments on another, or possibly the same, processor.

Sending messages and moving data constitute most of the overhead in a parallel program, and reducing the number of messages and the amount of data sent is critical to achieving performance and scalability. We will be investigating how Julia tackles this in a subsequent chapter.

Multiple dispatch

The choice of which method to execute when a function is applied is called dispatch.

Single dispatch polymorphism is a familiar feature in object-orientated languages where a method call is dynamically executed on the basis of the actual derived type of the object on which the method has been called.

Multiple dispatch is an extension of this paradigm where dispatch occurs by using all of a function's arguments rather than just the first.

Homoiconic macros

Julia, like Lisp, represents its own code in memory by using a user-accessible data structure, thereby allowing programmers to both manipulate and generate code that the system can evaluate. This makes complex code generation and transformation far simpler than in systems without this feature.

We met an example of a macro earlier in `@printf`, which mimics the C-like `printf` statements. Its definition is in given in the `base/printf.jl` file.

Interlanguage cooperation

We noted that Julia is often seen as a competitor to languages such as C, Python, and R, but this is not the view of the language designers and developers.

Julia makes it simple to call C and Fortran functions, which are compiled and saved as shared libraries. This is by the use of the in-built call. This means that there is no need for the traditional "wrapper code" approach, which acts on the function inputs, transforms them into an appropriate form, loads the shared library, makes the call, and then repeats the process in reverse on the return value. Julia's JIT compilation generates the same low-level machine instructions as a native C call, so there is no additional overhead in making the function call from Julia.

Additionally, we have seen that the PyCall package makes it easy to import Python libraries, and this has been seen to be an effective method of displaying the graphics from Python's `matplotlib`. Further, inter-cooperation with Python is evident in the provision of the IJulia IDE and an adjunction to IPython notebooks.

There is also work on calling R libraries from Julia by using the `Rif` package and calling Java programs from within Julia by using the `JavaCall` package. These packages present the exciting prospect of opening up Julia to a wealth of existing functionalities in a straightforward and elegant fashion.

Summary

This chapter introduced you to Julia, how to download it, install it, and build it from source. We saw that the language is elegant, concise, and powerful. The next three chapters will discuss the features of Julia in more depth.

We looked at interacting with Julia via the command line (REPL) in order to use a random walk method to evaluate the price of an Asian option. We also discussed the use of two interactive development environments (IDEs), Juno and IJulia, as an alternative to REPL.

In addition, we reviewed the in-built package manager and how to add, update, and remove modules, and then demonstrated the use of two graphics packages to display the typical trajectories of the Asian option calculation. In the next chapter, we will look at various other approaches to creating display graphics and quality visualizations.

2

Developing in Julia

Julia is a feature-rich language. It was designed to appeal to the novice programmer and purist alike. Indeed for those whose interests lie in data science, statistics and mathematical modeling, Julia is well equipped to meet all their needs.

Our aim is to furnish the reader with the necessary knowledge to begin programming in Julia almost immediately. So rather than begin with an overview of the language's syntax, control structures and the like, we will introduce Julia's facets gradually over the rest of this book. Over the next two chapters we will look at some of the basic and advanced features of the Julia core. Many of the features such as graphics and database access, which are implemented via the package system will be left until later.

If you are familiar with programming in Python, R, MATLAB and so on, you will not find the journey terribly arduous, in fact we believe it will be a particularly pleasant one.

At the present time Julia has not yet reached the version 1.0 status and some of the syntax may be deprecated and later changed. However, we believe that most of the material presented here will stand the test of time.

Integers, bits, bytes, and bools

Julia is a strongly typed language allowing the programmer to specify a variable's type precisely. However in common with most interpreted languages it does not require the type to be declared when a variable is declared, rather it infers it from the form of the declaration.

A variable in Julia is any combination of upper or lowercase letters, digits and the underscore (_) and exclamation (!) characters. It must start with a letter or an underscore _. Conventionally variable names consist of lowercase letters with long names separated by underscores rather than using camel case.

To determine a variable type we can use the typeof() function.

So typically:

```
julia>  x = 2;   typeof(x)  #  => gives Int64
julia>  x = 2.0; typeof(x) # => gives Float64
```

Notice that the type (see the preceding code) starts with a capital letter and ends with a number which indicates the number of bit length of the variable. The bit length defaults to the word length of the operating system and this can be determined by examining the built-in constant WORD_SIZE.

```
julia>WORD_SIZE  # => 64   (on my computer)
```

In this section, we will be dealing with integer and boolean types.

Integers

The integer type can be any of Int8, Int16, Int32, Int64 and Int128, so the maximum integer can occupy 16 bytes of storage and can be anywhere within the range of -2^{127} to $(+2^{127} - 1)$.

If we need more precision than this Julia core implements the BigInt type:

```
julia> x=BigInt(2^32); x^6
6277101735386680763835789423207666416102355444464034512896
```

There are a few more things to say about integers:

As well as the integer type, Julia provides the unsigned integer type Uint. Again Uint ranges from 8 to 128 bytes, so the maximum Uint is $(2^{128} - 1)$.

We can use the typemax() and typemin() functions to output the ranges of the Int and Uint types.

```
julia> for T = {Int8,Int16,Int32,Int64,Int128,Uint8,Uint16,Uint32,Uint64,
Uint128}println("$(lpad(T,7)): [$(typemin(T)),$(typemax(T))]")
end
```

```
    Int8: [-128,127]
   Int16: [-32768,32767]
   Int32: [-2147483648,2147483647]
   Int64: [-9223372036854775808,9223372036854775807]
  Int128: [-170141183460469231731687303715884105728,
```

170141183460469231731687303715884105727]

```
Uint8:   [0,255]
Uint16:  [0,65535]
Uint32:  [0,4294967295]
Uint64:  [0,18446744073709551615]
Uint128: [0,340282366920938463463374607431768211455]
```

Particularly notice the use of the form of the `for` statement which we will discuss when we deal with arrays and matrices later in this chapter.

Suppose we type:

```
julia> x = 2^32; x*x    # => the answer 0
```

The reason is that integer overflow 'wraps' around, so squaring 2^32 gives 0 not 2^64, since my `WORD_SIZE` is 64:

```
julia> x = int128(2^32); x*x   # => the answer we would expect
18446744073709551616
```

We can use the `typeof()` function on a type such as `Int64` to see what its parent type is.

So `typeof(Int64)` gives `DataType` and `typeof(Uint128)` also gives `DataType`.

The definition of `DataType` is 'hinted' at in the core file `boot.jl`; hinted at because the actual definition is implemented in C and the Julia equivalent is commented out.

The definitions of the integer types can also be found in `boot.jl`, this time not commented out. Typically:

```
abstract Number
abstract Real <: Number
abstract Integer <: Real
abstract Signed <: Integer
bitstype 64   Int64 <: Signed
```

Where the `<:` operator corresponds to a subclass of the parent and `bitstype` again is defined in the core, nominally as `#bitstype {32|64} Ptr{T}`.

If we type:

```
julia> x = 7; y = 5; x/y #   =>this gives 1.4
```

So division of two integers produces a real result. In interactive mode we can use the symbol `ans` to correspond to the last answer, that is, `typeof(ans)` gives `Float64`.

To get the integer divisor we use the function div(x,y) which gives 1 as expected and typeof(ans) is Int64. The remainder is obtained either by rem(x,y) or by using the % operator.

Julia has one curious operator the backslash, syntactically x\y is equivalent to y/x. So with x and y as before x\y gives 0.71428 (to 5 decimal places).

Logical and arithmetic operators

As well as decimal arguments it is possible to assign binary, octal, and hexadecimal ones using the prefixes 0b, 0o and 0x.

So x = 0b110101 creates the hexadecimal number 0x35 (that is, decimal 53) and typeof(ans) is Uint8, since 53 will 'fit' into a single byte. For larger values the type is correspondingly higher, that is x = 0b1000010110101 gives x = 0x10b5 and typeof(ans) is Uint16.

For operating on bits Julia provides the following: ~ (not), | (or), & (and) and $ (xor):

```
julia> x = 0xbb31; y = 0xaa5f; x$y # => 0x116e
```

Also we can perform arithmetic shifts using << (LEFT) and >> (RIGHT) operators. Note because x is of type Uint16 the shift operator retains that size, so:

```
julia> x = 0xbb31;  x<<8
```

This gives 0x3100 (the top two nibbles being discarded) and typeof(ans) is Uint16.

Arithmetic shifts preserve the sign bit. This is not relevant when dealing with unsigned integers but bit-wise operators can be applied to signed integers too. Logical and arithmetic left shifts produce the same result but right shifts do not. In this case Julia provides the >>> operator to apply a right logical shift:

```
julia> x = 0xbb31; y = int16(x)   # => 17615
```

y>>4 gives -1101 and y>>>4 gives 2995.

Booleans

Julia has the logical type Bool. Dynamically a variable is assigned a type Bool by equating it to the constant true or false (both lowercase) or to a logical expression such as:

```
julia> p = (2 < 3) # => true
julia> typeof(p) # => Bool
```

Many languages treat 0, empty strings, NULLS as representing false and anything else as true. This is NOT the case in Julia however, there are cases where a Bool value may be promoted to an integer in which case true corresponds to unity.

That is, an expression such as x + p (where x is of type Int and p of type Bool) will:

```
julia> x = 0xbb31; p = (2 < 3); x + p # => 0x000000000000bb32
julia>typeof(ans) # => Uint(64)
```

Arrays

An array is an indexable collection of (normally) homogeneous values such as integers, floats, booleans. In Julia, unlike many programming languages, the index starts at 1 not 0.

One simple way to create an array is to enumerate its values:

```
julia> A = [0, 1, 1, 2, 3, 5, 8, 13, 21, 34, 55, 89, 144, 233, 377];
15-element Array{Int64,1}
```

These are the first 15 values of the Fibonacci series and because all values are listed as integers the array created is of type Int64. The other number refers to the number of dimensions of the array, in this case 1.

In conjunction of loops in the Asian option example in the previous chapter, we meet the definition of a range as: start : [step] : end

```
julia> A = [1:10]; B = [1:3:15]; C =[1:0.5:5];
```

Here A is [1,2,3,4,5,6,7,8,9,10], B is [1,4,7,10,13] and C is [1.0,1.5,2.0,2.5,3.0,3.5,4.0,4.5,5.0]

Because the step in C is specified as a float value the array is of type Float64 not Int64.

Julia also provides functions such as zeros, ones and rand which provide array results. Normally these are returned a float-point value so a little bit of work is required to provide integer results.

```
julia> A = int(zeros(15)); B = int(ones(15)); C = rand(1:100,15);
```

Another method of creating and populating an array is by using a list comprehension. If we recall the first example of the Fibonacci series, we can get the same result by creating an uninitialized array of 15 integers by using `Array(Int64,15)` then by assigning the first couple of values and use the definition of the Fibonacci series to create the remaining values:

```
julia> A = Array(Int64,15); A[1]=0;A[2]=1;[A[i] = A[i-1] + A[i-2] for i = 3:length(A)]
```

Finally it is possible to create a completely empty array by using `Int64[]`. Since array sizes are fixed this would seem a little futile but certain functions can be used to alter the size of the array. In particular the `push!()` function can add a value to the array and increase its length by one:

```
julia> A = Int64[];
julia> push!(A,1); push!(A,2); push!(A,3)  # => [1,2,3]
```

The corresponding `pop!(A)` function will return the value 3, and result in A = `[1,2]`.

Note that the use of the tailing `!` borrows the syntax form Lisp-like conventions and is purely arbitrary. Since functions are first class variables this is the reason that `!` is an accepted character in variable names but it's a good idea to respect the convention and not use `!` in reference to common variables.

Consider the following two array definitions:

```
julia> A = [1,2,3];
3-element Array{Int64,1}
julia> A = [1 2 3];
1x3 Array{Int64,2}
```

The first, with values separated by commas, produces the usual one-dimensional data structure. The second, where there are no commas, produces a matrix or 1 row and 3 columns, hence the definition: `1x3 Array{Int64,2}`.

To define more rows we separate the values with semicolons as:

```
julia> A = [1 2 3; 4 5 6]
2x3 Array{Int64,2}
 1  2  3
 4  5  6
```

If we type:

```
for i in (1:length(A)) @printf("%1d: %1d\n", i, A[i]); end
1 : 1
2 : 4
3 : 2
4 : 5
5 : 3
6 : 6
```

In Julia indexing is in column order and the array/matrix can be indexed in a one-dimensional or two-dimensional.

```
julia> A[1,2] # => 2
julia> A[2] # => 4
julia> A[5]# => 3
```

In fact it is possible to reshape the array to change it from a 2x3 matrix to a 3x2 one:

```
julia> B = reshape(A,3,2)
3x2 Array{Int64,2}:
1   5
4   3
2   6
```

Operations on matrices

We will be meeting matrices and matrix operations through this book but let us look at the simplest of operations:

Taking A and B as defined previously the normal matrix rules apply.

We'll define C as the transpose of B so:

```
julia> C = transpose(B)
2x3 Array{Int64,2}:
1   4   2
5   3   6
julia> A + C
2x3 Array{Int64,2}:
```

```
2   6    5
9   8   12
julia> A*B
2x2 Array{Int64,2}:
15   29
36   71
```

Matrix division makes more sense with square matrices but it is possible to define the operations for non-square matrices too:

```
julia> A / C
2x2 Array{Float64,2}
0.332273   0.27663
0.732909   0.710652
```

Elemental operations

As well as the 'common' matrix operations, Julia defines a set which works on the elements of the matrix. So although A * C is not allowed because number of columns of A is not equal to number of rows of C but the following are all valid since A and C are the same shape:

```
julia> A .* C
2x3 Array{Int64,2}:
  1    8    6
 20   15   36
```

```
julia> A ./ C
2x3 Array{Float64,2}:
1.0   0.5       1.5
0.8   1.66667   1.0
```

```
julia> A .== C
2x3 BitArray{2}:
true    false   false
false   false   true
```

A simple Markov chain – cat and mouse

Suppose there is a row of five adjacent boxes, with a cat in the first box and a mouse in the fifth box. At each 'tick' the cat and the mouse both jump to a random box next to them. On the first tick the cat must jump to box 2 and the mouse to box 4 but on the next ticks they may jump to the box they started in or to box 3.

When the cat and mouse are in the same box the cat catches the mouse and the Markov chain terminates. Because there is an odd number of boxes between the cat and mouse it's easy to see that they will not jump past each other.

So Markov chain that corresponds to this contains the only five possible combinations of (Cat,Mouse).

State 1: (1,3) State 2: (1,5) State 3: (2,4) State 4: (3,5) State 5: (2,2), (3,3) & (4,4) # => cat catches the mouse

The matrix P = [0 0 .5 0 .5; 0 0 1 0 0; .25 .25 0, .25 .25; 0 0 .5 0 .5; 0 0 0 0 1] represents the probabilities of the transition from one state to the next and the question is how long has the mouse got before it's caught. Its best chance is starting in State 2 = (1,5).

The matrix P is a stochastic matrix where all the probabilities along any row add up to 1.

This is actually an easy problem to solve using some matrix algebra in a few lines in Julia and for a full discussion of the problem look at the Wikipedia discussion.

```
I = eye(4);
P = [0 0 .5 0; 0 0 1 0; .25 .25 0 .25; 0 0 .5 0];
ep = [0 1 0 0]*inv(I - P)*[1,1,1,1];
println("Expected lifetime for the mouse is $ep ticks")
Expected lifetime for the mouse is [4.5] ticks
```

Consider how this works:

1. The eye() function returns a square(real) matrix with leading diagonal unity and the other values of zero.

2. The matrix P can be reduced to 4x4 since when in state 5 the Markov chain terminates.

3. The inv(I - P)*[1,1,1,1] returns the expected lifetime (no disrespect) of the mouse in all states so multiplying with [0 1 0 0] gives the expectation when starting in state 2.0.

Char and strings

So far we have been dealing with numeric and boolean datatypes. In this section we will look at character representation and how Julia handles ASCII and UTF-8 strings of characters. We will also introduce the concept of regular expressions, widely used in pattern matching and filtering operations.

Characters

Julia has a built-in type `Char` to represent a character. A character occupies 32 bits not 8, so a character can represent a UTF-8 symbol and may be assigned in a number of ways:

```
julia> c = 'A'
julia> c = char(65)
julia> c = '\U0041'
```

All these represent the ASCII character capital A.

It is possible to specify a character code of `'\Uffff'` but char conversion does not check that every value is valid. However, Julia provides an `isvalid_char()` function:

```
julia> c = '\Udff3';
julia> is_valid_char(c; ) # => gives false.
```

Julia uses the special C-like syntax for certain ASCII control characters such as `'\b','\t','\n','\r',\'f'` for backspace, tab, newline, carriage return and form feed. Otherwise the backslash acts as an escape character, so int('\s') gives 115 whereas int('\t') gives 9.

Strings

The type of string we are most familiar with comprises a list of ASCII characters which, in Julia, are normally delimited with double quotes, that is:

```
julia> s = "Hello there, Blue Eyes"; typeof(s)
ASCIIString (constructor with 2 methods)
```

In fact a string is an abstraction not a concrete type and `ASCIIString` is only one such abstraction. Looking at `Base::boot.jl` we see:

```
abstract String
abstract DirectIndexString <: String
immutable ASCIIString <: DirectIndexString
```

```
        data::Array{Uint8,1}
    end
    immutable UTF8String <: String
        data::Array{Uint8,1}
    end
    typealias ByteString Union(ASCIIString,UTF8String)
```

In Julia (as in Java), strings are immutable: that is, the value of a `String` object cannot be changed. To construct a different string value, you construct a new string from parts of other strings.

ASCII strings are also indexable so from s as defined previously: `s[14:17]` gives `"Blue"`. The values in the range are inclusive and if we wish we can change the increment as `s[14:2:17]` which gives `"Bu"` or reverse the slice as `s[17:-1:14]` which gives `"eulB"`. Omitting the end of the range is equivalent to running to the end of the string: `s[14:]` which gives `"Blue Eyes"`.

However `s[:14]` is somewhat unexpected and gives the character B not the string upto and including B. This is because the `:` defines a 'symbol', and for a literal `:14` is equivalent to 14, so `s[:14]` is the same as `s[14]` and not `s[1:14]`.

Strings allow for the special characters such as `'\n'`, `'\t'`, and so on. If we wish to include the double quote we can escape it but Julia provides a `"""` delimiter. So `s = "This is the double quote \" character"` and `s = """This is the double quote"character"""` are equivalent:

```
julia> s = "This is a double quote \" character."; println(s);
This is a double quote " character.
```

Strings also provide the `$` convention when displaying the value of variable:

```
julia> age = 21; s =  "I've been $age for many years now!"
"I've been 21 for many years now!"
```

Concatenation of strings can be done using the `$` convention but also Julia uses the `*` operator (rather than `+` or some other symbol):

```
julia> s = "Who are you?";
julia> t = " said the Caterpillar."
```

The following two expressions are directly equivalent:

```
julia> s*t
"Who are you? said the Caterpillar."
julia> "$s$t"
"Who are you? said the Caterpillar."
```

Unicode support

We saw from the definition above that apart from ASCII strings Julia defines UTF-8 strings. In fact UTF-8 is not all that Julia supports and adding support for new encodings is quite easy. In particular, Julia also provides UTF16String and UTF32String types, constructed by the utf16(s) and utf32(s) functions respectively, for UTF-16 and UTF-32 encodings.

Julia provides a function endof() which can be used to used to determine the end of a string and a symbol end to denote the character in the last index position.

Because of variable-length encodings, the number of characters in a string which is given by length(s) is not always the same as the last index. If you iterate through the indices 1 through endof(s) and index into s, the sequence of characters returned when errors aren't thrown is the sequence of characters comprising the string. Thus we have the identity that length(s) <= endof(s), since each character in a string must have its own index:

```
julia> s = "\u2200 x \u2203 y"    # this is the mathematical expression
.....
julia>typeof(s) # =>  UTF8String
julia>endof(s)   # => 11
julia> length(s) # => 7
julia> s[end]    # => 'y'
```

In this case, since the string s has two UTF characters each occupying 3 bytes the only valid indices are s[1], s[4], s[5], s[6], s[7], s[11], so for example s[7] will return the character '\u2203'.

Regular expressions

Regular expressions (Regex) came to prominence with their inclusion in Perl programming.

There is an old adage: *"I had a problem and decided to solve it using regular expressions, now I have two problems"*.

Regular expressions are used for pattern matching, numerous books have been written on them and support is available in a variety of our programming languages post-Perl, notably Java and Python.

Julia supports regular expressions via a special form of string prefixed with an r.

Suppose we define the pattern `empat` as:

```
empat = r"^[_a-z0-9-]+(\.[_a-z0-9-]+)*@[a-z0-9-]+(\.[a-z0-9-]+)*(\.[a-z]
{2,4})$"
```

The following example will give a clue to what the pattern is associated with:

```
julia>ismatch(empat, "fred.flintstone@bedrock.net") # => true

julia>ismatch(empat, "Fredrick Flintstone@bedrock.net") # => false
```

The pattern is for a valid e-mail address and in the second case the space in `"Fredrick Flintstone"` is not valid so the match fails.

Since we may wish to know not only whether a string matches a certain pattern but also how it is matched, Julia has a function `match()`:

```
julia> m = match(r"@bedrock","barney,rubble@bedrock.net")

RegexMatch("@bedrock")
```

If this matches, the function returns a `RegexMatch` object, otherwise it returns `Nothing`:

```
julia>m.match # => "@bedrock"
```

```
julia>m.offset # => 14
```

```
julia>m.captures # => 0-element Array{Union(SubString{UTF8String},Nothi
ng),1}
```

Byte array literals

Another special form is the byte array literal: `b"..."` which enables string notation express arrays of `Uint8` values.

The rules for byte array literals are the following:

- ASCII characters and ASCII escapes produce a single byte
- `\x` and octal escape sequences produce the byte corresponding to the escape value
- Unicode escape sequences produce a sequence of bytes encoding that code point in UTF-8

Consider the following two examples:

```
julia> A = b"HEX:\xefcc" # => 7-element Array{Uint8,1}:[0x48,0x45,0x58,0x
3a,0xef,0x63,0x63]
```

```
julia> B = b"\u2200 x \u2203 y" #=> 11-element Array{Uint8,1}:[0xe2,0x88,
0x80,0x20,0x78,0x20,0xe2,0x88,0x83,0x20,0x79]
```

Version literals

Version numbers can easily be expressed with non-standard string literals such as `v"..."`.

Version number literals create `VersionNumber` objects which follow the specifications of semantic versioning (`http://semver.org`), and therefore are composed of major, minor and patch numeric values, followed by pre-release and build alpha-numeric annotations.

So a full specification typically would be: `v"0.3.1-rc1"`; the major version is `"0"`, minor version `"3"`, patch level `"1"` and release candidate is `1`. Only the major version needs to be provided and the others assume default values. So `v"1"` is equivalent to `v"1.0.0"`.

We met the use of version numbers previously when using the package manager to pin a package to a specific version: `Pkg.pin("NumericExtensions",v"0.2.1")`.

An example

Let us look at some code to play the game *Bulls and Cows*. A computer program *moo*, written in 1970 at MIT in the PL/I, was among the first Bulls and Cows computer implementation.

It is proven that any number could be solved for up to seven turns and the minimal average game length is 5.21 turns.

The computer enumerates a four digit random number from the digits 1 to 9, without duplication. The player inputs his/her guess and the program should validate the player's guess, reject guesses that are malformed, then print the 'score' in terms of number of bulls and cows.

The score is computed as follows:

- One bull is accumulated for each digit in the guess that equals the corresponding digit in the randomly chosen initial number
- One cow is accumulated for each digit in the guess that also appears in the randomly chosen number, but in the wrong position
- The player wins if the guess is the same as the randomly chosen number, and the program ends
- Otherwise the program accepts a new guess, incrementing the number of 'tries'

Coding it up in Julia:

```
function bacs ()
  bulls = cows = turns = 0
  A = {}
  srand(int(time()))
  while length(unique(A)) < 4
  push!(A,rand('1':'9'))
  end
  bacs_number = unique(A)
  println("Bulls and Cows")
  while (bulls != 4)
  print("Guess? ")
  if eof(STDIN)
  s = "q"
  else
  s = chomp(readline(STDIN))
  end
  if  (s == "q")
  print("My guess was "); [print(bacs_number[i]) for
  i=1:4]
  return
  end
  guess = collect(s)
  if  !(length(unique(guess)) == length(guess) == 4 &&
  all(isdigit,guess))
  print("\nEnter four distinct digits or q to quit: ")
  continue
  end
  bulls = sum(map(==, guess, bacs_number))
  cows = length(intersect(guess,bacs_number)) - bulls
  println("$bulls bulls and $cows cows!")
  turns += 1
  end
  println("You guessed my number in $turns turns.")
end
```

The preceding code can be explained as follows:

1. We define an array A as A = {} rather than A = []. This is because although arrays were described as homogeneous collections, Julia provides a type Any which can, as the name suggests, store any form of variable. This is similar to the Microsoft variant datatype.

    ```
    julia> A = {"There are ",10, " green bottles", " hanging on the
    wall.\n"}
    ```

```
julia> [print(A[i]) for i = 1:length(A)]
There are 10 green bottles hanging on the wall.
```

2. Integers are created as characters using the `rand()` function and pushed onto A with `push!()`.

3. The array A may consist of more than 4 entries so a `unique()` function is applied which reduces it to 4 by eliminating duplicates and this is stored in `bacs_number`.

4. User input is via `readline(STDIN)` and this will be a string including the trailing return (`\n`), so a `chomp()` function is applied to remove it and the input is compared with q to allow an escape before the number is guessed.

5. A `collect()` function applied is applied to return a 4-element array of type Char and it is checked that there are 4 elements and that these are all digits.

6. The number of `bulls` is determined by comparing each entry in guess and `bacs_number`. This is achieved by using a `map()` function to applying the `==` operator, if 4 bulls then we are done. Otherwise it's possible to construct a new array as the intersection of guess and `bacs_number` which will contain all the elements which match. So subtracting the number of 'bulls' leaves the number of cows.

Real, complex, and rational numbers

Now we will consider how to handle real and complex numbers in Julia and also introduce an alternate representation of fixed-point reals as a fraction comprising two integers, the `Rational` datatype.

Further we will discuss the use of the `Big()` function to handle integers and real numbers which are too large to be represented by the primitive Julia numeric types.

Reals

We have met real numbers a few times already. The generic type is `FloatingPoint` which is sub-classed from `Real`:

```
abstract Real <: Number
abstract FloatingPoint <: Real
bitstype 16 Float16 <: FloatingPoint
bitstype 32 Float32 <: FloatingPoint
bitstype 64 Float64 <: FloatingPoint
```

A float can be defined as `x = 100.0` or `x = 1e2` or `x = 1f2`; all represent the number `100`.

The first will be of the type equivalent to WORD_SIZE, the second of type Float64 and the third (using f rather than the e notation) of type Float32.

There is also a p notation which can be used with hexadecimals, that is x = 0x10p2 corresponds to 64.0.

Operators and built-in functions

Julia provides comprehensive operator and function support for real numbers. There is a wealth of mathematical functions built-in. In addition to the 'usual' ones such as exp(), log(), sin(), cos(), and so on, there is support for gamma, bessel, zeta and hankel functions and many others.

The reader should look at the section of the manual on *Mathematical Operations* (http://docs.julialang.org/en/release-0.3/manual/mathematical-operations/) for a comprehensive list.

One feature to note is that the multiplication operator * can be omitted in places where there is no ambiguity. If x is a variable 2.0x and 2.0*x are both valid. This is useful in cases when dealing with pre-defined constants such as pi, where 2pi is equal to 6.2831.

Special values

In dealing with real numbers Julia defines three special values Inf, -Inf and NaN. Inf and -Inf refer to values greater (or less) than all finite floating-point values and NaN is "not a number" which is a value not equal to any floating-point value (including itself). So 1.0/0.0 is Inf and -1.0/0.0 is -Inf, whereas 0.0/0.0 is NaN, as is 0.0 * Inf.

Observe that typemin(Float64) and typemax(Float64) are defined as -Inf and Inf respectively rather than the minimum/maximum representation.

BigFloats

Earlier, in regard to integers, we met BigInts.

Unsuprisingly, there are also BigFloats which can be used for arbitrary precision arithmetic:

```
julia>h_atoms_in_universe  = 1.0*10.0^82  # => 1.0e82

julia> x = BigFloat(h_atoms_in_universe)
9.999999999999999634067965630886574211027143225273567793680363843427086501542887e+81 with 256 bits of precision
```

The default precision, nominally 256, and rounding mode of `BigFloat` can be changed using `with_bigfloat_precision()` and `with_rounding()` functions.

Notice that it is also possible to apply the `big()` function to achieve a similar result and the function returns either a `BigInt` or `BigFloat`, corresponding to the type of its argument:

```julia
julia> k = big(7^7);       typeof(k); # => BigInt
julia> k = big(7.0^7);   typeof(k); # => BigFloat
```

Rationals

Julia has a rational number type to represent 'exact' ratios of integers. A rational is defined by use of the `//` operator, for example, 5//7. If the numerator and denominator has a common factor then the number is reduced to its simplest form, 21//35 # => 3//5.

Operations on rationals or on mixed rationals and integers return a rational result:

```julia
x = 3; y = 5//7;
x*y # => 15//7
y^2 # => 25/49
y/x # => 5//21;
```

The functions `num()` and `dem()` return the numerator and denominator of a rational and `float()` can be used to convert a rational to a float.

```julia
julia> x = 17//100;
num(x) # => 17
den(x) # => 100
float(x) # => 0.17
```

Complex numbers

There are two ways to define a complex number in Julia. First using the type definition Complex as its associated constructor `complex()`.

```julia
c = complex(1, 2); typeof(c) # => Complex{Float64};
```

Because the complex number consists of an ordered pair of two reals, its size is `complex128`. Similarly `complex64` has `Float32` arguments and `complex32` has `Float16` arguments.

The number `Complex(0.0,1.0)` corresponds to the imaginary number i, that is.`sqrt(-1.0)`, but Julia uses the symbol `im` rather the i to avoid confusion with a variable i, frequently used as an index, iterator.

Hence `Complex(1, 2)` is exactly equivalent to `1 + 2*im`, but normally the `*` operator is omitted and this would be expressed as `1 + 2im`.

The complex number supports all the normal arithmetic operations:

```
julia> c = 1 + 2im; d = 3 + 4im; c*d # => -5 + 10im
julia> c/d # => 0.44 + 0.08im
```

Also complex functions `real()`, `imag()`, `conj()`, `abs()`, and `angle()`.

`abs` and `angle` can be used to convert the complex arguments to polar form, that is:

```
julia> c = 1 + 2im; abs(c) # => 2.23606
julia> angle(c) # => 1.107148 (radians)
```

Complex versions of many mathematical apply:

```
julia> c = 1 + 2im;
julia> sin(c) = 3.1657 + 1.9596im;
julia>log(c) # => 0.8047 + 1.10715im;
Julia>sqrt(c) # => 1.272 + 0.78615im
```

Juliasets

The Julia documentation provides the example of generating a Mandelbrot set. Given the name of the language we will instead look at the code to create a related fractal - the Juliaset.

Both the Mandelbrot set and Julia set (for a given constant `z0`) are the sets of all z (complex numbers) for which the iteration `z → z*z + z0` does not diverge to infinity. The Mandelbrot set is those `z0` for which the Julia set is connected.

We create a file `jset.jl` and its contents define the function to generate a Julia set:

```
function juliaset(z, z0, nmax::Int64)
for n = 1:nmax
        if abs(z) > 2 (return n-1) end
        z = z^2 + z0
end
return nmax
end
```

Here z and z0 are complex values and nmax is the number of trials to make before returning. If the modulus of the complex number z gets above 2 then it can be shown that it will increase without limit.

The function returns the number of iterations until the modulus test succeeds or else nmax.

Also we will write a second file pgmfile.jl to handle displaying the Julia set:

```
function create_pgmfile(img, outf::String)
  s = open(outf, "w")
  write(s, "P5\n")
  n, m = size(img)
  write(s, "$m $n 255\n")
   for  i=1:n, j=1:m
     p = img[i,j]
   write(s, uint8(p))
  end
  close(s)
end
```

Although we will not be looking in any depth at graphics until *Chapter 7, Graphics* it is quite easy to create a simple disk file using the portable bitmap (netpbm) format. This consists of a "magic" number P1 - P6, followed on the next line by the image height, width and a maximum color value which must be greater than 0 and less than 65536; all of these are ASCII values not binary.

Then follows the image values (height x width) which may be ASCII for P1, P2, P3 or binary for P4, P5, P6. There are three different types of portable bitmap; B/W (P1/P4), Grayscale (P2/P5) and Colour (P3/P6).

The function create_pgmfile() creates a binary grayscale file (magic number = P5) from an image matrix where the values are written as Uint8. Notice that the for loop defines the indices i, j in a single statement with correspondingly only one end statement. The image matrix is output in column order which matches the way it is stored in Julia.

So the main program looks like:

```
include("jset.jl")
include("pgmfile.jl")
h = 400; w = 800; M = Array(Int64, h, w);
```

```
c0 = -0.8+0.16im;
pgm_name = "juliaset.pgm";

t0 = time();
for  y=1:h, x=1:w
  c = complex((x-w/2)/(w/2),  (y-h/2)/(w/2))
  M[y,x] = juliaset(c, c0, 256)
end
t1 = time();
create_pgmfile(M, pgm_name);
print("Written $pgm_name\nFinished in $(t1-t0) seconds.\n");
```

Consider how the previous code works:

1. We define an array M of type Int64 to hold the return values from the juliaset function.

2. The constant c0 is arbitrary, different values of c0 will produce different Julia sets.

3. The starting complex number is constructed from the (x, y) coordinates and scaled to the half width.

4. We 'cheat' a little by defining the maximum number of iterations as 256. This is because we are writing byte values (Uint8) and the value which remains bounded will be 256 and since overflow values wrap around will be output as 0 (black).

The script defines a main program in a function jmain():

```
julia>jmain
Written juliaset.pgm
Finished in 0.458 seconds # => (on my laptop)
```

The following screenshot shows the resulting image:

Composite types

A composition type is a collection of named fields, grouped together and treated as a single entity; these are termed records and structures in some programming languages.

If the type can also have functions (methods) associated with them the resulting collection is termed an object and the languages which support them (Java, C++, Python, Ruby, and so on) as object-oriented.

In Julia, functions are not bundled up with the data structures they operate on. The choice of the method a function uses is termed dispatch. When the types of ALL of a function's arguments are considered when determining the method employed, this is termed multiple dispatch and Julia uses this rather than the single dispatch we associated with object methods. We will be considering the implication of multiple dispatch in detail in the next chapter.

Composite type details are defined with the `type` keyword, followed by a list of field names, optionally annotated with the `::` operator and terminated with `end`. If the type of the field is not specified `Any` is assumed.

Consider a simple type definition for membership of a meetup group:

```
type Member
    fullname::ASCIIString
    email::ASCIIString
```

```
    meetup::ASCIIString

    age::Int

    organiser::Bool

    mobile::ASCIIString

end
```

me = ("Malcolm Sherrington", "malcolm@ljuug.org", "London Julia User Group", 55, true, "07777 555555")

julia> names(me)

6-element Array{Any,1}: # => [:fullname,:email,:group,:mobile,:organiser, :mobile]

julia>me.fullname #=> Malcolm Sherrington"

julia>me.mobile #=> "07777 555555"   (-- not really my number --

More about matrices

Previously we looked at simple operations with two-dimensional arrays and two-dimensional matrices.

In this section I will also discuss some further topics to cover multi-dimensional arrays, broadcasting and of handling sparse arrays but first I wish to introduce the concept of vectorized and devectorized code.

Vectorized and devectorized code

Consider the following code to add two vectors:

```
function vecadd1(a,b,c,N)
  for i = 1:N
    c = a + b
  end
end


function vecadd2(a,b,c,N)
  for i = 1:N, j = 1:length(c)
    c[j] = a[j] + b[j]
  end
end


julia> A = rand(2); B = rand(2); C = zeros(2);
```

```
julia> @elapsed vecadd1(A,B,C,100000000)
@elapsed vecadd1(A,B,C,100000000)  # => 18.418755286

julia> @elapsed vecadd2(A,B,C,100000000)
@elapsed vecadd2(A,B,C,100000000)  # => 0.524002398
```

Why the difference in timings? The function vecadd1() uses the array plus operation to perform the calculation whereas vecadd2() explicitly loops through the arrays and performs a series of scalar additions. The former is an example of vectorized coding and the latter devectorized, the current situation in Julia is that devectorized code is much quicker than vectorized.

With languages such as R, MATLAB, and Python (using NumPy) vectorized code is faster than devectorized but the reverse is the case in Julia. The reason is that in R (say) vectorization is actually a thin-wrapper around native-C code and since Julia performed is similar to C, calculations which are essentially concerned JUST with array operations will be comparable with those in Julia.

There is little doubt that coding with vector operations is neater and more readable and the designers of Julia are aware of the benefit of improving on timings for vector operations. That it has not been done is tantamount to the difficulty in optimizing code under all circumstances.

Multidimensional arrays

To illustrate the indexing and representation of arrays of higher dimensions, let us generate a three-dimensional array of 64 random numbers laid out in a 4 by 4 by 4 arrangement:

```
julia> A = rand(4,4,4)
4x4x4 Array{Float64,3}:
[:, :, 1] =
0.522564  0.852847  0.452363  0.444234
0.992522  0.450827  0.885484  0.0693068
0.378972  0.365945  0.757072  0.807745
0.383636  0.383711  0.304271  0.389717

[:, :, 2] =
0.570806  0.912306  0.358262  0.494621
0.810382  0.235757  0.926146  0.915814
0.634989  0.196174  0.773742  0.158593
```

```
0.700649   0.843975   0.321075   0.306428


[:, :, 3] =
0.638391   0.606747   0.15706     0.241825
0.492206   0.798426   0.86354     0.715799
0.971428   0.200663   0.00568161  0.0868379
0.936388   0.183021   0.0476718   0.917008


[:, :, 4] =
0.252962   0.432026   0.817504   0.274034
0.164883   0.209135   0.925754   0.876917
0.125772   0.998318   0.593097   0.614772
0.865795   0.204839   0.315774   0.520044
```

- Use of slice `:` to display the 3-D matrix
- Can reshape this into a 8x8 2-D matrix
- Values are ordered by the third index, then the second and finally the first

Notice that this can be recast into a two-dimensional array (that is, a matrix) by using the `reshape()` function:

```
julia> B = reshape(A,8,8)
8x8 Array{Float64,2}:
0.522564   0.452363    0.570806   0.358262   ...   0.15706      0.252962
0.817504
0.992522   0.885484    0.810382   0.926146         0.86354      0.164883
0.925754
0.378972   0.757072    0.634989   0.773742         0.00568161   0.125772
0.593097
0.383636   0.304271    0.700649   0.321075         0.0476718    0.865795
0.315774
0.852847   0.444234    0.912306   0.494621         0.241825     0.432026
0.274034
0.450827   0.0693068   0.235757   0.915814   ...   0.715799     0.209135
0.876917
0.365945   0.807745    0.196174   0.158593         0.0868379    0.998318
0.614772
0.383711   0.389717    0.843975   0.306428         0.917008     0.204839
0.520044
```

Similarly we can reshape the array A into a one-dimensional array:

```
julia> C = reshape(A,64); typeof(C) # => Array{Float64,1}
julia> transpose(C) ; # we can also write this as  C'
1x64 Array{Float64,2}:
0.522564  0.992522  0.378972  0.383636  …  0.876917  0.614772  0.520044
```

The reshaped array C is of a single dimension but its transpose has two. So the former is a vector and the latter a matrix.

Broadcasting

We saw earlier that it was possible to carry out binary operations on individual elements of two arrays by using the operators .+. .*, and so on.

It is sometimes useful to perform operations on arrays of different sizes, such as adding a vector to each column of a matrix. One way to do this is to replicate the vector to the size of the matrix and then apply a .+ operation but this becomes inefficient when the matrix is large.

Julia provides a function broadcast(), which expands singleton dimensions in array arguments to match the corresponding dimension in the other array without using extra memory and applies the given function element-wise.

The following code generates a 4x3 matrix of Gaussian random numbers, adds 1 to each element and then raises elements of each *row* to the power 1,2,3,4 respectively:

```
julia> P = randn(4,3)
4x3 Array{Float64,2}:
  0.859635  -1.05159   1.05167
  0.680754  -1.97133   0.556587
 -0.913965   1.05069  -0.215938
  0.165775   1.72851  -0.884942

julia> Q = [1,2,3,4];
4-element Array{Int64,1}:

julia> broadcast(^,P + 1.0,Q)
4x3 Array{Float64,2}:
  1.85963      -0.0515925  2.05167
```

2.82494	0.943481	2.42296
0.000636823	8.62387	0.482005
1.84697	55.4247	0.000175252

Sparse matrices

Normal matrices are sometimes referred to as 'dense', which means that there is an entry for cell[i,j]. In cases where most cell values are, say, 0 this is inefficient and it is better to implement a scheme of tuples: (i,j,x) where x is the value referenced by i and j.

These are termed sparse matrices and we can create a sparse matrix by:

```
S1 = sparse(I, J, X[, m, n, combine])
S2 = sparsevec(I, X[, m, combine])
S3 = sparsevec(D::Dict[, m])
```

Where S1 of will dimensions m x n and S[I[k], J[k]] = X[k].

If m and n are given they default to max(I) and max(J). The combine function is used to combine duplicates and if not provided, duplicates are added by default.

S2 is a special case where a sparse vector is created and S3 uses an associative array (dictionary) to provide the same thing. The sparse vector is actually an m x 1 size matrix and in the case of S3 row values are keys from the dictionary and the nonzero values are the values from the dictionary (see the section *Dictionaries, sets, and others* for more information on associative arrays).

Sparse matrices support much of the same set of operations as dense matrices but there are a few special functions which can be applied. For example spzeros(), spones, speye() are the counterparts of zeros(), ones(), and eye() and random number arrays can be generated by sprand() and sprandn():

```
julia> T = sprand(5,5,0.1)

# The 0.1 means only 10% for the numbers generated will be deemed as
nonzero

5x5 sparse matrix with 3 Float64 nonzeros:
    [1, 1]  =  0.0942311
    [3, 3]  =  0.0165916
    [4, 5]  =  0.179855


julia> T*T
```

```
5x5 sparse matrix with 2 Float64 non-zeros:
    [1, 1]  =   0.00887949
    [3, 3]  =   0.000275282
```

The function `full()` converts the sparse matrix to a dense one:

```
julia> S = full(T); typeof(S) # => 5x5 Array{Float64,2}
```

Data arrays and data frames

Users of R will be aware of the success of data frames when employed in analyzing datasets, a success which has been mirrored by Python with the `pandas` package. Julia too adds data frame support through use of a package `DataFrames`, which is available on GitHub, in the usual way.

The package extends Julia's base by introducing three basic types:

- `NA`: An indicator that a data value is missing
- `DataArray`: An extension to the `Array` type that can contain missing values
- `DataFrame`: A data structure for representing tabular datasets

It is such a large topic that we will be looking at data frames in some depth when we consider statistical computing in *Chapter 4, Interoperability*.

However, to get a flavor of processing data with these packages:

```
julia> Pkg.add("DataFrames")
# if not already done so, adding DataFrames will add the DataArray and
Blocks framework too.
julia> using DataFrames
julia> d0 = @data([1.,3.,2.,NA,6.])
5-element DataArray{Float64,1}:
 1.0
 3.0
 2.0
  NA
6.0
```

Common operations such as computing `mean(d)` or `var(d)` [variance] will produce `NA` because of the missing value in `d[4]`:

```
julia>isna(d0[4])   # => true
```

We can create a new data array by removing all the NA values and now statistical functions can be applied as normal:

```
julia> d1 = removeNA(d0) # => 4-element Array{Float64,1}
julia> (mean(d1), var(d1))  # => (3.0,4.66667)
```

Notice that if we try to convert a data array to a normal array, this will fail for d0 because of the NA values but will succeed for d1:

```
julia> convert(Array,d0) # =>MethodError(convert,(Array{T,N},[1.0,3.0,2.0
,NA,6.0]))
julia> convert(Array,d1) # => 4-element Array{Float64,1}:
```

Dictionaries, sets, and others

In addition to arrays, Julia supports associative arrays, sets and many other data structures. In this section we will introduce a few.

Dictionaries

Associative arrays consist of collections of (key, values) pairs. In Julia associative arrays are called dictionaries (Dicts).

Let us look at a simple datatype to hold a user's credentials: ID, password, e-mail, and so on. We will not include a username as this will be the key to a credential datatype. In practice this would not be a great idea, as users often forget their usernames as well as their passwords!

To implement this we use a simple module. This includes a type and some functions which operate on that type. Note the inclusion of the export statement which makes the type UserCreds and the functions visible.

```
moduleAuth

typeUserCreds
   uid::Int
   password::ASCIIString
  fullname::ASCIIString
  email::ASCIIString
  admin::Bool
end

function matchPwds(_mc::Dict{ASCIIString,UserCreds}, _
name::ASCIIString, _pwd::ASCIIString)
```

```
        return (_mc[_name].password == base64(_pwd) ? true : false)
    end

    isAdmin(_mc::Dict{ASCIIString,UserCreds}, _name::ASCIIString) = _mc[_
    name].admin;
    exportUserCreds, matchPwds, isAdmin;

    end
```

We can use this to create an empty authentication array (AA) and add an entry for myself. We will be discussing security and encryption later, so at present we'll just use the base64() function to scramble the password:

```
julia> using Auth

julia> AA = Dict{ASCIIString,UserCreds}();

julia> AA["malcolm"] = UserCreds(101,base64("Pa55word"),"Malcolm
Sherrington","malcolm@myemail.org",true);

julia>println(matchPwds(AA, "malcolm", "Pa55word") ? "OK" : "No, sorry")

OK
```

Adding the user requires the scrambling of the password by the user, otherwise matchPwds will fail.

To overcome this we can override the default constructor UserCreds() by adding an internal constructor inside the type definition - this is an exception to the rule that type definitions can't contain functions, since clearly it does not conflict with the requirement for multiple dispatch.

The using Auth statement looks for auth.jl in directories on the LOAD_PATH but will also include the current directory. On a Linux system where v"0.3" is installed on /opt typically would be:

```
julia>println(LOAD_PATH)

Union(UTF8String,ASCIIString)

["/opt/julia//usr/local/share/julia/site/v0.3","/opt/julia/usr/share/
julia/site/v0.3"]
```

We can add to the LOAD_PATH with push!:

```
Julia>push!(LOAD_PATH, "/home/malcolm/jlmodules); # => if we add this
statement to the startup file .juliarc.jlit will happen whenever Julia
starts up.
```

An alternative way to define the dictionary is adding some initial values:

```
julia> BB = ["malcolm" =>UserCreds(101,base64("Pa55word"),

"Malcolm Sherrington","malcolm@myemail.org",true)];
```

So the values can be referenced via the key:

```
julia> me = BB["malcolm"]
UserCreds(101,"UGE1NXdvcmQ=",

"Malcolm Sherrington","malcolm@myemail.org",true)
```

The . notation is used to reference the fields:

```
julia>me.fullname  # => "Malcolm Sherrington"
```

```
julia> for who in keys(BB) println( BB[who].fullname) end
Malcolm Sherrington
```

Attempting to retrieve a value with a key does not exist, such as AA["james"], will produce an error. We need to trap this in the module routines such as matchPwds and isAdmin using the try / catch / finally syntax.

So the isAdmin function in auth.jl could be rewritten as:

```
function isAdmin2(_mc::Dict{ASCIIString,UserCreds}, _
name::ASCIIString)
    check_admin::Bool = false;
    try
        check_admin = _mc[_name].admin
    catch
        check_admin = false
    finally
        return check_admin
    end
end
```

Sets

A set is a collection of distinct objects and the "Bulls and Cows" example earlier could have been implemented using sets rather than strings. Julia implements its support for sets in Base.Set (file: set.jl) and the underlying data structure is an associative array.

The basic constructor creates a set with elements of type `Any`, supplying arguments will determine (restrict) the `Set` type:

```
julia> S0 = Set(); # => Set{Any}()
julia> S1 = Set(1,2,4,2); # => Set{Int64}(4,2,1)
```

Elements can be added to a set using the `push!()` function; recall `!` implies that the data structure is altered:

```
julia> push!(S0,"Malcolm"); push!(S0,21); # => Set{Any}("Malcolm",21)
julia> push!(S1,"Malcolm"); # =>MethodError(convert,(Int64,"Malcolm") ,
since set elements need to be type {Int64}
```

The usual set operations apply such as union, intersection, difference (`setdiff()`) and complement. It is possible to test for subset, note that:

```
julia>  S0 = Set(1.0,2.5,4.0); S1 = Set(1.0); issubset(S1,S0) # => true
julia>  S0 = Set(1.0,2.5,4.0); S1 = Set(1); issubset(S1,S0)   # => false
```

When dealing with integers there is a special type of set `IntSet` which produces an ordered set:

```
julia> K = IntSet(2,2,3,1,5,13,7,3,11) # =>IntSet(1, 2, 3, 5, 7, 11, 13)
```

Normal sets of type `{Int}` can be mixed with an `{IntSet}` and the result is a regular set not an `IntSet`:

```
julia> L = Set(3,1,11)
julia>setdiff(K,L) # => 5-element Array{Int64,1}:  (2, 3, 7, 11, 13)
```

Other data structures

The package `DataStructures` implements a rich bag of data structures including deques, queues, stacks, heaps, ordered sets, linked lists, digital trees, and so on.

The `Deque` type is a double-ended queue with allows insertion and removal of elements at both ends of a sequence.

The `Stack` and `Queue` types are based on the `Deque` type and provide interfaces for FILO and FIFO access respectively. `Deques` expose the `push!()`, `pop!()`, `shift!()`, and `unshift!()` functions.

A stack will use `push!()` and `pop!()` to add and retrieve data, a queue will use `push!()` and `unshift!()`. Queues encapsulate these processes as `enqueue!()` and `dequeue!()`.

Consider the following simple example to illustrate using stacks and queues:

```julia
julia> usingDataStructures
julia> S = Stack(Char,100); # => Stack{Deque{Char}}(Deque [])
julia> Q = Queue(Char,100); # => Queue{Deque{Char}}(Deque [])
julia> greet = "Here's looking at you kid!";
julia> for i = 1:endof(greet)
  push!(S,greet[i])   enqueue!(Q,greet[i])end
julia> for i = 1:endof(greet) print(pop!(S)) end
!dikuoy ta gnikool s'ereH
julia> for i = 1:endof(greet) print(dequeue!(Q)) end
```

Here's looking at you kid!

Summary

In this chapter we began looking at programming in Julia with a consideration of various scalar, vector and matrix data types comprising integers, real numbers, characters and strings, as well as the operators acting upon them.

We then moved on to more data types such as rational numbers, big integers and floats and complex numbers.

Finally we looked at some complex data structures such as data arrays, data frames, dictionaries and sets.

The next chapter follows on with a discussion of user-defined data types and introduces the idea of multiple dispatch, which is a central feature within the Julia language.

3
Types and Dispatch

In this chapter and the next, we will discuss the features that make Julia appealing to the data scientist and the scientific programmer.

Julia was conceived to meet the frustrations of the principal developers with the existing programming languages; it is well designed and beautifully written. Moreover, much of the code is written in Julia, so it is available for inspection and change. Although we do not advocate modifying much of the base code (also known as *the standard library*), it is there to look at and learn from.

Much of this book is aimed at the analyst, with some programming skills and the jobbing programmer, so we will postpone the guts of the Julia system until the last chapter when we consider package development and contributing to the Julia community.

Functions

We have met functions in previous chapters and know how a `function()` ... `end` block works and that there is a convenient one-line syntax for the simplest of cases:

That is, `sq(x) = x*x` is exactly equivalent to the following:

```
function sq(x)
   y = x*x
   return y
end
```

The variable `y` is not needed (of course). It is local to the `sq()` function and has no existence outside the function call. So, the last statement could be written as `return x*x` or even just as `x*x`, since functions in Julia return their last value.

First-class objects

Functions are first-class objects in Julia. This allows them to be assigned to other identifiers, passed as arguments to other functions, returned as the value from other functions, stored as collections, and applied (mapped) to a set of values at runtime.

The argument list consists of a set of dummy variables, and the data structure using the () notation is called a tuple. By default, the arguments are of type {Any}, but explicit argument types can be specified, which aids the compiler in assigning memory and optimizing the generated code.

So, the preceding sq(x) function would work with any data structures where the * operator is defined as in the form sq(x::Int) = x*x and would only work for integers.

Surprisingly, perhaps, sq() does work for strings since the * operator is used for string concatenation rather than +.

```julia
julia> sq(x) = x*x
julia> sq(" Hello ") ; # =>" Hello Hello "
```

To apply a function to a list of values, we can use the map() construct. Let's slightly modify the sq() function by using the .* operator instead of *. For scalars, this has no effect, but we can now operate with vectors and matrices.

```julia
julia> sq(x) = x.*x
julia> map(sqAny[1, 2.0, [1,2,3]])
3-element Array{Any,1}:
1
4.0
[1,4,9]
```

Now, sq() will not work on strings, but since operators in Julia can be expressed in both infix and functional notations, the function can be easily rectified by defining the following:

```julia
julia> .*(s1::String, s2::String) = string(s1,s2)
.* (generic function with 25 methods)
```

Now, our revised sq() function will accept strings as well.

Notice the output from the operator overload: .* (generic function with 25 methods).

This is because before this call, there were 24 methods as defined by the standard library and possibly overloads due to package addition. We can list the methods of a function by using the methods() call:

```julia
julia> methods(.*)
# 25 methods for generic function ".*":
.*(x::Real,r::Ranges{T}) at range.jl:293
.*(r::Ranges{T},x::Real) at range.jl:294
.*{T<:Number,S<:Number}(r::Ranges{T<:Number},s::Ranges{S<:Number}) at range.jl:324
.*(x::Number,y::Number) at operators.jl:80
 .  .  .  .

 .  .  .  .

 .  .  .  .
.*(s1::String,s2::String) at none:1
```

We can see that not only does this list the methods for which .*() is defined, but it also lists the modules in which the definition occurs and the line number. Our definition for strings is there too but at the console not in a file.

It may well be that previously, we defined the sq() function in order to apply it to the vector. Julia has a special syntax to set up an anonymous function by using the -> operator.

```julia
julia> map(x -> x.*x, ([1 2 3]))
1x3 Array{Int64,2}:
 1 4 9
```

Let's finish this section with an example other than squaring data structures by defining a function that computes the Hailstone sequence of numbers.

These can be generated from a starting positive integer n by the following rules:

- If n is 1 then the sequence ends
- If n is even then the next n of the sequence = n/2
- If n is odd then the next n of the sequence = (3 * n) + 1

There is a conjecture according to Collatz, which states that the hailstone sequence for any starting number always terminates.

```
function hailstone(n)
  k = 1
  a = [n]
  while n > 1
    n = (n % 2 == 0) ? n >> 1 : 3n + 1
    push!(a,n)
    k += 1
  end

return (k,a)
end
julia> hailstone(17)
(13, [17,52,26,13,40,20,10,5,16,8,4,2,1])
julia> (m,s) = hailstone(1000)
(112, [1000,500,250,125,376,188,94,47,142  .  40,20,10,5,16,8,4,2,1])
julia> (m,s) = hailstone(1000000)
(153, [1000000,500000,250000,125000,62500,31250,  .  10,5,16,8,4,2,1])
```

There is no obvious pattern to the number of iterations in order to converge, but all integer values seem to do so eventually.

```
for i = 1000:1000:6000
  (m,s) = hailstone(i)
  println("hailstone($i) => $m iterations")
end
hailstone(1000) # => 112 iterations
hailstone(2000) # => 113 iterations
hailstone(3000) # => 49 iterations
hailstone(4000) # => 114 iterations
hailstone(5000) # => 29 iterations
hailstone(6000) # => 50 iterations
```

The function starts by creating an array with the single entry n and sets the counter (k) to 1. The `while` – end block will loop until the value of n reaches 1, and each new value is pushed onto the array. Since this effectively modifies the array, by increasing its length, the convention of using `!` is used.

The statement `(n % 2 == 0)? n >> 1 : 3n + 1` encapsulates the algorithm's logic.

`(condition) ? statement-1 : statement-2` is a shorthand for an `if else end` block, initially seen in C but borrowed by many languages including Julia.

`n >> 1` is a bitshift left, so it effectively halves n when n is even.

The sequence continues until an odd prime occurs, when it is tripled and one added, which results in a new even number and the process continues. While it is easy to see why the conjecture is true, the jury is still out on whether it has been proved or not.

It is worth noting that Julia orders its logical statements from left to right, so the operator or (`||`) is equivalent to `orelse` and the operator and (`&&`) to `andthen`.

This leads to another couple of constructs, termed short-circuit evaluation, becoming popular with Julia developers:

```
(condition) || (statement) # => if condition then true else statement
(condition) && (statement) # => if condition then statement else false
```

Notice that because the constructs return a value, this will be `true` for `||` if the condition is met and `false` for `&&` if it is not.

Finally, the function returns two values, namely the number of iterations and the generated array, which must be assigned to a tuple.

Passing arguments

Most function calls in Julia can involve a set of one or more arguments, and it is possible to designate an argument as being optional and provide a default value.

It is useful if the number of arguments may be of varying length and we may wish to specify an argument by name rather than by its position in the list.

How this is done is discussed as follows:

Default and optional arguments

In the previous examples, all arguments to the function were required and the function call was produced unless all were provided. If the argument type is not given, a type of Any is passed. It is up to the body or the function to treat an Any argument for all the cases, which might occur or possibly trap the error and raise an exception.

For example, multiplying two integers results in an integer and two real numbers in a real number. If we multiply an integer with a real number, we get a real number. The integer is said to be promoted to a real number.

Similarly, when a real number is multiplied with a complex number, the real number is promoted to a complex number and the result is a complex number.

When a real number and an array are multiplied, the result will be a real array, unless of course, it is an array of complex numbers.

However, when two arrays are multiplied, we get an exception raised, similar to the following:

```
julia> a = [1.0,2,3]; println(sq(a))
ERROR: '*' has no method matching *(::Array{Float64,1},
::Array{Float64,1})

 in sq at none:1
```

Typing of arguments is a good idea not only because it restricts function behavior but also because it aids the compiler. Just how this is done in Julia without overloading a function for every possible combination of argument types, we will see later in this chapter.

Sometimes, we wish for some (or all) of a function's argument to take default values if they are not provided. This is done by using an arg = value syntax, such as the following:

```
f(x, p = 0.0) = exp(p*x)*sin(x);
t = linspace(0.0,8pi);
w = zeros(length(t));
for i = 1:length(w) w[i] = f(t[i], 0.1) end
using PyPlot
plot (t, w)
```

The following figure shows a plot of this function (p = 0.1) using PyPlot to display the result. If p = 0.0 (default), clearly, we just get a sine wave:

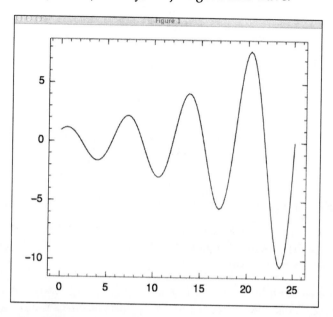

Notice in the call, p is given the value p=0.1; however, we could still pass a value such as p = 3 as this would be promoted in the function body.

Let us now look at the methods for f:

```
julia> methods(f)
# 2 methods for generic function "f":
f(x) at none:1
f(x,p) at none:1
```

In fact, we could pass a rational number or even a complex number:

```
julia> f(2.0,3//4);  # => 0.22313016
julia> f(2.0,2+3im); # => 0.01758613 + 0.0051176733im
```

Because of the complex argument, the result in the second case is a complex number too.

Optional arguments must come after the required ones as otherwise the meaning would be ambiguous. Further, when there are two optional parameters, values for the all preceding ones must be provided in order to specify the ones further down the list.

So, we define the following linear function: `f(x, y , a=2.5, b=4.0, c=1.0) =` `a*x + y *b +c`.

```
julia> f(1,1);      # =>7.5 : all parameters are defaulted
julia> f(1,1,2);    #=> 7.0 : sets equal to 2.0
julia> f(1,1,2.5,4.0,3.0); # => 9.5
```

This sets `c = 3.0`, but both `a` and `b` must be specified too.

 Therefore, for long argument lists, it is better to use named parameters rather than simple optional ones.

Variable argument list

First, we can look at the case where we wish to define a function that can take a variable number of arguments. We know that such a function exists, and plus (+) is an example of one such function.

The definition takes the following form: `g(a,b,c...)`, where `a` and `b` are required arguments but `g` can also take zero or more arguments represented by `c...` In this case, `c` will be returned as a tuple of values as the following code illustrates:

```
function g(a ,b, c...)
  n = length(c)
  if  n > 0 then
    x = zeros(n)
    for i = 1:n
       x[i] = a + b*c[i]
    end
      return x
  else
    return nothing
  end
end
julia> g(1.,2.); # => return 'nothing'
julia> g(1.,2.,3.,4.)
2-element Array{Float64,1}: #=> [ 7.0, 9.0 ]
```

The function needs to be sensible in terms of its arguments, but a call using rational numbers will work with this definition as they get promoted to real numbers:

```julia
julia> g(1.0, 2.0, 3//5, 5//7)
2-element Array{Float64,1}:
 2.2
 2.42857
```

Since functions are first-class objects these may be passed as arguments, so slightly modifying the definition of g gives a (very poor) map function:

```julia
function g(a ,b...)
   n = length(b)
   if n == 0 then
      return nothing
   else
   x = zeros(n)
   for i = 1:n
     x[i] = a(b[i])
   end
    return x
   end
end
julia> g(x -> x*x, 1. , 2., 3., 4.)
4-element Array{Float64,1}:
  1.0
  4.0
  9.0
 16.0
```

Note that in the cases where there were no variable arguments, I chose to return nothing. This is a special variable defined by Julia of type Nothing. We will meet another in the next chapter, NA.

Named parameters

Previously, we defined a linear function in two variables (x, y) with three default parameters (a, b, c) but met the problem that to set parameter c, we need to supply values for a and b.

To do this, we can use the following syntax:

```julia
julia> f(x, y; a=2.5, b=4.0, c=1.0) =  a*x + b*y + c;
julia> f(1.,1.,c=1.); # => 7.5
```

The only difference is that the final three arguments are separated from the first two by a semicolon rather than a comma. Now, a, b, and c are named parameters, and we can pass the value of c without knowing those of a and b.

We can combine variable arguments and named parameters in a meaningful way as follows:

```julia
function h(x...;  mu=0.0, sigma=1.0)
  n = length(x)
  (n == 0) ? (return nothing) : begin
    a = zeros(n);
    [a[i] = (mu + sigma*rand())*x[i] for i = 1:n]
    a
  end
end
julia> h(1.0,2.0,3.0, sigma=0.5)
3-element Array{Float64,1}:
 0.342006
 0.70062
 1.47813
```

So, h returns a Gaussian variable with mean mu and standard deviation sigma.

Scope

In the previous example, we used the ?: notation as a shorthand for if-then-else. However, it was necessary to wrap the code following the colon in begin-end.

This is a form of block, as are f statements and for and while loops. In fact, Julia signals the end of the most recent block by way of the end statement.

Other examples of blocks that we have met so far are those introduced by the `module`, `function`, and `type` definitions and by the `try` and `catch` statements.

The question we need to consider is as follows: If a variable is declared inside a block, is it visible outside it? This is controlled by Julia's scoping rules.

Since `if-then-else` or `begin-end` blocks do not affect a variable's visibility, it is better to refer to the current scope rather than the current block.

Certain constructs will introduce new variables into the current innermost scope. When a variable is introduced into a scope, it is also inherited by an inner scope unless the scope explicitly overrides it.

The following rules are reasonably clear:

- A `local` or `const` declaration introduces a new local variable
- A `global` declaration makes a variable in the current scope (and inner scopes) refer to the global variable of that name
- A function's arguments are introduced as new local variables into the scope of the function's body
- An assignment of x = 1 (say) introduces a new local variable x only if x is neither declared `global` nor introduced as `local` by any enclosing scope before or after the current line of code

Next, we clarify the last statement a function `f()` as follows:

```
function f()
   x = y = 0;
   while (x < 5)
      y = x += 1;
   end
   println(y)
end
f() ; # => 5


function f()
   x = y = 0;
   while (x <  5)
      local y = x += 1;
```

```
    end
    return y
end
f() ; # => 0 :
```

 Notice that the variable y in the while loop is local to it, and therefore, the value returned by the function is 0 not 5.

There is a further construct that Julia provides in passing anonymous function definitions as arguments, which is do - end and one that we will find convenient when working with the file I/O in the next chapter. Consider mapping an array to its squares when the value is 0.3 or more.

```
a = rand(5)
map(x -> begin
  if (x < 0.3)
    return(0)
  else
    return(x*x)
  end
end, a)
5-element Array{Real,1}:
# => [0.503944 , 0.711046, 0 , 0.214098 , 0]
map(a) do x
        if (x < 0.3)
          return(0)
        else
          return(x*x)
        end
end
5-element Array{Real,1}:
# => [0.503944 , 0.711046, 0 , 0.214098 , 0]
```

Both produce the same result, but the latter is cleaner and more compact. The use of the do x syntax creates an anonymous function with argument x and passes it as the first argument to map.

Similarly, do a,b would create a two-argument anonymous function and a plain do would declare that what follows is an anonymous function of the form () -> ....

 We should note that Julia does not (as yet) have a switch statement (as in C), which would be equivalent to successive if else statements. There is a package called Match.jl, which introduces a macro that will set up to generate multiple if else statements.

To illustrate this, let us consider the mathematicians' proof that all odd numbers are prime! We can code this concisely by using pattern matching as follows:

```
using Match

allodds(x) = @match x begin
  !isinteger(x) || iseven(x) || (x < 3) => "Not a valid choice"
  3 || 5 || 7 => "$x is prime"
  _ => "By induction all numbers are prime"
end
```

Running the preceding code on a select few gives the following:

```
for i in [1:2:9]
  @printf "%d : %s\n" i  allodds(i)
end

1 : Not a valid choice
3 : 3 is prime
5 : 5 is prime
7 : 7 is prime
9 : By induction all odd numbers are prime
```

The Queen's problem

Finally, I will introduce a function that we will use in the next chapter for timing macros. This is to solve the Queen's problem, which was first introduced by Max Bezzel in 1848, and the first solutions were published by Franz Nauck in 1850.

In 1972, Edsger Dijkstra used this problem to illustrate the power of what he called structured programming and published a highly detailed description of a depth-first backtracking algorithm.

The problem was originally to place 8 queens on a chessboard so that no queen could take any other, although this was later generated to *N* queens on an *N* × *N* board.

An analysis of the problem is given in Wikipedia. The solution to the case *N = 1* is trivial, and there are no solutions for *N = 2* or *3*. For a standard chessboard, there are 92 solutions, out of a possible 4.4 billion combinations of placing the queens randomly on the board, so an exhaustive solution is out of question.

The Julia implementation of the solution uses quite a few of the constructs that we have discussed:

```julia
qadd(board::Array{Vector{Int}},
  qrow::Vector{Int}) = push!(copy(board), qrow)


qhits(a::Array{Int}, b::Array{Int}) =
  any(a .== b) || abs(a-b)[1] == abs(a-b)[2]


qhit(qrow::Vector{Int}, board::Array{Vector{Int}}) =
any(map(x->qhits(qrow, x), board))


function qsolve(m, n=m, board=Array(Vector{Int}, 0))
  if n < 4
    return board
  end
  for px = 1:m
    for py = 1:m
      if !qhit([px, py], board)
        s = solve(m, n-1, qadd(board, [px, py]))
        s != nothing && return s
      end
    end
  end
  return nothing
end


qsolve(8)  # => 8-element Array{Array{Int64,1},1}:
  [1,1], [2,5], [3,8], [4,6], [5,3], [6,7], [7,2], [8,4]
```

The code has an array of vectors to represent the board but could be written using a matrix.

- `push!()`: This is used to recreate a copy of the board in `qadd()`
- `qhit()` uses `map()`: This is to apply an anonymous function to the board
- `qsolve()`: This is the main function that calls itself recursively and uses tree pruning to reduce the amount of computation involved

This computation slows down markedly with increasing n, and I'll use this function at the end of the chapter to give some benchmarks.

Julia's type system

Julia is not an object-oriented language, so when we speak of objects, they are a different sort of data structure from those in traditional O-O languages.

Julia does not allow types to have methods, so it is not possible to create subtypes that inherit methods. While this might seem restrictive, it does permit methods to use a multiple dispatch call structure rather than the single dispatch system employed in object-orientated ones.

Coupled with Julia's system of types, multiple dispatch is extremely powerful. Moreover, it is a more logical approach for data scientists and scientific programmers, and if for no other reason than exposing this to you, the analyst/programmer is a reason to use Julia. In fact, there are lots of other reasons as well, as we will see later.

A look at the rational type

The rational number type was introduced in the previous chapter, and like most of Julia, it is implemented in the language itself and the source is in `base/rational.jl` and is available to inspection. Because `Rational` is a base type, it does not need to be included explicitly and we can explore it immediately:

```
julia> names(Rational)
2-element Array{Symbol,1}:
 :num
 :den
```

The `names()` function lists what in object-orientated parlance would be termed properties but what Julia lists as an array of symbols. Julia uses the `:` character as a prefix to denote a symbol, and there will be much more to say on symbols when we consider macros.

`:num` corresponds to the numerator of the rational and `:den` to its denominator.

To see how we can construct `Rational`, we can use the `methods()` function as follows:

```
julia> methods(Rational)

# 3 methods for generic function "Rational":

Rational{T<:Integer}(n::T<:Integer,d::T<:Integer) at rational.jl:11

Rational(n::Integer,d::Integer) at rational.jl:12

Rational(n::Integer) at rational.jl:13
```

Obviously, we wish to construct rationals from integers not floating-point numbers, but in Julia, there are integers of different sizes ranging from `Int8` to `Int32`, and we have signed and unsigned types of integers.

Rather than providing a recipe for making a rational for every combination of these, Julia provides three ways that are generic and the `methods()` function helpfully lists the line in the source file in which they occur.

- `Rational(n::Integer)`: This is when there is a denominator of 1 (assumed not passed)
- `Rational(n::Integer, d::Integer)`: This is when both the numerator and the denominator are provided
- `Rational{T<:Integer}(n::T, d::T) = Rational{T}(n,d)`: This is called a parametric definition for all types, which are of the `Integer` (`Int8`, `Uint8`, ...) types

Parametric definitions are very useful for establishing the rules for manipulating types as we will see later.

The entire source is quite long, but the first few lines are informative and are reproduced here:

```
immutable Rational{T<:Integer} <: Real
  num::T
  den::T
  function Rational(num::T, den::T)
```

```
        num == den == 0 && error("invalid rational: 0//0")
        g = den < 0 ? -gcd(den, num) : gcd(den, num)
        new(div(num, g), div(den, g))
    end
end
Rational{T<:Integer}(n::T, d::T) = Rational{T}(n,d)
Rational(n::Integer, d::Integer) = Rational(promote(n,d)...)
Rational(n::Integer) = Rational(n,one(n))


//(n::Integer,  d::Integer ) = Rational(n,d)
//(x::Rational, y::Integer ) = x.num//(x.den*y)
//(x::Integer,  y::Rational) = (x*y.den)//y.num
//(x::Rational, y::Rational) = (x.num*y.den)//(x.den*y.num)
//(x::Complex,  y::Real     ) = complex(real(x)//y, imag(x)//y)
//(x::Real,     y::Complex ) = x*y'//real(y*y')


function //(x::Complex, y::Complex)
    xy = x*y'
    yy = real(y*y')
    complex(real(xy)//yy, imag(xy)//yy)
end
```

A rational number is defined using the `immutable` statement rather than `type`. This does not mean that a rational number once defined can't be changed, just that Julia makes it difficult.

```
Julia> r = 5//7; r.num = 3; println(r)
ERROR: type Rational is immutable
```

Although we said that type definitions can't contain methods: one that has the same name as the type is a special case and is called the (inner) constructor.

This is a recipe for how to build a datatype from its constituent parts. In the case of the rational, the constructor checks whether the denominator is zero, note the use of the short circuit form of evaluation terminating in an error statement (if true).

Otherwise, the constructor finds the **greatest common divisor** (GCD) of the denominator by the numerator in order to reduce the two numbers to their most primitive form. The special function called `new()` is called to return a value for the datatype.

Then, there are a number of outer constructors indicating the way to build rationals for different datatypes starting with the integer.

One other thing is that rational numbers can be defined for complex numbers as long as all of the real and imaginary parts of both complex numbers are integers. In fact, it is easy to achieve by multiplying the rational number with the complex conjugate of the denominator, which splits the number into a real (rational) and an imaginary (rational) part. Note that the use of `Real` in the definition refers to non-imaginary rather than floating-point numbers. Integers are a type of `Real` as are floats.

```julia
julia> (1+2im) / (3 + 4im) ;  # => 0.44 + 0.08im

julia> (1+2im) // (3 + 4im) ;  # => 11/25 + 2//25*im
```

The rest of the code in `rational.jl` deals with defining arithmetic operations on rationals. We will look at how this is done when discussing parametric types and multiple dispatch.

A vehicle datatype

Let us build a datatype from scratch, and as an example, let us look at data structures that describe vehicles and their ownership. This will be in a file called `vehicles.jl`, which needs to be added to the Julia environment by using the `include()` statement or encapsulated in a module.

```julia
type Contact
  name::String
  email::String
  phone::String
end
julia> methods(Contact)
# 1 methods for generic function "Contact":
Contact(name::String,email::String,phone::String)
```

All vehicles will have a person (or company) responsible for them. This provides the minimum information in terms of a name, e-mail, and phone number. All are strings and can be empty.

The definition creates default constructors that just define a new contact by supplying its arguments. To make some fields required or impose other restrictions on them, we need to provide an internal constructor.

```
function Contact(name::String, email::String, phone::String)
  length(name) == 0 && error("Need to provide a contact name")
  length(email) == 0 && length(phone) == 0 &&
    error("Need to provide either an email or a phone number")
  new(name, email, phone)
end
```

```
julia> methods(Contact)
# 1 method for generic function "Contact":
Contact(name::String,email::String,phone::String) at none:7
```

```
julia> me = Contact("","","")
ERROR: Need to provide a contact name
 in Contact at none:7
```

```
julia> me = Contact("malcolm","","")
ERROR: Need to provide either an email or a phone number
 in Contact at none:8
```

Now, we only have a single constructor and impose a compound rule that either the e-mail or the phone number must exist, as it is of little use to have a contact that we can't contact. Here, we could also impose maximum string lengths, which might be required if the data structure is eventually going to be saved as a database record.

```
abstract Vehicle
abstract Car <: Vehicle
abstract Bike <: Vehicle
abstract Boat <: Vehicle
abstract Powerboat <: Boat
```

This set of statements introduces a hierarchy of `abstract` types. These are types that do not have any attendant fields associated with them. At the top of the tree is `Vehicle`, and `Car`, `Bike`, and `Boat` are subtypes of `Vehicle`. Likewise, `Powerboat` is a subtype of `Boat` and implicitly of `Vehicle`.

The parent of any type can be shown by using the `super()` function and child types by using `subtypes()`:

```
super(Car); # => Vehicle
super(Powerboat) ; # => Boat
```

```
julia> subtypes(Vehicle)
3-element Array{Any,1}: ;# => [Bike, Boat, Car]
```

Subtypes in an `Any` array are only returned to one depth lower, so we do not know explicitly that a powerboat is a type of vehicle. We can use a different routine `subtypetree()`, which will provide the full breakdown of all subtypes not just the immediate children.

Now, we can start defining a few subtypes, which all define the actual makes of cars, bikes, and boats:

```
type Ford <: Car
  owner::Contact
  model::String
  fuel::String
  color::String
  engine_cc::Int64
  speed_mph::Float64
  function Ford(owner, model, engine_cc,speed_mph)
    new (owner,model,"Petrol","Black",engine_cc,speed_mph)
  end
end
type BMW <: Car
  owner::Contact
  model::String
  fuel::String
  color::String
  engine_cc::Int64
  speed_mph::Float64
```

```
  function BMW(owner,model,engine_cc,speed_mph)
    new (owner,model,"Petrol","Blue",engine_cc,speed_mph)
  end
end
type VW <: Car
  owner::Contact
  model::String
  fuel::String
  color::String
  engine_cc::Int64
  speed_mph::Float64
end
type MotorBike <: Bike
  owner::Contact
  model::String
  engine_cc::Int64
  speed_mph::Float64
end
type Scooter <: Bike
  owner::Contact
  model::String
  engine_cc::Int64
  speed_mph::Float64
end
type Yacht <: Boat
  owner::Contact
  model::String
  length_m::Float64
end
type Speedboat <: Powerboat
  owner::Contact
  model::String
  fuel::String
  engine_cc::Int64
  speed_knots::Float64
  length_m::Float64
end
```

These are called concrete types and are subclasses of the abstract type preceding them. However, further concrete types can't be obtained as subclasses from them.

All vehicles have an owner and a model, but these are defined in the concrete type rather than in the `Vehicle` type, as would be the case in an object-orientated language. Likewise, all cars have top speed, fuel type, engine capacity, etc., but these can't be inherited from `Car`.

The constructor for the `Ford` car imposes a restriction that the color (according to Henry Ford) has to be black and that the fuel is petrol. Further, we set the color of all BMWs as blue, which is not strictly true.

These are not immutable types, so they could be changed after they were constructed.

With these definitions, we can start to instantiate some variables corresponding to the vehicles and their owners.

```
malcolm = Contact("Malcolm","mal@abc.net","+44 7777 555999");

myCar = Ford(malcolm, "Model T", 1000, 50.0);

myBike = Scooter(malcolm, "Vespa", 125, 35.0);


james = Contact("James","jim@abc.net","+44 7777666888");

jmCar = BMW(james,"Series 500", 3200, 125.0);

jmCar.color = "Black";

jmBoat = Yacht(james,"Oceanis 44",14.6);

jmBike = MotorBike(james, "Harley", 850, 120.0);


david = Contact("David","dave@abc.net","+30 7777 222444");

dvCar = VW(david,"Golf", "diesel", "red", 1800, 85.0);

dvBoat = Speedboat(david,"Sealine 28","petrol", 600, 45.0, 8.2);
```

Note that James' BMW is black, so after creating the variable, I changed the color from blue to black by using the following code:

```
jmCar.color = "Black"
```

Given the type structure, we can already do something with these:

```
cs = [myCar, jmCar, dvCar]
3-element Array{Car,1}:
Ford(Contact("Malcolm","malcolm@abc.net","07777555999"),
    "Model-T","Petrol","Black",1000,50.0)
BMW(Contact("James","james@abc.net","07777666888"),
    "Series 500","Petrol","Black",3200,125.0)
VW(Contact("David","dave@abc.net","07777222444"),"Golf",
    "diesel","red",1800,85.0)
```

We can define the `cs` array since `Ford`, `BMW`, and `VW` are all subtypes of `Car`, and Julia creates the appropriate array and we can iterate over it as follows:

```
for c in cs
 who = c.owner.name
 model = c.model
 make = typeof(c);
 println("$who has a $make $model")
end
```

```
Malcolm has a Ford Model-T
James has a BMW series 500
David has a VW Golf
```

Similarly, we can define the vehicles that James owns as follows:

```
vs = [jmCar, jmBike, jmBoat]
```

This will create an `Any` array of the `Vehicle` type since it is the nearest common supertype, and we can use this array to list the vehicles as follows:

```
println("James owns the following:")
for v in vs
  model = v.model
  make = typeof(v)
  mtype = super(make)
  print("$mtype\t$make\t$model\n")
end
```

We can also define some functions using some of the type parameters. For example, we can find out if VW is quicker than BMW by defining the following function:

```
function isquicker(a::VW, b::BMW)
  if (a.speed_mph == b.speed_mph)
    return nothing
  else
    return(a.speed_mph > b.speed_mph ? a : b)
  end
end
```

Further, we can compare different types of vehicles, such as a boat and a bike, taking account of the fact that a boat's speed is expressed in knots and a bike's or a car's speed in miles per hour or kilometers per hour.

```
function isquicker(a::Speedboat, b::Scooter)
  const KNOTS_TO_MPH = 1.151
  a_mph = KNOTS_TO_MPH * a.speed_knots
  if (a_mph == b.speed_mph)
    return nothing
  else
    return(a_mph > b.speed_mph ? a : b)
  end
end
```

```
@printf "%s %s\n" isquicker(dvCar,jmCar) "has the faster car"
James has the faster car
```

```
@printf "The faster vehicle is the %s\n" isquicker(msBike,dsBoat)
The faster vehicle is the Sealine 28.
```

It is clear that there are a number of problems with this as it stands.

First although we can compare the speed of VW with BMW, we can't do this the other way round unless we define the following:

```
isquicker(a::BMW, b::VW) = isquicker(b,a)
```

Further, we are not able to compare two BMWs or two VWs nor any car with a Ford! While it would be possible to cover all the possibilities with only three types of car, it is hardly practicable to do this for all makes of car, let alone bikes and boats. Julia solves this by using parametric types that we will meet in the next section.

Secondly, we require all vehicles to have a speed field, and if defining rules by using parametric types, the speed field will need to be the same symbol (that is, have the same name) in each case.

Any defined function can check for the existence of a field before trying to use it, or alternatively, use a `try-catch` block to trap the error. The problem largely goes away if concrete types can inherit fields from their supertype(s).

The vehicle type and the accompanying constructors and function definitions are defined in the `vehicles.jl` file.

There is some merit in treating this as a module, and for this, we would add the following lines to the beginning of the file and terminate it with an `end` statement:

```
module Vehicles
export Contact, Vehicle, Car, MotorBike, Yacht, Powerboat, Boat
export Ford, BMW, VW, Scooter, Speedboat, isquicker
```

This is now accessed by means of the `using Vehicles` statement and will be picked up from the current folder or in a special array called `LOAD_PATH`.

Further, we can add our own folder(s) to this by using a `push!()` call as follows:

```
push!(LOAD_PATH,"/user/malcolm/jlmods).;  println(LOAD_PATH)
```

Putting this in the `.juliarc` file will ensure that it happens each time that Julia is started.

 Note that all the types and functions that we wish to be visible must be included in an `export` statement. This can come at the beginning of the module (as is usual) or the end, it does not matter.

Any function that is not exported can still be called and has to be explicitly referenced as follows: `Vehicles.islonger(jmBoat, dvBoat)`.

Modules can also have `using` statements, so the use of `myModule` implies that `myModule` will be available for resolving names as needed. It is possible to restrict this to a set of names such as `using myModule, myModule.fn2, myModule.fn3`, and this can be shortened to `using myModule: fn1, fn2, fn3`.

Modules can also use `import` statements to reference functions from other modules and `importall`, which will import all functions exported from a module rather than individual ones. The `import myModule: fn1, fn2, fn3` syntax is a shorthand for importing three functions from `myModule`.

Modules can also have `import` statements. All these support the same syntax as `using` but only operate on a single name at a time. Importing does not add modules to be searched the way using does and needs to have the functions to be imported with the `import` statement to be extended with new methods.

One last feature of incorporating our type system in a module is more a convenience than a necessity. When developing using the console REPL, any types defined are fixed, and once defined, we are cannot change them without restarting Julia and redefining them. However, modules can be reused and this will effectively redefine all that they contain including any defined types.

Typealias and unions

It is often convenient to introduce a new name for an already expressible type, and for this, Julia provides the `typealias` keyword. In terms of 1D and 2D arrays, we have seen the use of the `Vector` and `Matrix` terms; these are as follows:

```
typealias Vector{T} Array{T,1}
typealias Matrix{T} Array{T,2}
```

The `typealiase` keywords can be defined for parametric types `T`; these are discussed in the next section.

`Matrix{Float64}` is equivalent to writing `Array{Float64,2}`, and `Matrix` has as instances all `Array` objects where the second parameter (the number of dimensions) is 2, for all element types. In Julia, this allows one to write just `Matrix` for the abstract type including all 2D dense arrays of any element type.

Typealias is useful when defining the `umbrella` type as a union of simpler ones. Union types are extensively used in `Base`, and there are many examples in the code listing there. An example from `int.jl` is as follows:

```
typealias Signed64 Union(Int8,Int16,Int32,Int64)
typealias Unsigned64 Union(Uint8,Uint16,Uint32,Uint64)
typealias Integer64 Union(Signed64,Unsigned64)
```

Recall that in our vehicle type, we provided contact details as name, email, and phone type; however, alternatively, it might be more appropriate to use a postal address. To accommodate both, we can write the following:

```
type Address
  name::String
  street::String
  city::String
  country::String
  postcode::String
end


postal = Address("Malcolm Sherrington","1 Main Street",
  "London", "UK", "WC2N 9ZZ");


typealias Owner Union(Contact, Address)
```

The alias allows us to supply the owner field either as contact or postal details:

```
type Yacht <: Boat
  owner::Owner
  make::String
  length_m::Float64
end


y1 = Yacht(me,"Moody 36", 11.02)
Yacht(Contact("malcolm","malcolm@abc.com","07777555999"),
"Moody 36", 11.02)


y2 = Yacht(postal,"Dufour 44", 13.47)
Yacht(Address("Malcolm Sherrington","1 Main Street","London",
"UK","EC1A 9ZZ"), "Dufour 44". 13.47)
```

```
julia> c1.owner.name; # => "malcolm"

julia> c2.owner.name; # => "Malcolm Sherrington"


julia> c1.owner.email; # => "malcolm@abc.com"

julia> c2.owner.email
ERROR: type Address has no field email


julia> typeof(c1.owner); # => Contact

julia> typeof(c2.owner); # => Address

julia> isa(c1.owner,Contact); # =>   true

julia> isa(c1.owner,Address); # =>   false
```

Enumerations (revisited)

One problem with our vehicle type is that the fuel is defined as a string, whereas it would be better to restrict the choice to set of values. Previously, we discussed a macro that provides one approach to enumerations. In the absence of a preferred definition in Julia, various developers have adopted different strategies and I'll provide our own here.

First, we will use a vector of type {Any} to hold the enumerated values. This could be consts using integers or strings, but I'll restrict it to a list of symbols and create the vnum.jl file to hold the following:

```
typealias VecAny Array{Any,1}
function vnum(syms::Symbol...)
  A = {}
  for v in syms
    push!(A,v)
  end
  A
end
function vidx(A::VecAny, a::Symbol)
  for (i, v) in enumerate(A)
    if v == a then
      return (i - 1)
    end
    nothing
```

```
    end
  end
vin(A::VecAny, a::Symbol) = (vidx(A,a) >= 0 ? true : false)
```

vnum is created by pushing a variable list of symbols onto an empty `Any` vector. Additionally, there is a function called `vidx()`, which returns the position in the enumeration; holding with convention, this is zero-based, and a one-line `vin()` function checks whether a symbol is that of v-numeration.

We can use this to define our fuels types as follows:

```
fs = vnum(:NONE,:PETROL,:DIESEL,:LPG);
vidx(fs,:DIESEL);   # => 2
vin(fs,:NONE);      # => true
vin(fs,:GASOIL);    # => false
```

Further, we can now define a `Fuel` type to be used in `Vehicles` as follows:

```
type Fuel
  fuel
  function Fuel(fuel)
    fs = vnum(:NONE,:PETROL,:DIESEL,:LPG)
    vin(fs,fuel) ? new(fuel) : error(TypeError)
  end
end
```

Multiple dispatch

A function is an object that maps a tuple of arguments to a return value. In a case where the arguments are not valid, the function should handle the situation cleanly by catching the error and handling it or throw an exception.

When a function is applied to its argument tuple, it selects the appropriate method and this process is called dispatch. In traditional object-oriented languages, a method is chosen based only on the object type and this paradigm is termed single dispatch. With Julia, the combination of all function arguments determines which method is chosen; this is the basis of multiple dispatch.

To the scientific programmer, all this seems very natural. It makes little sense in most circumstances for one argument to be more important than the others. In Julia, all functions and operators (which are also functions) use multiple dispatch. The methods are chosen for any combination of operators.

For example, look at the methods of the power operator (^):

```
julia> methods(^)
# 43 methods for generic function "^":
^(x::Bool,y::Bool) at bool.jl:41
^(x::BigInt,y::Bool) at gmp.jl:314
^(x::Integer,y::Bool) at bool.jl:42
^{T<:FloatingPoint}(z::Complex{T<:FloatingPoint},
  p::Complex{T<:FloatingPoint}) at complex.jl:322
^{T<:Complex{T<:Real}}(z::T<:Complex{T<:Real},
  p::T<:Complex{T<:Real}) at complex.jl:369
^{T<:FloatingPoint}(z::Complex{T<:FloatingPoint},n::Bool)
  at complex.jl:431
^{T<:Integer}(z::Complex{T<:Integer},n::Bool)
  at complex.jl:432
^(A::Array{T,2},p::Number) at linalg/dense.jl:180
^(::MathConst{:e},x::AbstractArray{T,2}) at constants.jl:87
```

We can see that there are 43 methods for ^ and the file and line where the methods are defined are given too.

Because any untyped argument is designed to be of the Any type, it is possible to define a set of function methods such that there is no unique specific method applicable to some combinations of arguments.

```
julia> pow(a,b::Int64) = a^b;
julia> pow(a::Float64,b) = a^b;
Warning: New definition
pow(Float64,Any) at /Applications/JuliaStudio.app/Contents/Resources/
Console/Console.jl:1
is ambiguous with:
pow(Any,Int64) at /Applications/JuliaStudio.app/Contents/Resources/
Console/Console.jl:1.
To fix, define pow(Float64,Int64) before the new definition.
```

A call of pow(3.5, 2) can be handled by either function. In this case, they will give the same result because of the function bodies and Julia can't know that.

Although Julia does not disallow this, it does issue a warning and suggest a remedy. Sometimes, as a programmer, you will see such warnings when using a cocktail of packages. In many cases, they can be ignored, but you need to be aware of them.

Parametric types

Consider the following function definition: f{T}(x::T, y::T) = x + y*y.

We have seen this construct a few times already.

The f function will return its first argument added to the square of the second but only if the two arguments are of the same type.

f(1,2); # => 5

f(1.0,2.0); # => 5.0

f(1, 2.0)

ERROR: 'f' has no method matching f(::Int64, ::Float64)

This is not just true for integers and floats but also for all types provided that the function is valid. So, it would give an error for strings because the + operator is not defined, although the * operator is; overload +, and it will now work!

```
f(1+2im, 3+4im) ; # => -6 + 26im
f(1//2, 3//4); # =>  17//16
```

This function definition is in terms of the parametric type T. We can use parameter types for defining new types, and this is the situation in which it proves to be the most useful. Consider the definition of an ordered pair of numbers (x,y):

```
immutable OrdPair{T <: Integer}
  x::T;
  y::T;
end
```

Next, create a few ordered pairs:

```
julia> a = OrdPair(1,2); # => OrdPair{Int64}(1,2)1
julia> a = OrdPair(1.0,2.0);
ERROR: 'OrdPair{T<:Integer}' has no method matching ordpair{T<:Integer}
(::Float64, ::Float64)
```

The last case is clearly not what we want to happen. When creating an ordered pair of an integer and a float, we would like the result to be of two floats. Similarly, if we created a pair of a float and a complex, we would expect this to be a pair of two complex numbers.

Going up the type chain to the next common type is called promotion, and we will see how to do this later.

First, it would be a good idea to be able to do something with our ordered pairs, and the standard definitions of arithmetic operations seem to be a good place to start.

```
-(p::OrdPair) = OrdPair(-p.x, -ip.y)
+(p::OrdPair, q::OrdPair) = OrdPair(p.x + q.x, p.y + q.y)
-(p::OrdPair, q::OrdPair) = OrdPair(p.x - q.x, p.y - q.y)
*(p::OrdPair, q::OrdPair) =

  OrdPair (p.x * q.x - p.y * q.y, p.x * q.y  + p.y * q.x)
```

You will probably recognize from the multiplication rule that this is a redefinition of complex numbers in terms of order pairs. We could equally have used rationals in this example, but then, we would need to restrict it to only the integer types.

We would need to define division (/), which is trickier and the power operation (^). For this (continuing with the complex number parallel), we need to define some more elemental operations such as the `abs()` function and create a conjugate pair `conj()`.

```
abs2(p::OrdPair) = p.x*p.x + p.y*p.y
abs(p::OrdPair)  = sqrt(abs2(p))
conj(p::OrdPair) = OrdPair(p.x, -p.y)
```

We also need some logical function definitions, such as a way to assert that two ordered pairs are equal:

```
==(p::OrdPair, q::OrdPair) = (p.x == q.x) & (p.y == q.y)
```

Although we are well on the way to defining methods for working with ordered pairs, we can still not multiply these by a scalar real (integer of float) or by the more usual definition of a complex number. For this, we will need to be able to convert other numeric data types to ordered pairs and have (promotion) rules on how to apply such conversions.

Conversion and promotion

Conversion and promotion depend heavily on parameter typing and enable us to define a short set of rules rather than having to elucidate every possible combination of types.

The number hierarchy is defined in the `boot.jl` file (in base) as follows:

```
abstract Number
abstract Real   <: Number
abstract FloatingPoint <: Real
abstract Integer  <: Real
abstract Signed   <: Integer
abstract Unsigned <: Integer
```

So, with the exception of complex numbers, which we will treat as a special case, all types will be `Real`.

Conversion

To define a new conversion, simply provide a new method for the `convert()` function. Since our new type is tautologous with an ordered pair, the first rule is particularly easy.

```
convert(::Type{OrdPair}, z::Complex) =

  OrdPair(real(z),imag(z))
```

All we need to do is extract the real and imaginary parts of our complex number `z` and use them as the component parts in the `OrdPair()` constructor.

The `convert` function takes two arguments, namely `::Type{OrdPair}`, and the type of argument, which will be a real number as we have dealt with complex numbers previously.

There are three parametric rules:

```
convert{T<:Real}(::Type{OrdPair{T}}, x::Real)
  = OrdPair{T}(x,0)
convert{T<:Real}(::Type{OrdPair{T}}, p::OrdPair)
  = OrdPair{T}(p.x, p.y)
convert{T<:Real}(::Type{T}, p::OrdPair) =

isreal(p.x) ? convert(T,p.x) : throw(InexactError())
```

An ordered pair just maps to itself and a real number x to the pair (x, 0).

It is also necessary to cover the cases where a variable is not a real number (a string perhaps) by throwing an error.

Further, we supply a couple of generic (non-parametric) methods:

```
convert(::Type{OrdPair}, p::OrdPair) = p
convert(::Type{OrdPair}, x::Real) = OrdPair(x,0)
```

Promotion

Promotion refers to converting values of mixed types to a single common type. Although it is not strictly necessary, it is generally implied that the common type to which the values are converted can faithfully represent all of the original values.

Promotion to a common supertype is performed in Julia by the promote function, which takes any number of arguments and returns a tuple of the same number of values converted to a common type. If promotion is not possible (that is, not defined), the routine must throw an error.

```
promote(1, 2//3); # => (1//1, 2//3)
promote(1, 2.0 + 3.0im);  #=> (1.0 + 0.0im,2.0 + 3.0im)
```

In the second case, the first argument is promoted from an integer to a real number by an existing rule and then the whole pair is promoted to a complex number.

For this, we provide the code for the promote_rule() function:

```
promote_rule{T<:Real,U<:Real}(::Type{OrdPair{T}},
  ::Type{U}) = OrdPair{promote_type(T,U)}


promote_rule{T<:Real,U<:Real}(::Type{OrdPair{T}},
  ::Type{OrdPair{U}}) = OrdPair{promote_type(T,U)}
```

Here, we have two real numbers but have possibly different types, and we need to promote one of the real numbers to match the other.

A fixed vector module

Julia does not have a fixed array type, but in the source examples, there is an example of a 4-vector quaternion, which was defined by the great Irish mathematician William Rowan Hamilton in the nineteenth century. These have some odd properties, one of which is that multiplication is not commutative. Sadly for Hamilton, at the time, 4 vectors in the form of tensors proved much more useful, but recently, quarterions have been utilized in problems of computer vision.

We are going to finish this section by looking at a module to represent a more conventional 3-vector and provide a module to define it.

```
module Vectors3D
import Base.show, Base.convert, Base.abs, Base.dot
export Vector3D, getindex, phi
immutable Vector3D{T <: Real}
   x::T
   y::T
   z::T
end
+(u::Vector3D, v::Vector3D) = Vector3D(u.x + v.x, u.x + v.y, u.z + v.z)
-(u::Vector3D, v::Vector3D) = Vector3D(u.x - v.x, u.x - v.y, u.z - v.z)
*(a::Number, u::Vector3D) = Vector3D(a*u.x, a*u.y, a*u.z)
*(u::Vector3D, a::Number) = Vector3D(a*u.x, a*u.y, a*u.z)
/(a::Number, u::Vector3D) = Vector3D(u.x/a, u.y/a, u.z/a)
/(u::Vector3D, a::Number) = Vector3D(u.x/a, u.y/a, u.z/a)
show{T}(io::IO, u::Vector3D{T}) = print(io, "[$(u.x), $(u.y), $(u.z)]")

abs{T}(u::Vector3D{T}) = (u.x*u.x + u.y*u.y + u.z*u.z)^0.5
function phi(u::Vector3D, v::Vector3D)
  w0 = u.x*v.x + u.y*v.y + u.z*v.z
  w1 = abs(u)  * abs(v)
  try
    return atan(w0 / w1)
  catch
```

```
      error("Division by zero")
   end
end
dot(u::Vector3D, v::Vector3D) = u.x*v.x + u.y*v.y + u.z+v.z
getindex(u::Vector3D, i) = (i == 1 ? u.x : (i==2 ? u.y : u.z))
convert(::Type{Vector3D}, u::Array{Float64,1}) =
   Vector3D(u[1],u[2],u[3])
end
```

The 3D vector is written as a module Vectors3d, so using or require() will find it on LOAD_PATH and any types defined in it can be redefined in the REPL by reloading it.

We need to provide rules for the standard arithmetic operations (+, -, *, and /). These are written in a functional form, for example, +(vec1, vec2) = ...

In order to overload some routines from the base to be able to print the vector (show), convert a normal vector and take the modules (abs) and the **dot** product of the two vectors. We would also wish to compute other metrics such as the **cross** product (which Julia denotes as the times() function).

In addition to the modulus, we will compute the angle between the vectors as the function phi(). Since this is not an extension to the base, the routine needs to be exported along with the Vector3D type. Recall that any routine not exported can still be called by fully qualifying it as Vectors3D.phi().

Further, it is necessary to provide a routine for returning a component of the 3D vector getindex() and we need to also be able to set components by using setindex() and iterate over a collection of vectors by providing three routines start(), next(), and end(), whose meanings are clear.

 For a more complete definition of the 3D vector type, see the code samples accompanying this book.

Summary

In this chapter, we looked at how the Julia type system defines common numeric and string types and the role that multiple dispatch plays in creating an efficient mechanism for calling functions.

We developed a set of types for a class of vehicle types and then added data to create and manipulate some specific instances.

Finally, we discussed the topic of parametric types and developed a numeric example of an ordered pair as an alternate formulation of complex numbers.

In the next chapter, we will complete our survey of coding in Julia, looking at how it encompasses interoperability with other programming languages and how it is simple to utilize functions and methods in these languages, such as C, Python, and R, from Julia.

We will also introduce concepts of homoiconicity and metaprogramming and how this leads to the definition and the use of runtime macros in Julia and will see how this simplifies the execution of code asynchronously.

Finally, we will see how it is possible to interface with the underlying operating system, to spawn and run tasks, chaining these by pipelining and to process the results within the Julia environment.

4
Interoperability

In this chapter, we focus on the cooperation between Julia and other languages and with the underlying operating system.

Developers of Julia naturally focused on calling from Julia, and most of the discussions will be concerned with that; however, handles were provided to go the other way and call Julia from C and hence, incorporate it into foreign code, and a brief overview of this is given at the end of this chapter.

Interfacing with other programming environments

Julia has a rich and varied syntax, but it was always known that a vast wealth of code existed in object libraries covering a wide range of specialities. So, a simple mechanism to call functions from these libraries would prove to be useful, and a one-line native instruction call `ccall()` was added.

This has led to the development of packages that effectively wrap code around the existing application programming interfaces (APIs). An example would be to access a database that exposes an API to perform functions such as those to establish a database connection, to create and update records, and to execute queries.

Another major area of interoperability has been between Julia and Python, and we have already shown some evidence of that in using Python for displaying graphs and using the IPython system as a proxy IDE.

There is also some further work on interfacing with R, Java, and MATLAB, and I'll present a brief overview of this too later.

Calling C and Fortran

One of Julia's strengths is that it makes calling code written in C, and by implication Fortran, very easy. The code to be called must be available as a shared library rather than just a standalone object file.

Most C and Fortran libraries are compiled into shared libraries and are distributed as such. On Unix/Linux systems, these (usually) have the extension .so; on Mac OS X, .dylib; and on Windows, .dll. To assemble your own C code, it is necessary to make it position independently by compiling with the –shared and –fPIC switches.

Sometimes, the differences in operating systems make it necessary to segment the code and Julia provides a base set of functions in osutils.jl, which incorporate macros such as @unix, @osx, and @windows to facilitate such differentiation.

The C-interface comprises of three functions in Julia (Base.ccall), namely ccall, cglobal, and cfunction. The first is the most common and we will focus on its use here.

The most common syntax for ccall is as follows:

```
ccall((symbol, library), RetType, (ArgType1, ...), Arg1, ...)
```

The first argument is a tuple consisting of the function to be called (passed as a symbol by prefixing it with a colon) and the second component is the shared library in which the function is to be found.

The second is the return type of the function call. The return type, which may be any bits type, including Int32, Int64, Float64, or Ptr{T}, the last being a pointer to the values of type {T}. For (void) functions, that is, ones that do not return a value, Julia uses the Ptr{Void} construct.

The next argument is another tuple of the types of arguments to pass to the function. This is written as a literal tuple, not a tuple-valued variable or expression.

Julia's type system is very rich and is exposed to you, so it is possible to create any type of data structure here. If passing by reference (rather than by value), a pointer to the data structure will be passed.

Finally, there is a list of variables, written individually, not a tuple, matching the data types provided in the third argument.

As the first example, we will look at the generation of random numbers using the standard library on Linux. It should be noted that Julia does not use this method for its own generation of random numbers (in `random.jl`). This is written in Julia by using the Mersenne Twister method, but the randomization starting seed does use calls to system libraries and because of the difference in operating systems, it makes use of the underlying operating system and the macros mentioned previously. These are defined in the base file called `osutils.jl`.

Here, we are also going to call the `rand()` function from the `libc` library. This is a very simple function to call as it takes no input argument and returns a 32-bit integer, which corresponds to an integer in the range of `[0:2^31]`. This will not work in Windows where we will have to use the Windows Advanced Services API (`advapi32.dll`).

```
x = ccall( (:rand, "libc"), Int32, ())   ;# => 16807
x = ccall( (:rand, "libc"), Int32, ())   ;# => 282475249
```

To look at a more exacting usage, the following pair of calls retrieves a user's home folder given by the environment variable `$HOME` and pushes a folder of my Julia modules on to `LOAD_PATH`, which is an array of folders. Using `push!()` will put the folder at the end of the folder chain; `unshift!()` will put it at the beginning:

```
home = ccall( (:getenv, "libc"), Ptr{Uint8},
  (Ptr{Uint8},), "HOME")
Ptr{Uint8} @0x00007fa5dbe73fe5
jmods = string(bytestring(home),"/julia/mymods");
push!!(LOAD_PATH, jmods);
println(LOAD_PATH)
3-element Array{Union(UTF8String,ASCIIString)
"/usr/local/Julia/local/share/julia/site/v0.3"
"/usr/local/Julia/share/julia/site/v0.3"
"/home/malcolm/julia/mymods"
```

The second of the places listed above is a convenient place to add system-wide folders, which will be available to all. Notice that Julia defines `LOAD_PATH` in terms of the system version number, which may well be a good practice to adopt with our modules, while the language is still under rapid development.

The `getenv` routine returns a pointer to a null-terminated C-style string, and the call to `bytestring()` converts this into a Julia string.

Mapping C types

Julia has corresponding types for all C types; refer to the Julia online documentation (http://docs.julialang.org/) for a full list. One caveat is that the Char type in Julia is 32-bit, so C characters must be passed as Uint8.

Since ccall requires a tuple of argument types, Julia is able to convert any passed variables implicitly rather than the programmer needing to do so explicitly.

Julia automatically inserts calls to the convert function to convert each argument to the specified type, so it is not necessary for the programmer to explicitly make a call to a library function.

Calling a replacement power function such as pow(3,3) in libmymath will function correctly:

```
ccall((:pow,"libmymath"),Float64,(Float64,Int32),x,n)
```

```
pow(x,n) = ccall((:pow,"libmymath"),Float64,(Float64,Int32),
```

```
(convert(Float64,x),convert(Int32,n))
```

Array conversions

When an array is passed to C as a Ptr{T} argument, it is never converted; Julia simply checks that the element type of the array matches T and the address of the first element is passed. This is done in order to avoid copying arrays unnecessarily.

Therefore, if an array contains data in the wrong format, it will have to be explicitly converted using a call such as int32(a).

To pass array A as a pointer of a different type without converting the data beforehand (for example, to pass a Float64 array to a function that operates on uninterpreted bytes), you can either declare the argument as Ptr{Void} or you can explicitly call convert(Ptr{T}, pointer(A)).

Type correspondences

On all currently supported operating systems, basic C/C++ value types may be translated into Julia types. Every C type also has a corresponding Julia type with the same name, prefixed by C.

This can help in writing portable code and remembering that int in C is not necessarily the same as Int in Julia.

In particular, characters in C are 8-bit and in Julia 32-bit, so Julia defines typealiases:

```
(unsigned) char # => typealias cuchar  Uint8
(signed)   short # => typealias cshort  Int16
```

We met pointer types in `ccall` to the `libc` function `getenv()`, and these follow the same scheme, but they are not C typealiases:

```
char*              => Ptr(Uint8)
char** or *char[]  => Ptr{Ptr{Uint8}}
```

In addition, the Julia API, discussed in the following sections, defines C-type `j_type_t*` as `Ptr{Any}`.

For a comprehensive list of C-types versus Julia-types, the reader is referred to the Julia documentation.

Calling a Fortran routine

When calling a Fortran function, all inputs must be passed by reference.

The prefix & is used to indicate that a pointer to a scalar argument should be passed instead of the scalar itself.

For example, to compute a dot product using the **basic linear algebra system (BLAS)** by calling a function from the LAPACK library, use the following code:

```
function compute_dot(DX::Vector{Float64},DY::Vector{Float64})
  assert(length(DX) == length(DY))
  n = length(DX)
  incx = incy = 1
  product = ccall((:ddot, "libLAPACK"),
    Float64,
    (Ptr{Int32}, Ptr{Float64}, Ptr{Int32},
    Ptr{Float64}, Ptr{Int32}),
    &n, DX, &incx, DY, &incy)
  return product
end
```

The function requires, and sets, three scalars, namely n, incx, and incy, and two 1D arrays DX and DY. The arrays are passed by reference (by default), and this is also required for the scalars.

Notice the use of the assert(condition) statement to check that both arrays are of the same size. This has no action if the condition is true but produces an error otherwise. The function calls the ddot() routine in the LAPACK library, which returns a 64-bit float.

Calling curl to retrieve a web page

For a slightly longer example, I have included a set of calls to the libcurl library to grab a webpage, in this case, the Julia home page. We need to define a couple of constants to be sure that the curl request follows the relocation status. The full list of constants can be found in the curl.h file.

Then, it is a four-step process:

1. Initialize curl and return a pointer to a data structure to use in the remaining calls.

2. Set up the options, the most important of them being passed the URL of the page to be retrieved.

3. Perform the HTTP get operation.

4. Tidy up by release of the memory grabbed in step 1.

Notice that the final call passes a single argument, the address of the memory to be freed, but this must be given as a tuple. So, this is written as (Ptr(Unit8},) with the trailing comma necessary to distinguish it as a tuple rather than a simple bracketed expression.

```
const CURLOPT_URL = 10002
const CURLOPT_FOLLOWLOCATION = 52;
const CURLE_OK = 0
jlo = "http://julialang.org";
curl = ccall( (:curl_easy_init, "libcurl"), Ptr{Uint8}, ())
ccall((:curl_easy_setopt, "libcurl"), Ptr{Uint8},
   (Ptr{Uint8}, Int, Ptr{Uint8}), curl, CURLOPT_URL, jlo.data)
ccall((:curl_easy_perform,"libcurl"),
   Ptr{Uint8}, (Ptr{Uint8},), curl)
ccall((:curl_easy_cleanup,"libcurl"),
Ptr{Uint8},(Ptr{Uint8},), curl);
```

Here are the first eight lines of the result:

```
<!DOCTYPE html>
<html xmlns="http://www.w3.org/1999/xhtml" xml:lang="en-us" lang="en-us">
<head>
<meta http-equiv="content-type" content="text/html; charset=utf-8" />
<title>The Julia Language</title>
<meta name="author" content="Jeff Bezanson, Stefan Karpinski, Viral Shah,
Alan Edelman, et al." />
<link rel="stylesheet" href="/css/syntax.css" type="text/css" />
<link rel="stylesheet" href="/css/screen.css" type="text/css"
media="screen, projection" />
```

Python

PyCall is a package authored by Steve Johnson at MIT, which provides a `@pyimport` macro that mimics a Python `import` statement.

It imports a Python module and provides Julia wrappers for all the functions and constants including automatic conversion of types between Julia and Python. Type conversions are automatically performed for numeric, boolean, string, and I/O streams plus all tuples, arrays, and dictionaries of these types.

Python submodules must be imported by a separate `@pyimport` call, and in this case, you must supply an identifier to use in them.

After adding it via `Pkg.add("PyCall")`, an example of its use is as follows:

```
julia> using PyCall
julia> @pyimport scipy.optimize as so
julia> @pyimport scipy.integrate as si
julia> so.ridder(x -> x*cos(x), 1, pi); # => 1.570796326795
julia> si.quad(x -> x*sin(x), 1, pi)[1]; # =>  2.840423974650
```

In the preceding commands, the Python optimize and integrate modules are imported, and functions in these modules are called from the Julia REPL.

One difference imposed on the package is that calls using the Python object notation are not possible from Julia, so these are referenced using an array-style notation `po[:atr]` rather than `po.atr`, where `po` denotes a `PyObject` and `atr` represents an attribute.

It is also easy to use the Python `matplotlib` module to display simple (and complex) graphs:

```
@pyimport matplotlib.pyplot as plt
x = linspace(0,2*pi,1000); y = sin(3*x + 4*cos(2*x));
plt.plot(x, y, color="red", linewidth=2.0, linestyle="--")
1-element Array{Any,1}:
PyObject<matplotlib.lines.Line2D object at 0x0000000027652358>
plt.show()
```

Notice that keywords such as `color`, `linewidth`, and `linestyle` can also be passed in the preceding code.

The resulting plot is shown in the following figure:

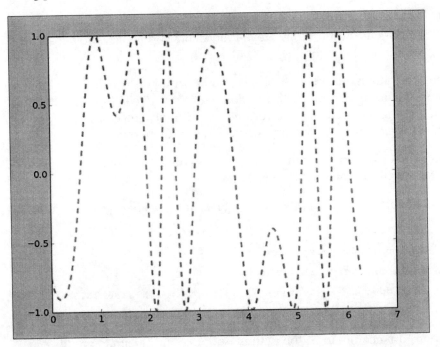

Plotting using `matplotlib` is encapsulated in another package from Steve Johnson called PyPlot, which was introduced in *Chapter 1, The Julia Environment*, and will be considered in more detail when discussing visualization in *Chapter 7, Graphics*.

Further, when looking at IDEs for Julia, we meet IJulia, now incorporated as the part of the Jupyter project.

The latter is a package that provides a backend for IPython. Recall that the IJulia package needs to be installed, and Python with `matplotlib` has to be executable from the system path. A convenient way is to use an Anaconda bundle as this not only adds Python and IPyton but also a large set of modules, including NumPy, SciPy, and Matplotlib. Other modules can be added using `easy_install`.

Once set up, IJulia is accessed by adding a profile option to an IPython notebook as follows:

```
ipython notebook -profile julia
```

Some others to watch

Python is by no means an exceptional case in providing inter-language cooperation hooks and since Julia is exposing such a wealth of riches to the developer, it is not surprising that packages are being written to link Julia to languages too. All packages are available on GitHub, and an overview can be found on `pkg.julialang.org`.

Four such packages are listed here:

- **R** (`Rif.jl`): This provides a link to the R interpreter and hence, the wealth of libraries available within R. There are a couple of caveats: in order to use this, R must be compiled as a shareable image using `-enable-R-shlib` (most distros are not built as shareable) and R must be available on the execution path. In addition, there is a recent package called `Rcall.jl` that permits an instance of R to be embedded in Julia provided that both R and RScript are on the execution path.

- **Java** (`JavaCall.jl`): This permits access to Java classes from within Julia by means of the **Java Native Interface (JNI)**, which in turn calls the **Java Virtual Machine (JVM)**. The package uses a `jcall()` function similar to `ccall()` and has been used to access an Oracle database via JDBC.

- **MATLAB** (`Matlab.jl`): This permits communication with MATLAB™ engine sessions. It is necessary to have a licensed copy of MATLAB installed, so it would be interesting to extend this to open source clones such as GNU Octave.

- **Mathematica** (`Mathematica.jl`): This likewise provides an interface for using Wolfram Mathematica™, and as with `Matlab.jl`, a licensed copy of Mathematica needs to be installed and executable.

All approaches will impose restrictions on Julia, and it is clearly better to work with the native language where possible. However, they do allow us to work with legacy code and the links to JVM will not have the limitations on speed that the others may have.

The Julia API

Julia is written in Julia, but not all of it. For speed and (sometimes) necessity, some of the implementation is coded in C and in LISP/Scheme, which requires Julia to have a runtime macro evaluation as we will see in the next section.

boot.jl (in base) comments out many of the types and functions that fall into this class and will use ccall to get them from the API. Note that ccall() has an alternate form when referencing these by using a symbol not a tuple.

Calling API from C

It is possible to access Julia from other languages by making calls to the Julia API, which is provided by the shared library called libjulia. This is created when Julia is built from source and will be located in a folder such as $JULIA_HOME/usr/lib/julia on Linux/OS X. On Windows, it is a DLL and is in the same folder (bin) as the Julia executable.

The library must be included in any linkage and locatable at runtime. Under Linux (say), this means using ld.config or adding the library to LD_LIBRARY_PATH:

Here is an example to print the Julia constant PI: pi.c

```
#include <julia.h>
#define LIBEXEC "/home/malcolm/julia/usr/lib"
int main() {
  jl_init(LIBEXEC);
  JL_SET_STACK_BASE;
  jl_eval_string("println(pi)");
  return 0;
}
```

It is necessary to include C-definitions in julia.h, and the program needs to know where the Julia system image (sys.ji) is located, which I've defined as LIBEXEC.

We build a version of Julia from source on CentOS 6.5 Linux by using the following commands:

```
export JH=/home/malcolm/julia
export LD_LIBRARY_PATH=$JH/usr/lib
gcc -o pi -I$JH/src  -I$JH/src/support
            -I$JH/usr/include -L$JH/usr/lib -ljulia pi.c

./pi ; # =>  π = 3.1425926535897 …
```

If we wish to call Julia functions and pass C-variables, we need convert these to the Julia type. This is termed as **boxing,** and the generic `jl_value_t` is used with the appropriate box function for the C-type to be passed.

Here is a program that uses the Julia power operator (^) to compute the values of the square of PI (recall that ^ is a function in Julia).

```
#include <stdio.h>
#include <math.h>
#include <julia.h>
#define LIBEXEC "/home/malcolm/julia/usr/lib"
int main() {
  jl_init(LIBEXEC);
  JL_SET_STACK_BASE;
  jl_function_t  *powf = jl_get_function(jl_base_module, "^");
  jl_value_t *arg1 = jl_box_float64(M_PI);
  jl_value_t *arg2 = jl_box_float64(2.0);
  jl_value_t *rtv  = jl_call2(powf,arg1,arg2);
  JL_GC_PUSH1(&rtv);
  if (jl_is_float64(rtv)) {
    double e_pi = jl_unbox_float64(rtv);
    printf("pi (squared) is %f\n", e_pi);
  }
  else {
    printf("Oops, an error occurred!\n");
  }
  JL_GC_POP();
  return 0;
}
```

Building and executing gives the following: `pi (squared) is 9.869604.`

Notice the following points when calling the Julia API:

- We needed `stdio.h` for doing some C-based I/O (which we did not do previously)
- Further, `math.h` was included, just to pick a value for PI
- `jl_box_float64` was used to switch the C value to a Julia one float
- `jl_value_t` is a C-structure that contains the Julia type and a pointer to the data value; see `julia_internals.h` for its definition
- ^ is a function in base and has two arguments, so call `jl_call2` to apply the function to the arguments

- We needed to check whether the return value is float64 (might be an error)
- If all was OK, the return value was an *unboxed* (to a C-value) value and printed

Julia is responsible for its own garbage collection, which is cleaning up any allocated memory when variables are defined or go out of scope. This can be triggered by the programmer by using the gc() function, but normally, this is not advisable.

When calling from C, it is not a good idea to assume that any memory allocated will be freed, so the purpose of JL_GC_PUSH1 and JL_GC_POP C-macros is to indicate that the return value from the Julia call needs to be destroyed before the program exits.

Metaprogramming

Julia has been designed to tackle problems arising in science and statistics. It follows the route of traditional imperative languages. It is not a functional language, such as Haskell, OCaml, and Clojure, but since it incorporates a Scheme interpreter, it is possible to create runtime macros rather than the preprocessor style ones found in C/C++.

Macros are useful in efficiently generating boilerplate code, and we have already made use of the @printf macro, which emulates the C-style printf() function.

If a true functional approach is required, the reader is directed to the Lazy.jl package, which implements lazily evaluated lists plus a library of functions to use them and many well-designed macros. So, to get a grasp of Julia metaprogramming, you could do no better than looking at the source code in the Lazy package.

To generate macros, a language needs to have the property of homoiconicity. This means that the primary representation of program code is also a data structure in a primitive type of the language itself.

The obvious example is LISP, which only has the single data structure of a list, and a LISP program is also expressed in lists. This means that the interpreter is also able to parse and execute code as well as working with the underlying data.

In Julia, it is not clear how this is achieved, but before we look at this, we need to explore the Julia symbols in more detail.

Symbols

Consider the simple operation of multiplying two variables and adding the result to a third:

```
julia> ex = :(a+b*c)
:(a + b * c)
```

The use of the colon (:) operator in front of (a + b*c) results in the expression being saved in ex rather than being evaluated.

In fact, the expression would clearly fail unless all the variables had values.

The colon (:) operator creates a symbolic representation, and this is stored in a data structure Expr and is saved in ex rather than being evaluated.

```
julia> typeof(ex); # => Expr
```

If we now initialize the variables a, b, and c, the expression can be evaluated as follows:

```
julia> a = 1.0;  b = 2.5;  c= 23 + 4im;
julia> eval(ex)
58.5 + 10.0im
```

So, this process effectively splits the calculation into two parts, storing the expression and then evaluating it.

Expr consists of a vector of three symbols:

```
julia> names(Expr)
3-element Array{Symbol,1}:
 :head
 :args
 :typ
```

Further, if we look at the arguments of the expression ex, this is an array of symbols:

```
julia> ex.args
3-element Array{Any,1}:
 :+
 :a
 :(b * c)
```

The third element is interesting since it is an *n* arithmetic expression and can be further reduced as follows:

```julia
julia> ex.args[3].args
3-element Array{Any,1}:
 :*
 :b
 :c
```

The other components of the `Expr` type are more straightforward:

```julia
julia> ex.head   ; # => :call
julia> ex.typ;   ; # => Any
```

More complex expressions would be difficult to store by means of the `:()` mechanism, so Julia provides a `quote ... end` block mechanism for storing code expressions. This two-stage evaluation forms the basis of Julia's macro capabilities.

Macros

The basis of Julia macros is in the incorporation of a LISP-style interpreter in its runtime. This allows code to be constructed, stored, and then initialized at a later stage and *spliced* inline.

Quite complex snippets of Julia, which would require considerable boilerplating, can be reduced to the use of a macro called from a single line of code.

Macros are constructed by using the `macro()` function, which has a name and takes a variable number of arguments: macro `name(ex1, ex2, ex3 ...)`.

It is called with `@name`, and there are no commas between arguments as follows: `@name ex1 ex2 ex3`.

One of the simplest macros calculates the execution time of a Julia function. This merely requires recording the time before the function is started and noting the time at the end of the execution of the function.

To write our own version of this, we can use the system library to return the Unix() systime which is the number of seconds since 1/1/1970. This is 32-bit value, so we are OK until 19/01/2038 when the time will overflow, a little after 3 am. For this, we will use a native call to the `time` function in `libc.so`:

```julia
systime() = ccall( (:time, "libc"), Int32, ());
macro uxtime(ex)
```

```
quote
    t0 = systime()
    $(esc(ex))
    t1 = systime()
    println("Time taken was $(t1 - t0) sec.")
  end
end
```

The code is too large for a single symbolization, so it is defined in a quote block. The expression/function to be timed is executed using the `$()` construct, and the use of `esc()` ensures that there is no name clash with the existing namespace.

The granularity of this macro is only to the nearest second, so in Julia, it is difficult to get routines that are computationally complex to "trouble to the scorers." However, the Queen's routine developed earlier for an 8 × 8 board on my i5-based computer takes a little time:

```
include('queens.jl')
@uxtime   qsolve(8)
Time taken was 53 sec.
```

Of course, Julia has its own timing macro called `@elapsed`, similar to ours to the nanosecond rather than the second. This is defined in base in the `util.jl` file and to achieve this, makes a call to a routine in the Julia API: `ccall(:jl_hrtime, Uint64, ())`, which returns an unsigned 64-bit value.

The `macroexpand()` function can be used to show the code produced from a macro call. Consider a timing function `hangabout()` defined as follows:

```
function hangabout(n)
  s = 0.0
  for i = 1:n
    s += i/(i+1)^2
  end
  s
end
```

```
julia> hangabout(1_000_000_000) ; # => 17.35296236700634
julia> @elapsed hangabout(1_000_000_000); # => 5.786654631
```

This function is written to loop over an integer range and evaluate the
(floating point) sum of 1/4, 2/9, 3/16, ...; this series does not converge
but increases very slowly.

Running this a billion times takes around 5.8 s on my laptop:

```
macroexpand(quote @elapsed hangabout(1_000_000_000) end)
quote  # none, line 1:
  begin  # util.jl, line 68:
    local #173#t0 = Base.time_ns() # line 69:
    local #174#val = hangabout(1_000_000_000) # line 70:
    Base./(Base.-(Base.time_ns(),#173#t0),1.0e9)
  end
end
```

Expanding the macro gives a reference to the file where it is defined and you will
see that it is very similar to our own. The first two lines of code create a copy of local
variables to store the start time and the return value of hangabout().

The third line looks a little odd, but note that Base./ is a fully qualified call to the
division operator, and likewise, Base.- is a call to subtraction. As noted, time_ns()
returns the time in nanoseconds to the line corresponding to (t1 - t0) / 1.0e+9.

To time a command, we will write a macro called @benchmark, which calls @elapsed
10 times and returns the mean.

```
macro benchmark(f)
  quote
    $(esc(f))
    mean([@elapsed $(esc(f)) for i = 1:10])
  end
end
```

This macro calls @elapsed, which will be expanded inline in the normal fashion.
Further, the f() function is called once before the timing loop so that it will be
compiled, if not already done so; therefore, the compilation time is not taken into
account in the timing. The use of esc() is to avoid any possible name clashes while
expanding the macro in the user's program context.

```
macroexpand(quote @benchmark hangabout(1_000_000_000) end)
quote  # none, line 1:
  begin  # none, line 3:
```

```
hangabout(1000000000) # line 4:
mean($(Expr(:comprehension, quote  # util.jl, line 68:
    local #176#t0 = Base.time_ns() # line 69:
    local #177#val = hangabout(1000000000) # line 70:
    Base./(Base.-(Base.time_ns(),#176#t0),1.0e9)
  end, :(#175#i = 1:10))))
end
end
```

Lines 6–8 correspond to the `@elapsed` expansion; this is wrapped up as a list comprehension, and the whole is passed to the `mean()` function.

Not all macros are as simple as timing ones, and while in base, you may well look at an old favorite `@printf` in `printf.jl`. For an example of a cleverly constructed macro in terms of a number of helper functions, we advise you to look at the macro source code and the expansion of (say): `macroexpand(quote @printf "%s %\n"` `"The answer is " x end)`.

Package authors too make good use of macros and provide a good reference source. Often, the principal aim may be to define the main macro, as is the case in point with the PyCall package and `@pyimport`, which we met earlier.

Testing

Julia is a rapidly developing language, so it is very important to ensure that all code works and continues to work. All packages, in addition to an `src` folder, contain a test and in this are placed unit tests that can be run to assert that the package is not broken.

We have seen that Julia defines the `assert()` function (`error.jl`), which raises an "assert exception" if a condition is not met but does nothing otherwise. Also provided is an assert macro (`@assert`), which will evaluate a condition and output a custom message if given; otherwise, a default one.

Assert macros are often used to raise problems within a package where exceptions can be dealt with at runtime. For unit testing, it is more usual to utilize the functionality of a different base file: `test.jl`.

The simplest usage is the `@test` macro, as follows:

```
julia> using Base.Test
julia> x = 1;
```

```
julia> @test x == 1
julia> @test x == 2
ErrorException("test failed: :((x==2))")
```

This will throw an error if the test fails. However, sometimes, we may wish to check for a particular type of error while reporting many others; this is done using `@test_throws`.

`@test_throws`

```
julia> a =  rand(10);
julia>  @test_throws BoundsError a[11] = 0.1
julia>  @test_throws DomainError a[11] = 0.1
ERROR: test failed: a[11] = 0.1
 in error at error.jl:21
 in default_handler at test.jl:19
 in do_test_throws at test.jl:55
```

As floating-point comparisons can be imprecise conditions, such as $sin(pi) == 0.0$, they may fail. In these cases, additional macros exist, which will take care of numerical errors.

Consider the following cases:

```
julia> @test_approx_eq 0.0 sin(pi)
ERROR: assertion failed: |0.0 - sin(pi)| <= 2.4651903288e-28
  0.0 = 0.0
  sin(pi) = 1.2246467991473532e-16
```

This still fails as the value retuned from $sin(pi)$ is above the (default) permitted value of the macro call. However, it is possible to specify the allowable level.

```
julia> @test_approx_eq_eps 0.0 sin(pi) 1.0e-10
julia> @test_approx_eq_eps 0.0 sin(pi) 1.0e-20
ERROR: assertion failed: |0.0 - sin(pi)| <= 1.0e-20
  0.0 = 0.0
  sin(pi) = 1.2246467991473532e-16
  difference = 1.2246467991473532e-16 > 1.0e-20
```

It is worth noting that a de facto standard testing framework is now provided by the use of the FactCheck.jl package. The reader is referred to the final chapter of this book when we will return to the question of testing in a more general discussion of package development.

Error handling

A handler is a function defined for three types of arguments: Success, Failure, and Error.

It is possible to specify different handlers for each separate case by using the with_ handler() function.

```
julia> using Base.Test
julia> my_handler(r::Test.Success) =
 println("I'm OK with $(r.expr)");
julia> my_handler(r::Test.Failure) =
error("Error from my handler: $(r.expr)")
julia> my(r::Test.Error) = rethrow(r)
```

Test.Success and Test.Failure have a single parameter called expr, which is the expression, whereas Test.Error is a little more complex as it returns an error status and backtrace reference:

```
julia> names(Test.Error)
3-element Array{Symbol,1}:
 :expr
 :err
 :backtrace

julia> my_handler(r::Test.Failure) =
println("$(r.expr): Yep, As expected!");
julia> my_handler(r::Test.Success) =
  println("$(r.expr): I'm OK with this");
julia> my_handler(r::Test.Error) = rethrow(r);
```

It is possible to overwrite the `Error` status as well as `Success` and `Failure`, but normally, it is a good idea to rethrow the expression and let Julia report it. So, we use our handlers as follows:

```
Test.with_handler(my_handler) do
  x = 1;
  @test x == 1
  @test x == 2
  @test x / 0
end
x == 1: I'm OK with this
x == 2: Yep, As expected!
ERROR: test error during x / 0
```

The enum macro

When looking at our vehicle types, we constructed a simple representation from an enumeration, and I commented that the Julia language does not yet provide an enum type although various approaches have been suggested (and adopted) in dealing with problems that incorporate enumerations such as interfacing with database systems.

The examples section of Julia provides one such solution in terms of an `@enum` macro, and I'm going to close this section by having a look at it.

First, let's use it to define four possible status returns from a system call from informational to fatal, which perhaps might be inserted into a system log.

```
@enum STATUS INFO WARNING ERROR FATAL
::Type{enum STATUS (INFO, WARNING, ERROR, FATAL)}

INFO; # => INFO
STATUS(0); # => INFO
STATUS(1); # => WARNING
typeof(INFO); # => enum STATUS (INFO, WARNING, ERROR, FATAL)
```

`typeof(INFO)` looks a bit strange, so to see how this occurs, let us look at the definition of the enum macro:

```
macro enum(T,syms...)
  blk = quote
```

```
    immutable $(esc(T))
       n::Int32
       $(esc(T))(n::Integer) = new(n)
  end
  Base.show(io::IO, x::$(esc(T))) = print(io, $syms[x.n+1])
  Base.show(io::IO, x::Type{$(esc(T))}) = print(
io,
$(string("enum ", T, ' ', '(', join(syms, ", "), ')')))
  )
  end
  for (i,sym) in enumerate(syms)
    push!(blk.args, :(const $(esc(sym)) = $(esc(T))($(i-1))))
  end
  push!(blk.args, :nothing)
  blk.head = :toplevel
  return blk
end
```

Looking at this macro definition, we note the following:

- Using @enum is going to generate and splice the preceding code
- The symbolic representation in blk = quote … end creates an immutable type based on the first argument T and defines the way to display it (Base. show) as the word enum followed by T and a join of the other arguments enclosed by brackets
- Looping through the arguments (syms…), which are passed as a tuple, creates a constant for each one, which is zero-based: $(esc(T))($(i-1))
- These are pushed onto the macro's argument stack, and the process is terminated with the symbol (:nothing)
- The macro head is assigned to :toplevel
- This is similar in construct to our simple version in the previous section in that the symbols (in blk.args) are enumerated and pushed onto blk itself as the macro return via the push!() call
- Notice the overloading of Base.show(), which allows the enumeration to be displayed

The following code snippet illustrates the use of the enum macro:

```
require("Enum")
@enum MSGSTAT INFO WARN ERROR FATAL
typealias MsgStatus typeof(INFO)
enum MSGSTAT (INFO, WARN, ERROR, FATAL) (constructor with 1 method)

using Calendar
type LogMessage
   stamped::CalendarTime
   msgstat::MsgStatus
   message::String
end

import Base.show
show(m::LogMessage) =
print("$(m.stamped): $(m.msgstat) >> $(m.message)")

msg = LogMessage(Calendar.now(), WARN, "Be very afraid")
show(msg)
28 Aug 2014 09:55:33 BST: WARN >> Be very afraid!
```

Therefore, we can see the following:

- This snippet uses require() to find enum.jl. It's the routine used by using a package and will find the file in the current folder or on LOAD_PATH

- The type generated by the @enum macro is rather unwieldy, so typeassert is defined to the typeof(): anyone of the enum's values

- LogMessage has a timestamp of the CalendarTime type provided by the Calendar package, which also has the now() function to get the current (local) time

- Adding a show() routine for displaying log messages needs Base.show to be imported

Tasks

Tasks (aka co-routines) form the basis for Julia's provision of parallel processing. They are sometimes referred to as lightweight or green threads. When some code is executed as a task, it is possible to suspend it and switch to another task. The original task can be resumed and will continue from where it was suspended.

Tasks cooperate by using a producer-consumer mechanism. A producer task will halt at a point where it has some values, which need to be consumed, and a separate task will be able to access these values. Producer and consumer tasks can both continue to run by exchanging values as necessary.

```
function fibs(n = 10)
  fib = int64(zeros(n))
  fib[1] = 1
  produce fib[1]
  fib[2]
  produce fib[2]
  for i = 3:n
    fib[i] = fib[i-1] + fib[i-2]
    produce(fib[i])
  end
  produce(-1)
end
```

This function computes the first 10 numbers in the Fibonacci series. When this function is used to create a task, it will halt at each `produce()` statement until the value being signaled is consumed. The function sends (-1) as its last value to indicate that it is ending.

```
p = Task(fibs); #=> Task
consume(p); # => 1
. . . . . . . . . . . . . . . . . . . . .
. . . . . . . . . . . . . . . . . . . .
consume(p); # => 55
consume(p); # => -1
```

A task is an iterable object, so the values produced can be used in a loop as follows:

```
for x in p
  if x < 0
    break
  else
    @printf "%d " x
  end
end
1 1 2 3 5 8 13 21 34 55
```

Parallel operations

Julia provides a multiprocessing environment based on message passing. The programmer only needs to explicitly manage one processor in a two-processor operation. The operations involve high-level function calls rather than traditional message send and message receive operations.

To do this, Julia introduces a remote reference; this is an object that can be used to refer to any process on a particular processor.

Associated with remote references are remote calls. These are requests to call a function with a given set of arguments on a specific processor (possibly its own) and return a remote reference to the call. In the case where the remote call fails, an exception is raised; otherwise, it runs asynchronously with the remote task. It is possible to wait for the remote task to finish by using its remote reference, and the value of the result can be obtained by using `fetch()`.

There are a few ways to set up a multiprocessor system. First, Julia can be started using the following: `julia -p n`, which will create n separate processors on the same computer. If the computer is multi-core, then each processor will run a separate core, so it is sensible to choose n to reflect this.

Separate files can also be preloaded on multiple processes at startup, and the main script can be used to control the overall process:

```
julia -p 2 -L file1.jl -L file2.jl  main.jl
```

Each process has an associated identifier. The process providing the interactive Julia prompt always has an ID equal to 1, as would the Julia process running the main script in the preceding example. The processes used by default for parallel operations are referred to as workers. When there is only one process, process 1 is considered a worker. Otherwise, workers are considered to be all processes other than process 1.

Alternatively, it is possible to create extra processors from a running system by using `addproc(n)`. Since there is already a process running, the number n should now be chosen as one less than the number of cores:

```
julia> addprocs(3); # => equivalent to startup as:  julia -p 4
julia> nprocs(); #=> 4
```

`nprocs()` confirms that four processors are now available.

An `nworkers()` call returns the number of workers available, which is one less than `nprocs()` in a multiprocessor environment; otherwise, it is 1.

After adding the workers, we can select one of them to execute some code, as follows:

```
r = remotecall(2, randn, 5)
fetch(r) ;# => [0.094615,0.339905,0.422061,0.790972,0.552309 ]
```

In a distributed setup, an alternative form of `addprocs(machines)` is available where `machines` is a vector with items taking the following form: `user@host:port`.

The user defaults to the current user and the port to SSH, so only the host is required. In the case of multihomed hosts, `bind_addr` may be used to explicitly specify an interface.

This form of `addprocs()` has three additional keyword arguments:

- `tunnel = false`: If true then SSH tunneling will be used to connect to the worker

- `dir = JULIA_HOME`: Specifies the location of the Julia binaries on the worker nodes

- `sshflags`: Specifies additional SSH options, for example, `sshflags='-i / home/malcolm/key.pem'`

In the era of big data, this aspect of Julia's parallelism makes it very attractive. Worker processes can also be spawned on arbitrary machines quite transparently in a cluster environment, and it is possible to use the `ClusterManager` interface to provide our own way to specify, launch, and manage worker processes.

Parallel execution is added via a set of macros such as `@async`, `@spawn`, and `@spawnat`.

Let us run the Fibonacci series again but now using a recursive definition. This can be computationally expensive due to the double recursion unless defined by a tail-recursive scheme.

```
addprocs(3)
@everywhere fib(n) =   (n < 2) ? n : (fib(n-1) + fib(n-2))
```

The `@everywhere` macro ensures that the function definition is available on all processors:

```
julia> @elapsed fib(40); # => 1.311472619
julia> r = @spawn @elapsed fib(40); # => RemoteRef(4,1,17)
julia> fetch(r); # => 1.272693849
```

The `@spawn` macro ran the command on one of the workers chosen randomly, in this case, worker 4. The macro returned `RemoteRef`, and this was used to get the elapsed time.

It is possible to use `@spawnat`, which specifies which worker to select, and using the syntax `@spawnat 1 <args...>` will run the command on active processor (1) rather than a worker.

I'll look at spawning processes after we consider distributing our data.

Distributed arrays

When using a process on multiple computers, it is also desirable to be able to make use of the remote machine's memory. For this, Julia provides a DArray (distributed array). In order to create a DArray, there are functions such as `dzeros()`, `dones()`, `dfill()`, `drand()`, and `drandn()`, all of which function in a fashion similar to that of their non-distributed counterparts.

DArrays have been removed from Julia Base library as of v0.4, so it is now necessary to import the `DistributedArrays` package on all spawned processes.

If you are working with v0.4 or greater, please refer to the details on GitHub for information.

```
julia> addprocs(3);
julia> d = drand(100000);
julia> typeof(d) ; # => DArray{Float64,1,Array{Float64.1}}
```

This processes a distributed array of 100,000 random numbers distributed over the three workers but not the active machine.

The metadata associated with d is provided in a 5-element array of the special type Any.

As the name suggests, this is an array whose elements can be a mixture of types, integers, real numbers, strings, other arrays, and user-defined objects:

```
julia> names(d)
5-element Array{Symbol,1}:
 :dims
```

```
:chunks

:pmap

:indexes

:cuts
```

The chunks parameter provides the remote references, and the indexes parameter provides the ranges on a per worker basis. Therefore, the length of either chunks or indexes gives the number of workers holding the data:

```
julia> d.cuts
1-element Array{Int64,1},1}:
 [1,33334,66668,100001]
julia> d.chunks
3-element Array{RemoteRef,1}:
 RemoteRef(2,1,5)
 RemoteRef(3,1,6)
 RemoteRef(4,1,7)
julia> length(d.chunks); # => 3


julia> d.indexes
3-element Array{(UnitRange{Int64},),1}:
 (1:33333,)
 (33334:66667,)
 (66668:100000,)
```

Notice that the dims parameter gives a vector of the dimensions of the array rather than how it has been sliced and diced:

```
d0 = dzeros(100,200,300) ; d.dims ;  # = > (100,200,300)
```

The data can be treated similar to any "normal" array.

For example, we can compute the frequency histogram and estimate the bias in the random number generator from the standard error of the mean:

```
julia> (r, fq) = hist(d,10)
(0.0:0.1:1.0,
[10047,10008,10004,9982,9892,9850,10023,10007,10142,10045])


julia> stdm(fq,  mean(fq)); #  =>  81.3388
```

A simple MapReduce

As an example of processing, let's generate a matrix of 300 × 300 normally distributed random numbers with a zero mean and unit standard deviation using three workers.

```
addprocs(3);
d   = drand(300,300);
nd = length(d.chunks)
```

To work with data on an individual worker, it is possible to use the `localpart()` function. We need to apply the function to all the workers, which hold data, and for our purposes, this is a calculation of the values of the mean and standard deviation.

`procs()` provides an iterable array of workers, which can be used in the `@spawnat` macro. Finally, we wait for each process to yield results by using `fetch()` to map this over all workers and reduce the result by simple summation.

The total computation results in two lines of code:

```
µ = reduce(+, map(fetch,
Any[@spawnat p mean(localpart(d)) for p in procs(d) ]))/nd;
0.001171701
σ = reduce(+, map(fetch,
Any[@spawnat p std(localpart(d)) for p in procs(d) ]))/nd;
1.001011265
```

> Hint: Julia supports unicode characters and REPL can use these as normal variables. Therefore, to display (and use) the variables µ and σ within Julia, you would type \mu<TAB> and \sigma<TAB>, respectively.

Executing commands

We saw in the first chapter that it is possible to shell out of the console REPL to the operating system by using the `;` command. In addition, Julia provides a number of built-in functions so that scripts can interactive with the OS and its filesystem. Most of these commands mirror the standard Unix commands. For Windows users, they will be familiar to those who have used the MINGW or similar shells.

Two familiar ones are pwd() and cd():

```
julia> pwd();
"/Users/malcolm/Packt/Chapter-4"
julia> cd("../../Work");
julia> pwd();
"/Users/malcolm/Work"
```

The pwd() command indicates where we are now (print working folder), and of course, cd() is used to change the folder. This can be relative to the current location or an absolute if the file specification starts with /.

It is also possible to create new folders with mkdir() subject to your access permissions. Files may be copied cp(), moved mv(), or deleted rm().

Folders are also deleted using the rm() command, which has a recursive argument (default: false) to remove a folder tree, with the caveat that the folder needs to be empty before it can be removed.

There is also the useful download(url, [localfile]) command, which can get a remote file via HTTP. If the second argument is supplied, the download is saved to a disk file.

Commands not built into the language are easily added using the ccall() mechanism. For example, we saw that it is possible to find the value of an environmental variable by using a function, as follows:

```
function getenv(evar::String)
  s = ccall( (:getenv,"libc"),Ptr{Uint8}, (Ptr{Uint8},),evar)
    bytestring(s)
  end
```

This can be used to locate the home folder and navigate from there. In the following examples, we have a (top-level) folder containing some of the poems of Lewis Carroll in the *Alice* books, and to get there, we can use the function as follows:

```
home_dir = getenv("HOME"));
alice_dir = string(home_dir, "/Alice");
cd(alice_dir)
```

Running commands

For executing operating system commands, Julia uses a back tick convention, similar to Perl and Ruby. However, Julia does not run the command immediately, rather a Cmd object is returned, which can then be run later.

```
osdate = 'date';  typeof(osdate);  # => Cmd

run(osdate)

Sun 31 Aug 2014 09:26:02 BST
```

Having the ability to store commands in this manner gives great flexibility. Instead of using run() as mentioned previously, we can use readall() to capture the output:

```
julia> pwd(); # =>  "/Users/malcolm/Alice"


julia> ls = readall('ls -lnoSr')
"total 112\n-rw-r--r— 501 1   813 28 Aug 15:37 voice-of-the-lobster.txt\n-
rw-r--r— 501 1   968 28 Aug 15:37 jabberwocky.txt\n-rw-r--r-- 501 1 1182
28 Aug 15:37 lobster-quadrille.txt\n-rw-r--r-- 501 1 1455 28 Aug 15:37
father-william.txt\n-rw-r--r-- 501 1 1887 28 Aug 15:37 mad-gardeners-
song.txt\n-rw-r--r-- 501 1 2593 28 Aug 15:37 aged-aged-man.txt\n-rw-r-
-r-- 501 1 3415 28 Aug 15:37 walrus-and-carpenter.txt\n-rw-r--r—501 1
25225 28 Aug 15:37 hunting-the-snark.txt\n"
```

This is a listing of the Alice folder obtained from the ls command, which is returned as a string. It looks a little odd until we realize that the lines are delimited by line feed characters (\n), and so, we can split the output on these to produce a separate array of strings:

```
julia> split(ls,"\n")
8-element Array{SubString{ASCIIString},1}:
"total 112"
"-rw-r--r-- 501 1    813 28 Aug 15:37 voice-of-the-lobster.txt"
"-rw-r--r-- 501 1    968 28 Aug 15:37 jabberwocky.txt"
"-rw-r--r-- 501 1   1182 28 Aug 15:37 lobster-quadrille.txt"
"-rw-r--r-- 501 1   1455 28 Aug 15:37 father-william.txt"
"-rw-r--r-- 501 1   1887 28 Aug 15:37 mad-gardeners-song.txt"
"-rw-r--r-- 501 1   2593 28 Aug 15:37 aged-aged-man.txt"
"-rw-r--r-- 501 1   3415 28 Aug 15:37 walrus-and-carpenter.txt"
"-rw-r--r-- 501 1 25225 28 Aug 15:37 hunting-the-snark.txt"
```

Often, we wish to do more than just capture the output of the command as a string. It is possible to do this by opening the standard output (STDOUT) and working within a do – end block.

For example, in the spirit of "Through the Looking Glass," here are the first four lines of Jabberwocky as Alice first saw them:

```
open('cat jabberwocky.txt',"r",STDOUT) do io
  for i = 1:4
    s = readline(io)
    println(reverse(chomp(s)))
  end
end
sevot yhtils eht dna ,gillirb sawT'
:ebaw eht ni elbmig dna eryg diD
,sevogorob eht erew ysmim 11A
.ebargtuo shtar emom eht dnA
```

Revisiting an earlier example where we interfaced with libcurl to get a copy of the Julia homepage, this can be done easily by using an OS command:

```
Julia> jlo = readall('curl -L "http://www.julialang.org"');
julia> [println(jlo[i]) for i = 1:8];

<!DOCTYPE html>
<html xmlns="http://www.w3.org/1999/xhtml" xml:lang="en-us" lang="en-us">
<head>
<meta http-equiv="content-type" content="text/html; charset=utf-8" />
<title>The Julia Language</title>
<meta name="author" content="Jeff Bezanson, Stefan Karpinski, Viral Shah,
Alan Edelman, et al." />
<link rel="stylesheet" href="/css/syntax.css" type="text/css" />
<link rel="stylesheet" href="/css/screen.css" type="text/css"
media="screen, projection" />
```

Working with the filesystem

We should note that when using commands in Julia, the shell expansions do not work. In particular, it is not possible to run expressions containing wild cards such as `ls *.txt` since * will be interpreted literally.

Julia has a `readdir()` function, which will return a folder listing as an array of strings, so using the `wc` command to get a line/word/character count for the files in Alice:

```
julia> run('wc  $(readdir())')
        4        43        255 README.1st
       92       502       2593 aged-aged-man.txt
       38       280       1455 father-william.txt
      734      4423      25225 hunting-the-snark.txt
       33       168        968 jabberwocky.txt
       19       221       1182 lobster-quadrille.txt
       68       331       1887 mad-gardeners-song.txt
       16       157        813 voice-of-the-lobster.txt
      124       626       3415 walrus-and-carpenter.txt
     1128      6751      37793 total
```

Most of the files have the .txt extension, but there is a README file, and later, we will be producing other files as a result of some text processing for which I will deliberately use a different extension.

In order to work on the contents of the poems alone, we will need to filter the list by applying a regular expression-based pattern match.

```
function filter(pat::Regex, dir=".")
  a = []
  for fl in readdir(dir)
    ismatch(pat, fl) && push!(a, fl)
  end
  a
end
```

This function is a very simple wrapper around `readdir()`, which grabs the listing and tests it for a match against a regex (regular) expression. Regex was introduced in *Chapter 2, Developing in Julia*, and you might recall that these are strings delimitated by r"...".

Using our filter function, we can pick out all the titles with the word `the` in them. Note that we will also get `father-william` as it has `the` in `father`:

```
julia> run('wc $(filter(r"the"))')
    38       280     1455 father-william.txt
   734      4423    25225 hunting-the-snark.txt
    16       157      813 voice-of-the-lobster.txt
   788      4860    27493 total
```

However, we still have a problem using this (and `readdir()`) as the `wc` command will stall if the filter function does not produce an output, so we need to check for this before running the command.

Looking for files beginning with `h`, we find one `.txt` file but no log file, so we use the following code:

```
aa = filter(r"^h\.log"); length(aa) > 0 && run('wc -l $(aa)')

aa = filter(r"^h\.txt"); length(aa) > 0 && run('wc -l $(aa)')
   734      4423    25225  hunting-the-snark.txt
   734      4423    25225  total
```

It is worthy to notice that there is a Unix command that will handle wildcard `find`. This is because `find` mimics the shell rather than utilizing it. The wildcard `*` needs to be preceded by a backslash; otherwise, it is interpreted literally:

```
julia> run('find "/Users/Malcolm" -name \*.1st');
/Users/Malcolm/Alice/README.1st
```

This can be very useful as it produces a recursive list of fully qualified files. Further, `find` has a great number of other options to enhance the file search; see the Unix manual for a description of the full syntax.

Redirection and pipes

A consequence of Julia not using the Unix shell for its command processing is that the conventional chaining of commands using pipes will not work.

Instead, Julia provides its own pipe operator (| >) to chain *separate* Julia command objects:

```
julia> run('echo "Don't Panic!"' |> 'rev')
!cinaP t'noD
```

The pipe operator has been depreciated as of version v0.4, and while continuing to be valid, it will produce deprecation warnings.

We are working with the current stable version v0.3.x and will use this notation, but the alternate accepted form for future versions will now be the following use of the pipe() function:

```
julia> run(pipe('echo "Don't Panic!"','rev'))
```

Assuming that we are in the `Alice` folder, the following searches (using `grep`) for all lines containing the word beaver in "The Hunting of the Snark":

```
julia> pwd();  # =>  "/Users/malcolm/Alice"
julia> wc(f) = isfile(f) && run('wc $f');
julia> txtfile = "hunting-the-snark.txt";
julia> logfile = "hunting-the-snark.log";
julia> run('grep -i beaver $txtfile' |> logfile);
julia> wc(logfile)
    19         138         821   hunting-the-snark.log
```

- The `grep -i` command enforces a case-insensitive search
- The `wc()` function just encapsulates the Unix `wc` command for a given file, checking first whether the file exists
- If the command chain is terminated by a string, Julia will write the output to a file of that name; otherwise, to STDOUT

Note that using `|>` in this fashion will always create a new file. To append the output to an existing file, the `>>` operator is used as follows:

```
julia> run('grep -i bellman $txtfile' >> logfile);
julia> wc(logfile)
    49         371        2022   hunting-the-snark.log
```

Therefore, to check for lines containing both `Bellman` and `Beaver`, we can double `grep` through a pipe as follows:

```
julia> run('grep -i bellman snark.log' |> 'grep -i beaver')
He could only kill Beavers. The Bellman looked scared,
He could only kill Beavers. The Bellman looked scared,
```

That the line occurs twice is confirmation that `>>` has appended to the file. It was added once when using grep for beaver and again when using grep for bellman.

Perl one-liners

As a devotee of Perl, I still find it one of the best languages for munging data. Perl is famous (among other things) for what can be achieved on a single line so much so that books are devoted just to Perl one-liners.

The following command reverses the lines in a file and applying it to the Jabberwocky:

```
julia> cp0 = 'perl -e 'print reverse <>'';
julia> run('cat jabberwocky.txt' |> cp0
|> 'tee jabberwocky.rev' |> 'head -4')
And the mome raths outgrabe
All mimsy were the borogoves,
Did gyre and gimble in the wabe:
'Twas brillig, and the slithy toves
```

This creates a file on disk (via `tee`) and displays the first four lines of the output (that is, the last four lines of the poem reversed).

```
julia> run('find . -name \*.rev');
./jabberwocky.rev
```

Use of Perl's one-liners adds considerable text processing capabilities to Julia without exiting the language.

```
tfl = "hunting-the-snark.txt";
cp1 = 'perl -pne 'tr/[A-Z]/[a-z]/' $(tfl)';
cp2 = 'perl -ne 'print join("\n",
            split(/ /,$_)); print("\n")'';
run(cp1 |> cp2 |>'sort'|>'uniq -c'|>'sort -rn'|>'head -8')
 889
 299 the
 153 and
 123 a
 105 to
  91 it
  82 with
  76 of
```

This lists counts the words (case insensitive) listed in a descending numerical order. Not surprisingly <space> ranks the highest, followed by common words such as the and and.

As with all text, processing punctuation does present its problems; for example, looking for the number of times bellman appears in the Jabberwocky gives the following:

```
run(cp1|> cp2|>'sort'|>'uniq -c'|>'sort -rn'|>'grep bellman')
25 bellman
 4 bellman,
 1 bellman's
```

In general, shell commands can just be dropped into the Julia syntax, and the back tick will take care of it with few problems. Cases that we need to be aware of are the contexts in which special characters such as $ and @ are used as these are interpreted differently by Julia and Perl; normally, this requires not getting single and double quotes confused.

To finish, here are a couple of examples of using "The Walrus and the Carpenter":

```
julia> tfl = "walrus-and-carpenter.txt";
julia> ofl = "walrus-and-carpenter.out"
julia> run('wc $tfl' |> 'tee $ofl')
    124     626    3291 walrus-and-carpenter.txt
```

We have created a file (using tee) of the line /word/character counts in the poem and can now define a command that will find all integer numbers and increment them by 1.

```
julia> cp0 = 'perl -pe 's/(\d+)/ 1 + $1 /ge' $ofl'
julia> run(cp0)
    125     627    3292 walrus-and-carpenter.txt
```

Finally, here is another approach to reverse the lines in a file, which we implemented earlier on the Jabberwocky by using a line-by-line read in an open-do-end block. This is a one-liner applied this time to the first verse (6 lines) of "Walrus and the Carpenter":

```
julia> cp1 = 'perl -alne 'print "@{ [reverse @F] }"''
'perl -alne 'print "@{ [reverse @F] }"''
julia> run('head -6 $tfl' |> cp1)
```

```
sea, the on shining was sun The
might: his all with Shining
make to best very his did He
-- bright and smooth billows The
was it because odd, was this And
night. the of middle The
```

Summary

This chapter marks the end of our overview of some of the more unusual features of the Julia language. We have discussed the way Julia can interface directly with routines written in C and Fortran and how it is possible to use modules from other programming languages such as Python, R, and Java.

Further, we looked at the homoiconity nature of Julia and how this leads to the ability to define genuine runtime macros.

Finally, we introduced the running of separate tasks and pipelining and how the use of macros creates boilerplate code to greatly simplify the execution of the code on parallel processors.

In the subsequent chapters, we will be looking at individual topics that are of particular interest to analysts and data scientists, with a discussion of the I/O system and how to process data stored in disk files.

5

Working with Data

In many of the examples we have looked at so far, the data is little artificial since it has been generated using random numbers. It is now time to look at data held in files.

In this chapter, I'm going to concentrate on simple disk-based files, and reserve discussions of data stored in databases and on the Web for later chapters. Also, we will look at some of the statistical approaches in Julia that are incorporated both into the Julia base and into some of the growing number of packages covering statistics and related topics.

Basic I/O

Julia views its data in terms of a byte stream. If the stream comes from a network socket or a pipe, it is essentially asynchronous but the programmer need not be aware of this as the stream will be blocked until cleared by an I/O operation.

The primitives are the read() and write() functions which deal with binary I/O. When dealing with formatted data, such as text, a number of other functions are layered on top of these.

Terminal I/O

All streams in Julia have at least a read and a write routine. These take a Julia stream object as their first argument. In common with most systems, Julia defines three special terminal streams: standard-in (STDIN), standard-out (STDOUT) and standard-error (STDERR). The first is read-only and the latter two, write-only.

The special streams are provided by calls to the Julia API (libjulia) that links to the underlying operating system. Their definitions -- in terms of ccalls() -- along with the functions to operate on them, are part of the Base::streams.jl file.

There are a number of other files in Base for the curious to look at, notable among them are io.jl and fs.jl. However, to the analyst all the inner workings of the I/O system are relatively straightforward and follow a normal pattern of POSIX-based operating systems.

Consider some simple output to STDOUT:

```
julia> write(STDOUT, "Help ME!!!\n")
Help Me!!!
11
```

11 is the number of bytes written, including the newline character. Due to the asynchronous nature of the I/O, the REPL outputs the string before the number of characters that were written.

We have seen earlier that using the print function, rather than write, absorbs the byte count. Also, if not provided, the STDOUT stream is taken as default. So print(STDOUT, "Help ME!!!\n") and print("Help ME!!!\n") will both produce identical output. Also, conveniently the println() function will append more.

To format output, we saw that Julia employs the macro system for generating the boilerplate. In fact, the whole system is so complex that it warrants its own module in Base, printf.jl. Also, included in the module is a @sprintf macro which will print formatted output to a string rather than to an output stream.

> Julia does not have a @fprintf macro to write to a file, instead it uses an extended form of @printf as we will see later.

Now, let's look at how to get input from STDIN. Julia uses the read() function that takes two arguments. The Julia stream object as the first argument and the second being the datatype to input:

```
julia> read(STDIN,Char)   # => Typing a return (®) gives 'a'
```

But all is not immediately obvious, try for instance:

```
julia> read(STDIN,Int32)   # => Typing 1234® gives 875770417
```

Although this seems bizarre, the behavior is easily explained as:

```
julia> read(STDIN,Uint32)  # => Typing 1234 ® gives 0x34333231
```

So the result (875770417) is the ASCII representation of 1234 in reverse order!

To get the expected behavior, we need to use `readline()` instead of `read()`. This will consume the entire line and give the output as a string in the correct order:

```
julia> a = readline()   # => Typing 1234 ® gives a = "1234\n"
```

A couple of points to note are that `readline` includes the final return character, so to strip it off use the `chomp(readline())` construct.

Also, the routine returns a string where we probably expected an integer. The easiest way to deal with this is by just casting (converting) the string to the required datatype, in this case: `int(chomp(readline()))`.

Of course, the conversion will fail unless the input is parsed correctly as an integer.

This will raise an exception error, unless trapped with a `try/catch` block. So a function such as the following would clean up the input:

```
function getInt()
  a = chomp(readline())
  try
    return int(a)
  catch
    return Nothing
  end
end
```

Finally, it is possible to use the `readbytes(STDIN,N)` function to read N bytes into a `Uint8` array as:

```
julia> readbytes(STDIN,4)
abcd
#=> 4-element Array{Uint8,1}: [0x61, 0x62, 0x63, 0x64]
```

Disk files

Files on disk are accessed or created using the `open()` function. There are various flavors of open statements that can be listed using the `methods(open)` command. Here, I'll deal with the usual type where a file name is passed as an argument to `open()`, these are to be found in `iostream.jl`:

```
open(fname::String)
open(fname::String [,r::Bool,w::Bool,c::Bool,t::Bool,f::Bool])
open(fname::String, mode::String)
```

In all cases, `fname` is the name of the file to be opened. This may be relative to the current location or can be a fully qualified path name and successful opening of the file returns an `IOStream` object.

The first variant is the most straightforward. This opens the file for reading and if the file does not exist, or the current user process can't access the file due to insufficient privileges, an error (trappable) is raised.

The second form consists of the file name followed by five optional boolean parameters. The first corresponds to opening the file for reading or writing, if both are true it is open for both reading and writing. The third parameter will specify that the file will be created, if it does *not* exist, and the fourth indicates that it will be truncated, if it *does* exists. The final parameter indicates that any writes will be appended to the end of the current file. When no flags are specified the default is `r` . If this is true and the rest are false, then that the file is opened read-only.

Not all of the combinations of the flags are logically consistent, so it is more common to employ the third form of open where the mode is passed as an ASCII string having the following possible values:

```
+-------+------------------------------------------+
| r     | read                                     |
+-------+------------------------------------------+
| r+    | read, write                              |
+-------+------------------------------------------+
| w     | write, create, truncate                  |
+-------+------------------------------------------+
| w+    | read, write, create, truncate            |
+-------+------------------------------------------+
| a     | write, create, append                    |
+-------+------------------------------------------+
| a+    | read, write, create, append              |
+-------+------------------------------------------+
```

These will be familiar to any Unix readers as they are the same as those used by the Unix standard library.

Since opening a file, doing something to its contents, and finally closing it again is a very common pattern, there is another option that takes a function as its first argument and filename as its second. This opens the file, calls the function with the file as an argument, applies the function to the file contents and then closes it again.

For example, suppose we take the file consisting of the first four lines of the Jabberwocky from the previous chapter in the `/Users/malcolm/Alice/jabber4.txt` file.

Then, we can capitalize the text using the following:

```
function capitalize(f::IOStream)
  return uppercase(readall(f))
end
```

```
open(capitalize, "/Users/malcolm/Alice/jabber4.txt")
 "Twas brillig, and the slithy toves\nDid gyre and gimble in the wabe:\
nAll mimsy were the borogoves,\nAnd the momeraths outgrabe.\n"
```

In this example, the entire file is input into a string using `readall()` and since uppercase will operate on the entire string, the function is pretty lightweight.

For more complex processing, we will open the file and work on individual parts of the file. So the example of reversing the lines of text, which we performed using Perl in the previous chapter, could be written natively in Julia as:

```
f = open("/Users/malcolm/Alice/jabber4.txt")
while (!eof(f))
  println(reverse(chomp(readline(f))))
end
close(f)
sevot yhtils eht dna ,gillirb sawT'
:ebaw eht elbmig dna eryg diD
,sevogorob eht erew ysmim llA
.ebargtuo shtar emom eht dnA
```

Notice that `readline()` again returns a string including a return character, but because we are reversing the line we need to strip it off and output the line with `println()`. Again, this `open/process/close` construct is so common that it can be written in an alternative form using a do block as:

```
open("/Users/malcolm/Alice/jabber4.txt") do f
  while (!eof(f))
    println(reverse(chomp(readline(f))))
  end
end
```

Text processing

Use of functions such as `read()`, `readline()`, and `readall()` provides us with the tools to implement text processing routines without having to resort to the sort of operating system tricks we employed in the previous chapter.

Consider the basis of the standard Hadoop example of counting the number of words in a file. We can start with a basic `word_count()` function that splits an arbitrary line of text in to individual words.

```
function wordcount(text)
  wds = split(lowercase(text),
    [' ','\n','\t','-','.',',',':',';','!','?','\'','"'];
      keep=false)
  d = Dict()
    for w = wds
      d[w]=get(d,w,0)+1
    end
    return d
end
```

This function converts the input text to lowercase so as not to differentiate between cases such as `The` and `the`. It splits the text on the basis of whitespace and various punctuation marks, and creates a `d` dictionary (hash) to hold the word count.

The `get()` function returns the value for the `w` word from the `d` dictionary or a `0` if the word is not yet present. After processing all the text, the function returns.

We can apply this to our `jabber4` file. Rather than using the full file specification, I've used the `getenv()` function we created earlier to get the `HOME` directory and changed it into the `Alice` subdirectory.

```
cd (getenv("HOME")*"/Alice");
open("jabber4.txt") do f
  c = wordcount(lowercase(readall(f)))
  print(c)
end
{"'twas"=>1,"gyre"=>1,"and"=>3,"brillig"=>1,"raths"=>1,"in"=>1,"mome"=>1,
"toves"=>1,"mimsy"=>1,"did"=>1,"the"=>4,"borogoves"=>1,"were"=>1,"all"=>1
,"wabe"=>1,"outgrabe"=>1,"slithy"=>1,"gimble"=>1}
```

Coupled with the `readdir()` function, it is possible to work on collections of files in a specific directory on the filesystem. Combine this with regex style pattern matching and all processing of text can be coded natively in Julia.

So if we wish to compute the word count for all the files with `.txt` extension in the Alice directory, we can refine the word count routine to take a dictionary and return the number of words processed as:

```
function wordcount(dcnts,text)
total = 0
words = split(lowercase(text),
[' ','\n','\t','-','.',',',':',';','!','?','\'','"','(',')']; 
keep=false)
for w = words
  dcnts[w] = get(dcnts,w,0)+1
    total += 1
end
return total
end
```

Applying this to all the text (txt) files in the directory is relatively easy:

```
d = Dict();
for fname in filter!(r"\.txt$", readdir())
  open(fname) do f
    n = wordcount(d, readall(f))
    @printf "%s: %d\n" fname n
  end
end
```

Running the preceding code gives the following output:

```
aged-aged-man.txt: 512
father-william.txt: 278
hunting-the-snark.txt: 4524
jabber4.txt: 23
jabberwocky.txt: 168
lobster-quadrille.txt: 231
```

```
mad-gardeners-song.txt: 348
voice-of-the-lobster.txt: 158
walrus-and-carpenter.txt: 623
```

The highest word count is for the stop words such as: the, and, a.

More interestingly, we can see the number of times a particular word, such as "snark", occurs from the following:

```
wd = ["bellman", "boots", "gardener", "jabberwock", "snark"];
for w in wd
  @printf "%12s  => %4d\n" w d[w]
end
      bellman # =>    30
        boots # =>     3
     gardener # =>     2
   jabberwock # =>     3
        snark # =>    32
```

Binary files

Julia can handle binary files as easily as text files using readbytes() and write().

In the first chapter, we created a simple grayscale image for a Julia set. It's possible to add some color using the following algorithm for each pixel value:

```
function pseudocolor(pix)
  if pix < 64
    pr = uint8(0)
    pg = uint8(0)
    pb = uint8(4*pix)
  elseif pix < 128
    pr = uint8(0)
    pg = uint8(4*(pix-64))
    pb = uint8(255)
  elseif pix < 192
    pr = uint8(0)
    pg = uint8(255)
```

```
      pb = uint8(4*(192 - pix))
    else
      pr = uint8(4*(pix - 192))
      pg = uint8(4*(256 - pix))
      pb = uint8(0)
    end
    return (pr , pg,  pb)
  end
```

Recall that the magic number of a binary colored NetPBM image is `"P6"`:

```
img = open("juliaset.pgm");
magic = chomp(readline(img));    # => "P5"
if magic == "P5"
  out = open("jsetcolor.ppm", "w");
  println(out, "P6");
  params = chomp(readline(img));   # => "800 400 255"
  println(out, params);
  (wd, ht, pmax) = int(split(params));
  for i = 1:ht
    buf = readbytes(img, wd);
    for j = 1:wd
      (r,g,b) = pseudocolor(buf[j]);
      write(out,r); write(out,g); write(out,b);
    end
  end
  close(out);
else
  error("Not a NetPBM grayscale file")
end
close(img);
```

We use `readline()` to grab the magic number and check that it is a PGM file. In this case, we open a file to hold the colored image and write `"P6"`, the PPM magic number.

The next line has the width, height and maximum pixel values. Because we are keeping byte values, we can write this back as it is. Also, we will need to decode the width and height in order to process all the pixels in the image.

I have applied the `pseudocolor()` function on a line-by-line basis.

This could have been easily done by reading individual bytes or grabbing all the bytes with a single `readbytes(wd*ht)` call. The latter has the merit of reducing file read/writes since the image will easily fit into available memory.

The result can be displayed using an image processing program that can read NetPBM images:

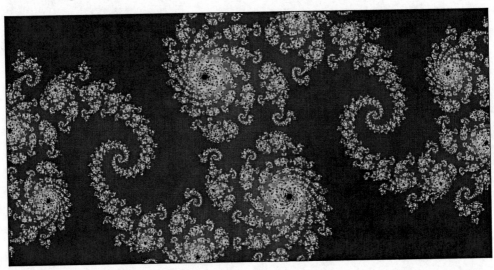

Structured datasets

In this section, we will look at files that contain metadata, the way that data is arranged as well as the values themselves. This includes simple delimited files and also files with additional metadata such as XML and HDF5.

Also, we will introduce the important topic of data arrays and frames in Julia, which is familiar to all R users and also implemented in Python via the `pandas` module.

CSV and DLM files

Data is often presented in table form as a series of rows representing individual records and fields corresponding to a data value for that particular record. Columns in the table are consistent, in the sense that they may be all integers, floats, dates, and so on,, and are to be considered as the same class of data. This will be familiar to most as it maps similar to the way data is held in a spreadsheet.

One of the oldest forms of such representation of such data is the **Comma-Separated-Value (CSV)** file. This is essentially an ASCII file in which fields are separated by commas (,) and records (rows) by a newline.

There is an obvious problem if some of the fields are strings containing commas, so CSV files use quoted text (normally using a ") to overcome this. However, this gives rise to the new question of how to deal with text fields that contain a " character.

In fact, the CSV file was never defined as a standard and a variety of implementations exist. However, the principle is clear that we require a method to represented involving a field separator and a record separator together with a way to identify any cases where the field and record separators are to be interpreted as regular characters.

This generalization is termed a **delimited file (DLM)** and an alternative to the CSV file is a **tab-separated file (TSV)** where the comma is replaced by a tab.

Julia has a built-in function called `readdlm()` that can open and read an entire disk file. Its source can be found in `base/datafmt.jl`.

The general form of the call is:

```
readdlm(source, delim::Char, T::Type, eol::Char; opts... )
```

Each line; is separated by `eol` and the fields separated by `delim`. The source can be a text file, stream, or byte array. Memory-mapped files can be used by passing the byte array representation of the mapped segment as source.

If `T` is a numeric type, the result is an array of that type with any non-numeric elements as `NaN` for floating-point types, or zero; other values for `T` can be `ASCIIString`, `String`, and `Any`.

A simpler form of `readdlm(source; opt)` will assume a standard end-of-line separator (`'\n'`) and that fields are delimited by whitespace. This can encompassed TSV files, if consisting of all numeric data, but if some of the fields are text containing spaces, it is necessary to specify `delim = '\t'` explicitly.

For comma-separated files, there is a separate `readcsv(source; opt...)` call where the delimiter is a comma (`delim = ','`).

The optional arguments are as follows:

```
header=false, skipstart=0, skipblanks=true, use_mmap, ignore_invalid_
chars=false, quotes=true, dims, comments=true, comment_char='#'
```

- If header is true, the first row of data will be read as header and the (`data_cells`, `header_cells`) tuple is returned instead of only `data_cells`.
- Specifying `skipstart` will ignore the corresponding number of initial lines from the input; if `skipblanks` is true, blank lines in the input will be ignored.
- If `use_mmap` is true, the file specified by source is memory mapped for potential speedups. The default is true except on Windows, for which we may want to specify true if the file is large and has to be read only once and not written to.
- If `ignore_invalid_chars` is true, bytes in source with invalid character encoding will be ignored. Otherwise an error is thrown indicating the offending character position.
- If `quotes` is true, column enclosed within double quote (`''`) characters are allowed to contain new lines and column delimiters. Double quote characters within a quoted field must be escaped with another double quote.
- Specifying `dims` as a tuple of the expected rows and columns (including header, if any) may speed up reading of large files.
- If `comments` is true, lines beginning with `comment_char` and text following `comment_char` in any line are ignored.

In the `Work` directory, we have a CSV file of the Apple share prices from 2000 to 2002. This has a header line and six fields, and we can read it into an array as:

```
(aapl,cols) = readcsv("AAPL.csv"; header=true);
```

The `aapl` matrix contains the data and the `head` vector contains the column information:

```
julia> cols
1x13 Array{String,2}:
"Date" "Open" "High" "Low" "Close" "Volume"
"Ex-Dividend" "Split Ratio"
"Adj. Open"  "Adj. High"  "Adj. Low"  "Adj. Close"  "Adj. Volume"
```

We see that there are 13 fields per row comprising the date, opening, high, low, and closing prices, and the volume traded (both actual and adjusted) as well as the ex-dividend and split ratio values. Nominally these will be `0.0` and `1.0` respectively unless there is a day on which a dividend is paid or a rights issue in effect.

The data consists of a matrix of 752 rows and 13 columns:

```julia
julia> typeof(aapl)     # => Array{Any,2}
```

The data is in the form of an {Any} array; looking at the first 6 columns:

```julia
julia> aapl[:, 1:6]
 "2002-12-31"   14.0    14.36   13.95   14.33   3584400
 "2002-12-30"   14.08   14.15   13.84   14.07   2768600
 "2002-12-27"   14.31   14.38   14.01   14.06   1429200
 "2002-12-26"   14.42   14.81   14.28   14.4    1525400
 "2002-12-24"   14.44   14.47   14.3    14.36   702500
 "2002-12-23"   14.16   14.55   14.12   14.49   2246900
 "2002-12-20"   14.29   14.56   13.78   14.14   5680300
 "2002-12-19"   14.53   14.92   14.1    14.2    6250700
 "2002-12-18"   14.8    14.86   14.5    14.57   2691100
```

Since the date is a non-numeric field, this is input as a string and results in the {Any} typing. Also, notice that the dates are in descending order.

So in order to get the closing prices, we will need to slice the matrix along the fifth column, convert to `float64`, and reverse the array order as:

```julia
aa_close = float64(reverse(aapl[:,5]));
```

Since the dates are not arranged linearly, due to weeks and bank holidays, we need to transform the dates as an offset from some reference date for which we will take the minimum date as `2000-01-01`.

We can compute the days from this reference and use the indexing of the list comprehension to reverse the date order as:

```julia
using Date
d0 = Date("2000-01-01")
naapl = size(aa_date)[1]
aa_date = zeros(naapl)
```

```
[aa_date[1+n-i] = int(Date(aapl[i,1]) - d0) for i = 1:nappl]
```

```
using Winston
plot(aa_date, aa_close)
```

The resulting graph is shown in the following figure:

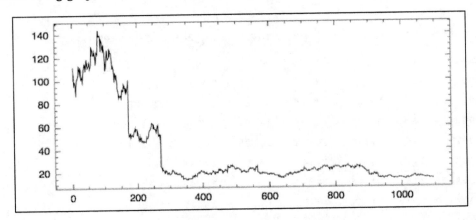

The first year (2000) was clearly a volatile one with a rapid decline in value, although the current value of Apple stocks is more than 500 percent of the peak price here.

On two occasions we can see a fall of over $20 in a single day, so looking for these days:

```
for i in 2:(size(aapl)[1] - 1)
  if abs(aapl[i,5] - aapl[i-1,5]) > 20.0
    println(i+1, " : ", aapl[i+1,1:8])
    println(i,     " : ", aapl[i,1:8])
    println(i-1, " : ", aapl[i-1,1:8])
  end
end
```

This code produces the following output:

```
635 : Any["2000-06-20" 98.5 103.94 98.38 101.25 4.4767e6 0.0 1.0]
634 : Any["2000-06-21" 50.5 56.94 50.31 55.62 8.75e6 0.0 2.0]
633 : Any["2000-06-22" 55.75 57.62 53.56 53.75 8.352e6 0.0 1.0]
```

```
566 : Any["2000-09-27" 51.75 52.75 48.25 48.94 7.1832e6 0.0 1.0]
565 : Any["2000-09-28" 49.31 53.81 48.12 53.5 1.74926e7 0.0 1.0]
564 : Any["2000-09-29" 28.19 29.0 25.38 25.75 1.325293e8 0.0 1.0]
```

The stock price from close of 20/06/2000 to open of 21/06/2000 has roughly halved but this is explained by the Split Ratio = 2.0; so in fact there was a 2 for 1 script issue following the close of 20/06/2000.

For the second sharp fall on 28/09/2000, there is no obvious cause but there are very high volumes on this day and more so on the following day, indicating a rapid sell off of Apple stocks.

If we wish to look at the price spreads over individual days, we need to look at the differences between the opening and closing prices, which is easily achieved as:

```
aa_diff = float64(reverse(aapl[:,2] - aapl[:,5]));
plot(aa_date[1:250], aa_diff)
```

This plot is displayed in the following figure:

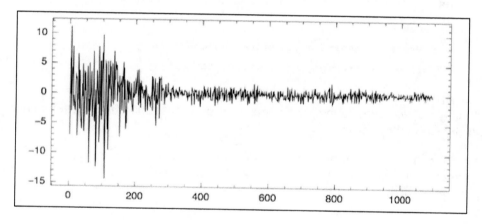

HDF5

HDF5 stands for **Hierarchical Data Format v5**. It was originally developed by the NCSA in the USA and is now supported by the HDF Group. It was developed to store large amount of scientific data that are exposed to a user as groups and datasets that are akin to directories and files in a conventional filesystem.

Version 5 was developed to overcome some of the limitations of the previous version (v4) and Julia, in common with languages such as Python, R, MATLAB/Octave, has extensions to be able to access files in HDF5 format.

HDF5 also uses attributes to associate metadata with a particular group or dataset, and ASCII names for these different objects. Objects can be accessed by UNIX-like pathnames, such as, `/projects/juno/tests/first.h5` where `projects` is a top-level group, `juno` and `tests` are subgroups, and `first.h5` is a dataset.

Language wrappers for HDF5 may be viewed as either low-level or high-level. The `hdf5.jl` Julia package contains both levels. At the low level, it directly wraps HDF5's functions, copying their API, and making them available from within Julia. At the high level, it provides a set of functions that are built on the low-level wrapper in order to simplify the usage of the library.

For simple types (scalars, strings, and arrays), HDF5 provides sufficient metadata to know how each item is to be interpreted while representing the data in a way that is agnostic to computing architectures.

Plain HDF5 files are created and/or opened in Julia with the `h5open` command:

```
fid = h5open(filename, mode)
```

In the preceding command, `mode` can be any one of the following:

`"r"`   `read-only`

`"r+"` `read-write, preserving any existing contents`

`"w"`   `read-write, destroying any existing contents`

This returns an object of the `PlainHDF5File` type, a subtype of the `HDF5File` abstract type. *Plain* files have no elements (groups, datasets, or attributes) that are not explicitly created by the user.

The `HDF5.jl` package also provides a **Julia Data format (JLD)** to accurately store and retrieve Julia variables. It is possible to use plain HDF5 for this purpose, but the advantage of the JLD module is that it preserves the exact type information of each variable.

The Julia implementation of the HDF5 is very comprehensive and the reader is encouraged to look at the excellent online documentation on HDF and JLD in the `HDF5.jl` GitHub repository.

Here, I will concentrate on the JLD module. This is very convenient for interchanging the Julia data between sites.

As an example, we will store the `aa_date` APPL and the `aa_close` data that we created in the previous section as:

```
jdlopen(/Users/malcolm/Work/aapl.jld, "w") do fid
  write(fid, "aa_date", aa_date)
  write fid  "aa_close", aa_close)
end
close(fid)
```

This creates a `aapl.jld` file and adds datasets for `aa_date` and `aa_close`.

Alternatively, the same process can be achieved using:

```
save("/Users/malcolm/Work/aapl.jld",
  "aa_date", aa_date. "aa_close", aa_close)
```

There are also macro versions that assume the dataset name is the same as the variable such as:

```
@save "/Users/malcolm/Work/aapl.jld" aa_date aa_close
```

Reading back the data is relatively straightforward:

```
fid = jldopen("/Users/malcolm/Work/aapl.jld")
ac = read(fid, "aa_close")
ad = read(fid, "aa_date")
```

We can check that the re-read data matches the original:

```
typeof(ad); # => 752-element Array{Float64,1}:


[assert(ad[i] == aa_date[i]) for i = 1:size(ad)[1]];
```

Because JLD is a special case of HDF5, we can use the routines from the latter module. For example, the structure of the file we can use `dump()`, the first few lines are the most enlightening:

```
dump(fid)
JldFile
  plain: HDF5File len 3
    _require: HDF5Dataset () : UTF8String[]
    aa_close: HDF5Dataset (752,) : [111.94,102.5,104.0,95.0,
    aa_date: HDF5Dataset (752,) : [2.0,3.0,4.0,5.0,
```

In the previous example, we wrote the AAPL data in its own file. However, it is easy to create a file, and create an `aapl` group to hold the datasets:

```
fid = jldopen("/Users/malcolm/Work/mydata.jld", "w")

g = g_create(fid, "aapl")

g["aa_date"] = aa_date

g["aa_close"] = aa_close
```

We can check the structure has changed as:

```
dump(fid)
JldFile
  plain: HDF5File len 2
    _require: HDF5Dataset () : UTF8String[]
    aapl: HDF5Group len 2
      aa_close: HDF5Dataset (752,) : [111.94,102.5,104.0,95.0,
      aa_date: HDF5Dataset (752,) : [2.0,3.0,4.0,5.0,
```

The datasets can be retrieved by either of the following:

```
g = fid["aapl"];  ad = g["aa_date"]

ad = fid["aapl/aa_date"]
```

XML files

Alternative data representations are provided using XML and JSON. We will consider data handling again in *Chapter 8, Databases* and *Chapter 9, Networking*, when we look at JSON and discuss networking, web, and REST services.

In this section, we will look at XML file handling and the functionality available in the `LightXML` package.

To assist we will use the `books.xml` file, which contains a list of ten books. The first portion of the file is:

```
<?xml version="1.0" encoding="UTF-8" ?>
<catalog>
  <book id="bk101">
    <author>Gambardella, Matthew</author>
    <title genre='Computing'>XML Developer's Guide</title>
    <price currency='GBP'>44.95</price>
    <publish_date>2000-10-01</publish_date>
    <description>An in-depth look at creating applications
    with XML.</description>
  </book>
</catalog>
```

`LightXML` is a wrapper of `Libxml2`, which provides a reasonably comprehensive high-level interface covering the most functionalities:

- Parse a XML file or string into a tree
- Access XML tree structure
- Create an XML tree
- Export an XML tree to a string or an XML file

Here, I will cover parsing an XML file as it is probably the most common procedure:

```
cd(); cd ("Work")
using LightXML
xdoc = parse_file("books.xml");
xtop = root(xdoc);
println(name(xtop));  # => catalog
```

To read the file into memory, we use the `parse_file()` function. To traverse the entire tree, we start by getting a reference to the top element: `catalog`. The following finds all the element nodes and the `title` child element. This element has an attribute corresponding to the `genre` element and the code prints out all ten books and their genre.

```
for c in child_nodes(xtop)
  if is_elementnode(c)
    e = XMLElement(c)
    t = find_element(e, "title")
    title = content(t)
    genre = attribute(t, "genre")
    @printf "%20s :%s\n" title genre
  end
end
XML Developer's Guide  : Computing
Midnight Rain          : Fantasy
Maeve Ascendant        : Fantasy
Oberon's Legacy        : Fantasy
The Sundered Grail     : Fantasy
Lover Birds            : Romance
Splish Splash          : Romance
Creepy Crawlies        : Horror
```

```
Paradox Lost              : SciFi
.NET Programming Bible : Computing
```

Finally, we look for all the computing books and print out the full details. The publication date is in the format YYYY-MM-DD, so I've used the Dates package to create a more readable string.

Notice that, as I have pointed out earlier, this book is using the current stable version of Julia (v0.3.x). There is an important change in v0.4, here the Dates package is incorporated into the Base and this is likely to be the stable version at the time of reading.

```
using Dates
for c in child_nodes(xtop)
  if is_elementnode(c)
    e = XMLElement(c)
    t = find_element(e, "title")
    genre = attribute(t, "genre")
    if genre == "Computing"
      a = find_element(e,"author")
      p = find_element(e,"price")
      curr = attribute(p, "currency")
      d = find_element(e,"publish_date")
      dc = DateTime(content(d))
      ds = string(day(dc)," ",monthname(dc)," ",year(dc))
      desc = find_element(e,"description")
      println("Title: ", content(t))
      println("Author: " ,content(a))
      println("Date: " ,ds)
      println("Price: " ,p ," (", curr, ")")
      println(content(desc),"\n");
    end
  end
end
Title:      XML Developer's Guide
Author:     Gambardella, Matthew
```

Date: 1 October 2000

Price: 44.95 (GDP)

An in-depth look at creating applications with XML.

Title: .NET Programming Bible

Author: O'Brien, Tim

Date: 9 December 2000

Price: 36.95 (GBP)

Microsoft's .NET initiative is explored in detail in this deep
programmer's reference.

DataFrames and RDatasets

When dealing with tabulated datasets there are occasions when some of the
values are missing. One of the features of statistical languages is that they can
handle such situations.

In Julia, the DataFrames package has been developed in order to treat such cases
and this is the subject of this chapter.

The DataFrames package

The package extends the Julia base by adding three new types:

- NA is introduced in order to represent a missing value. This type only has
  one particular value NA.

- DataArray is a type that emulates Julia's standard Array type, but is able
  to store missing values in the array.

- DataFrame is a type that is capable of representing tabular datasets such
  as those found in typical databases or spreadsheets. The concept of the
  data frame is most evident in R language and is one of the cornerstones
  of its popularity.

Except for its ability to store NA values, the DataArray type is meant to behave
exactly as Julia's standard Array type. In particular, DataArray provides two type
aliases called DataVector and DataMatrix that mimic the Vector and Matrix type
aliases for 1D and 2D array types.

The `DataArray` is included as part of the `DataFrames` package, so in order to introduce it and the `NA` type we type: `using DataFrames`.

Creating a data array is via the `@data` macro:

```
using DataFrames
da = @data([NA, 3.1, 2.3, 5.7, NA, 4.4])
```

This creates a `6-element DataArray` of the `Float64` type with the first and fifth elements being `NA`.

If we take a simple statistical metric such as the `mean(da)` command, this gives a `NA` value.

In order to get a meaningful value for the mean, we need to ignore (`drop`) the NA values:

```
mean(dropna(da))  ; # => 3.875
```

This effectively sums up all non-NA values, and computes the mean of 4 values and not 6. The `dropna()` function can also be used to convert the data array to a regular array as:

```
aa = convert(Array,dropna(da))
4-element Array{Float64, 1} #= => [3.1, 2.3, 5.7, 4.4]
```

It is also possible to substitute missing (NA) values for a default value:

```
aa = array(da, 0)
4-element Array{Float64, 1} #=> [0.0, 3.1, 2.3, 5.7, 0.0, 4.4]
```

```
mean(aa); # => 2.5833
```

The mean value is now different as we have 6 elements rather than 4.

DataFrames

`NA` and `DataArray` provide mechanisms for handling missing values for scalar types and arrays, but most real-world datasets have a tabular structure that do not correspond to a simple `DataArray` type.

Columns of tabular datasets may be of different types, normally scalars such as lengths integers or reals, strings or booleans (such as `Yes`/`No`). Also they may be values within enumerated set.

However, apart from the possibility of absence of a value in any particular position in a column all values will be of the same type and the columns will be of equal length.

This description will be familiar to anyone who has worked with R's `dataframe` type, Pandas' `DataFrame` type, an SQL-style database, or Excel spreadsheet.

We can create a data frame consisting of two columns: x being linear spaced between `0` and `10`, and y being an equivalent number of normally distributed values. This can be done as:

```
df = DataFrame(X = linspace(0,10,101), Y = randn(101))
101x2 DataFrame
```

```
| Row | X   | Y          |
|-----|-----|------------|
| 1   | 0.0 | -0.0929538 |
| 2   | 0.1 | 0.56163    |
| 3   | 0.2 | -1.23955   |
| 4   | 0.3 | -1.19571   |
| 5   | 0.4 | -0.66432   |
```

The names of the columns are now part of the `DataArray` type structure and so we use the symbol (`:Y`) in the `df[:Y]` notation as a shorthand for `df[: , 2]`.

Recalling that this is a set of randomly spread data values, we can look at the basic statistic metrics of mean, standard deviation, median and covariance:

```
mean(df[:Y]);    # => 0.0568417959105659    (expected 0.0)
var(df[:Y]);     # => 0.9609662097467784    (expected 1.0)
```

The package has a `readtable()` function similar to `readcsv()` we saw earlier, but rather than returning any existing header row as part of the data or as a separate vector it is now part of the data frame structure.

There is also a `writetable()` function to export data to a file, typically:

```
writetable(fname, df; opts...)
```

`readtable()` and `writetable()` take a pragmatic view to opening the file; if the extension is `csv`, the file type is assumed to be comma-separated, if it's `tsv` then tab-separated, and if `wsv`, it is white-space separated.

Otherwise, it is possible to use the optional argument (separator =) to indicate the field separator character.

There are a number of other options, a useful one is header = that takes the false value if there is no header row and true (default) otherwise.

Using our APPLE share data: aapl = readtable("AAPL.csv")

```
752x13 DataFrame
```

(Looking at the first 6 columns):

Row	Date	Open	High	Low	Close	Volume
1	"2002-12-31"	14.0	14.36	13.95	14.33	3.5844e6
2	"2002-12-30"	14.08	14.15	13.84	14.07	2.7686e6
3	"2002-12-27"	14.31	14.38	14.01	14.06	1.4292e6
4	"2002-12-26"	14.42	14.81	14.28	14.4	1.5254e6
5	"2002-12-24"	14.44	14.47	14.3	14.36	702500.0

The base provides a few basic statistical functions, such as the mean() used previously. Tying these all together to define a description() routine, we have:

```
function describe(aa)
   println("Mean       : " , mean(aa))
   println("Std. Devn. : " , std(aa))
   println("Median     : " , median(aa))
   println("Mode       : " , mode(aa))
   println("Quantiles  : " , quantile(aa))
   println("# samples  : " , length(aa))
end


julia> describe(aapl[:Close])
Mean       : 37.12550531914894
Std. Devn. : 34.118614874718254
Median     : 21.49
Mode       : 19.5
Quantiles  : [13.59,17.735,21.49,31.615,144.19]
```

We can calculate the correlation and covariance between opening and closing prices as:

```
cor(aapl[:Open], aapl[:Close]);  # => 0.9982147046681757
cov(aapl[:Open], aapl[:Close]);  # => 1162.2183466395873
```

If we can create a vector of the daily spreads, using the `hist()` function computes an histogram with (default) 10 intervals:

```
spread = aapl[:High] - aapl[:Low];
hist(spread); # => (0.0:2.0:18.0,[557,70,50,41,13,14,3,3,1])
```

`hist()` returns a tuple of two elements, range, and frequency vector.

The following figure is a plot of the spreads and histogram. The histogram figure was created using `Winston` with the following code:

```
using Winston

p = FramedPlot()

add(p,Histogram(hist(spread)...))
```

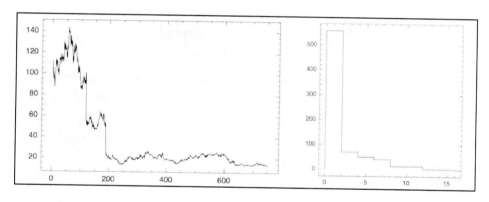

RDatasets

The Julia `RDatasets` package is a part of the Rdatasets *repo* authored by Vincent Arelbundock. These are taken from many standard R packages and are located on GitHib at https://github.com/vincentarelbundock/Rdatasets.

Installing `RDatasets.jl` places all the datasets in a number of subdirectories that are under a data directory, which we refer to as data group. The individual data is provided as either compressed CSV (`.csv.gz`) or R datafile (`.rda`) format.

There are over 700 packages in 34 groups. A full list of the groups can be found at `https://github.com/johnmyleswhite/RDatasets.jl`.

In order to load any of the datasets, the `DataFrames` package needs to be installed.

To load data we use the `dataset()` function, which takes two arguments, the name of the data group and the specific dataset, and returns a data frame of the underlying data:

```
using DataFrames, RDatasets
mlmf = dataset("mlmRev","Gcsemv")
```

`mlmRev` is a group of datasets from multilevel software review and `Gcsemv` refers to GSCE exam scores.

A complete list of all datasets can be obtained by `RDatasets.available_datasets()`.

For an individual group such as `mlmRev`, the related data is listed with `RDatasets.datasets("mlmRev")`.

Subsetting, sorting, and joining data

We will look at the `Gcsemv` dataset in the `mlmRev` group.

This covers the GCSE results from 73 schools both in examination and course work. The data is not split by subject (only school and pupil) but the gender of the student is provided:

```
julia> mlmf = dataset("mlmRev","Gcsemv");
julia> summary(mlmf); # =>  "1905x5 DataFrame"
julia> head(mlmf)
```

Row	School	Student	Gender	Written	Course
1	"20920"	"16"	"M"	23.0	NA
2	"20920"	"25"	"F"	NA	71.2
3	"20920"	"27"	"F"	39.0	76.8
4	"20920"	"31"	"F"	36.0	87.9
5	"20920"	"42"	"M"	16.0	44.4
6	"20920"	"62"	"F"	36.0	NA

There are 5 columns, the school code, student code, gender, and the written and course work percentages.

Notice that some of the data values are marked as NA (not available). We can select the data for a particular school as:

```julia
julia> mlmf[mlmf[:School] .== "68207", :]
5x5 DataFrame
```

Row	School	Student	Gender	Written	Course
1	"68207"	"7"	"F"	32.0	58.3
2	"68207"	"84"	"F"	25.0	41.6
3	"68207"	"101"	"F"	23.0	62.9
4	"68207"	"126"	"F"	26.0	57.4
5	"68207"	"167"	"M"	NA	50.0

We can group the data by school as:

```julia
julia> groupby(mlmf, :School);
GroupedDataFrame 73 groups with keys: [:School]
```

So let's list all schools with results from more than 50 students and compute the mean examination and course work scores:

```julia
for subdf in groupby(mlmf, :School)
  (size(subdf)[1] > 40) &&
    @printf "%6s : %4d : %6.2f : %6.2f\n" subdf[:School][1] size(subdf)
[1] mean(dropna(subdf[:Written])) mean(dropna(subdf[:Course]))
end
22520 :   65 :  35.84 :   56.45
60457 :   54 :  53.34 :   85.61
68107 :   79 :  44.41 :   74.19
68137 :  104 :  28.92 :   62.62
68321 :   52 :  52.00 :   78.64
68411 :   84 :  40.96 :   59.21
68809 :   73 :  42.68 :   70.98
```

We can sort the dataset in ascending examination scores:

```
julia> sort!(mlmf, cols=[:Written])
1905x5 DataFrame
```

Row	School	Student	Gender	Written	Course
1	"22710"	"77"	"F"	0.6	41.6
2	"68137"	"65"	"F"	2.5	50.0
3	"22520"	"115"	"M"	3.1	9.25
4	"68137"	"80"	"F"	4.3	50.9
5	"68137"	"79"	"F"	7.5	27.7
6	"22710"	"57"	"F"	11.0	73.1

We can see that, in general, marks for course work seem higher than for examination.

So computing the differences and some basic metrics:

```
diff = dropna(mlmf[:Course] - mlmf[:Written]);
```

mean(diff) is 26.9 with SD of 15.58.

minimum(diff) is -43.5 and maximum(diff) is 76.0.

A histogram tells us more:

```
hh = hist(diff)
(-50.0:10.0:80.0, [2,1,6,16,53,125,251,408,361,211,78,10,1])
```

hh is a tuple where hh[1] is the range and hh[2] is an array containing the frequency counts. There are 5 bins for negative and 8 for positive ones.

```
julia> sum(hh[2][1:5]) ;    # => 78
julia> sum(hh[2][6:13]);  # => 1445
```

So in only 78 cases (out of 1523) is the examination mark greater than that of the course work.

Finally, let's compute the correlation coefficient between the two sets of marks.

We need to select only rows with no NA values, one method would be to use a logical condition such as:

```
!(isequal(mlmf[:Written][i], NA) || isequal(mlmf[:Course][i], NA))
```

However, there is an easier way using the `complete_cases()` function to create a subsetted data frame.

```
df = mlmf[complete_cases(mlmf[[:Written, :Course]]), :]
cor(df[:Written],df[:Course]); => 0.4742
```

So the correlation between the written and course work is only 0.48.

The Julia base also has a `linreg()` linear regression function that will fit a least squares line through the data values:

```
linreg(array(df[:Written]), array(df[:Course]));
# => 2-element Array{Float64,1}: [ 17.9713, 0.388884 ]
```

The following figure is a scatterplot of the written and course work scores, together with the least squares linear regression line:

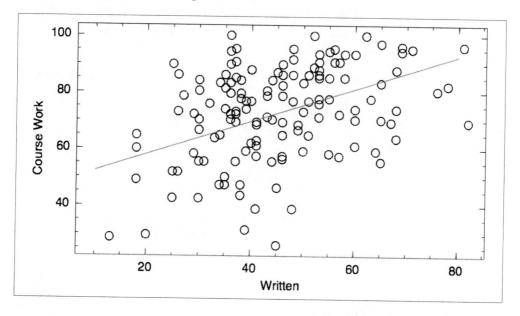

Statistics

The Julia community has begun to group packages and developers together where there is some significant common functionality. One of the most prolific is the JuliaStats group that, as the name suggests, is concerned with statistical matters.

Although Julia was initially conceived as a replacement for slow scientific languages such as MATLAB and its clones, the success of the language in a wide variety of disciplines, including statistics, makes it attractive for a much wider audience.

JuliaStats has its own web page on GitHub (`https://github.com/JuliaStats`) that list links to various packages. The group is concerned with machine learning as well as basic and advanced statistics. Many packages provide documentation at `http://readthedocs.org` in addition to the markdown README file in the package itself.

In this section, I will be looking at some of the features provided by the Julia base and in `StatsBase.jl`, the full documentation of the latter is at `http://statsbasejl.readthedocs.org`.

This enhances the base with a series of statistics-related mathematical and empirical functions and covers the following topics:

- *Mean and Counting Functions*
- *Scalar and Summary Statistics*
- *Ranking and Correlation*
- *Sampling and Empirical Estimation*

Most of the popular `pandas.py` Python module is now covered by the combination of `DataFrames` and `StatsBase` and the goal of the group is to extend this to (at least) all of `pandas`.

There is also a `Pandas.jl` wrapper package that interfaces with the pandas API, which uses `PyCall` and so needs a working version of Python with `pandas` installed. I will look at this package briefly later.

There are many modules provided by R and it is possible to use `Rif.jl` to access these. Although, this is out of the scope of this book, the reader is directed to the GitHub sources for more details.

Simple statistics

We will return again to the Apple share prices from 2000 to 2002. In addition to the full CSV file, I have provided a short version with just the first 6 columns, that is, up to `Volume`.

Uptil now we have used simple statistics in Julia base, now we will investigate this data further.

```
using DataFrames, StatsBase
aapl = readtable("AAPL-Short.csv");


naapl = size(aapl)[1]
m1 = int(mean((aapl[:Volume]))); # => 6306547
```

The data is read into a `DataFrame` and we can estimate the mean (`m1`) as before. For the volume, I've cast this as an integer as this makes more sense.

As we have seen, there are 3 years of data and we wish to give more data to the recent years than earlier ones. We can do this by creating a weighting vector:

```
using Match
wts = zeros(naapl);
for i in 1:naapl
  dt = aapl[:Date][i]
  wts[i] = @match dt begin
    r"^2000" => 1.0
    r"^2001" => 2.0
    r"^2002" => 4.0
    _        => 0.0
  end
end;


wv = WeightVec(wts);
m2 = int(mean(aapl[:Volume], wv)); # => 6012863
```

In addition, by computing weighted statistical metrics it is possible to trim off the outliers from each end of the data.

Returning to the closing prices:

```
mean(aapl[:Close]);           # => 37.1255
mean(aapl[:Close], wv);       # => 26.9944
trimmean(aapl[:Close], 0.1);  # => 34.3951
```

`trimean()` is the trimmed mean where 5 percent is taken from each end.

```
std(aapl[:Close]);            # => 34.1186
skewness(aapl[:Close])        # => 1.6911
kurtosis(aapl[:Close])        # => 1.3820
```

As well as second moments such as standard deviation, `StatsBase` provides a generic `moments()` function and specific instances based on this such as for `skewness` (third) and `kurtosis` (fourth).

It is also possible to provide some summary statistics:

```
summarystats(aapl[:Close])
```

```
Summary Stats:
Mean:          37.125505
Minimum:       13.590000
1st Quartile:  17.735000
Median:        21.490000
3rd Quartile:  31.615000
Maximum:       144.190000
```

The `1st` and `3rd` quartiles are related to 25 percent and 75 percent percentiles. For a finer granularity we can use the `percentile()` function:

```
percentile(aapl[:Close],5);   # => 14.4855
percentile(aapl[:Close],95);  # => 118.934
```

Samples and estimations

Let's now return to look at the GCSE scores we loaded from the `mlmRev` collection from `RDatasets`:

```
julia>  using RDatasets

julia>  mlmf = dataset("mlmRev","Gcsemv");
```

Recall that we can reduce the data to cases where there are no available values (NA) as:

```
df = mlmf[complete_cases(mlmf[[:Written, :Course]]), :];
mean(df[:Written]); # => 46.5023
std(df[:Written]);  # => 13.4775
sem(df[:Written]);  # =>  0.3454
```

`sem()` standard error of the mean.

Let's compute 10 samples, each with 100 data values, from the written scores and estimate it ourselves:

```
n = 10;

mm = zeros(n);

[mm[i] = mean(sample(df[:Written], 100))  for I on 1:10];
 # => [47.67. 45.15, 47.48, 45.94, 47.49, 44.89, 45.71, 46.48, 45.47,
45.79]

mean(mm);      # => 46.2062
std(mm);       # => 1.020677
```

The mean value of the samples approaches the population mean of 46.5 and our estimate of the standard error is found by dividing the sample standard deviation by the square root of the number of samples:

```
std(mm) / sqrt(n) ; #   =>  0.3328
```

Pandas

As we stated earlier, much of functionality in the `pandas` Python module is now in `DataFrames` and `StatsBase` packages. However, calling Python via `PyCall` makes the entire module accessible from Julia.

Let's look at our reduced dataset of Apple share prices using `Pandas`:

```julia
julia> aapl = read_csv("AAPL-short.csv");
julia> aapl
```

	Date	Open	High	Low	Close	Volume
0	2002-12-31	14.00	14.36	13.95	14.33	3584400
1	2002-12-30	14.08	14.15	13.84	14.07	2768600
2	2002-12-27	14.31	14.38	14.01	14.06	1429200
3	2002-12-26	14.42	14.81	14.28	14.40	1525400

Notice that the row count starts at 0 rather than 1, this is because the `Pandas` module automatically switches between the zero-based indexing in Python and the 1-based indexing in Julia.

The other main difference is that the method calls in Python are again transformed to function calls in Julia:

```julia
mean(aapl[:Close]); # => 37.1255
std(aapl[:Close]);  # => 34.1186
```

We can find the row values for the minimum and maximum closing prices as:

```julia
idxmin(aapl[:Close]); # => 57
aapl[:Close][57];     # => 13.59


idxmax(aapl[:Close]); # => 696
aapl[:Close][696]   ; # => 144.19
```

Also, we can use the pandas `describe` the entire dataset:

```julia
julia> describe(aapl)
```

	Open	High	Low	Close	Volume	
count	752.00000	752.00000	752.00000	752.00000	7.520000e+02	
mean	37.142168	38.252460	36.069840	37.125505	6.306547e+06	
std	34.124977	35.307115	33.020107	34.118615	6.154990e+06	
min	13.540000	13.850000	13.360000	13.590000	7.025000e+05	25%
	17.730000	18.280000	17.250000	17.735000	3.793100e+06	
50%	21.45000	22.03000	20.81000	21.49000	5.103250e+06	
75%	32.53250	33.67250	30.38250	31.61500	7.165525e+06	
max	142.44000	150.38000	140.00000	144.19000	1.325293e+08	

Selected topics

The JuliaStats group lists a variety of packages to tackle both statistics and machine learning.

Worthy of mention are:

- `MultivariateAnalysis.jl`: Data analysis, dimension reduction and factor analysis
- `Clustering.jl`: A set of algorithms for data clustering
- `MCMC.jl`: Monte Carlo Markov Chain algorithms

I am going to conclude this chapter by looking briefly at four other packages, but a reader who is new to Julia is encouraged to look at the JuliaStats' GitHub site for more information, and download the packages exploring the examples and tests provided.

Time series

Time series are often used in analysis of financial data where we wish to even out daily market fluctuations to view underlying trends.

For this section, I will return again to Apple share prices between 2000 and 2002 and will use the *short* CSV, which comprises the first six fields, that is, upto the nonadjusted trading volumes.

One of the problems we encountered previously while working with the dates was that they were returned as strings and the dataset was presented in descending date order. So we needed to compute a day difference and reverse the order of underlying data.

The `TimeArray` data structure (defined in `TimeSeries.jl`) solves this problem by encapsulating the dataset in separate parts:

```
timestamp::Union(Vector{Date}, Vector{DateTime})
values::Array{T,N}
colnames::Vector{UTF8String}
```

- `timestamp` can be either `Date` or `DateTime`
- `values` holds the actual data
- `colnames` is a string vector of column names

DateTime is depreciated in favor of Date in v0.4. The Date type does not include hours:minutes:seconds, whereas DateTime does and both the Date and DateTime types are defined in the new Dates package incorporated in the base. While it is possible to set up a TimeArray using the constructor defined in the package, TimeSeries also provides a readtimearray() function that makes a good attempt at 'finding' the time data.

Note that the TimeSeries package supports both date types and is likely to do so in the foreseeable future:

```
using TimeSeries
cd(); cd("Work") ;
```

```
ta = readtimearray("AAPL-Short.csv")
752x5 TimeArray{Float64,2} 2000-01-03 to 2002-12-31
```

	Open	High	Low	Close	Volume
2000-01-03	104.88	112.5	101.69	111.94	4.7839e6
2000-01-04	108.25	110.62	101.19	102.5	4.5748e6
2000-01-05	103.75	110.56	103.0	104.0	6.9493e6
2000-01-06	106.12	107.0	95.0	95.0	6.8569e6
2002-12-26	14.42	14.81	14.28	14.4	1.5254e6
2002-12-27	14.31	14.38	14.01	14.06	1.4292e6
2002-12-30	14.08	14.15	13.84	14.07	2.7686e6
2002-12-31	14.0	14.36	13.95	14.33	3.5844e6

If you wish to look at current stock prices, these can be obtained from the Quandl.jl package using aapl = quandl("GOOG/NASDAQ_AAPL").

The date order and associate values are now in ascending order and the data values are now Float64 (not Any). Also, the show() function for the time array gives the date range.

The ta.colnames parameter can also be listed using a convenient colnames(ta) function and likewise for the timestamp and values parameters:

```
julia> colnames(ta)
5-el Array{UTF8String,1}: "Open" "High" "Low" "Close" "Volume"
```

Let's look at the year 2000. We have to extract the data and create a new `Time Array`. To do this, we can use the `from()` and `to()` functions:

```
ta0 = from(to(ta,2000,12,31), 2000,1,1)
252x5 TimeArray{Float64,2} 2000-01-03 to 2000-12-29
```

This is now a `252` array containing just the values for the year `2000`.

We can look at the lag (previous values) and lead (future values):

```
lag(ta0["Close"],30)[1]; # => 2000-02-15 | 111.94
lead(ta0["Close"],30)[1] # => 2000-01-03 | 119.0
```

The lag starts at `2000-02-15` as earlier values are outside the dataset. Note that these are `30` values not thirty days. Also, we may wish to apply a function to a series of values, and we can do this using `moving()`.

So to compute the moving average:

```
moving(ta0["Close"],mean,30)
223x1 TimeArray{Float64,1} 2000-02-14 to 2000-12-29
             Close
2000-02-14 | 105.24
2000-02-15 | 105.47
2000-02-16 | 105.86
2000-02-17 | 106.22
```

Rather than working with a fixed number of values, we may wish to take a period such as a calendar month:

```
collapse(ta["Close"], mean, period=month)
12x1 TimeArray{Float64,1} 2000-01-31 to 2002-12-31
             Close
2000-01-31 | 103.36
2000-02-29 | 111.64
2000-03-31 | 128.5
```

Also, we can compute the change from the previous values by looking for the maximum and taking absolute values to account for fails as well as rises:

```
maximum(abs(values(percentchange(ta0["Close"])))); # => 0.5187
```

Recall that this corresponds to the script issue of 2 for 1.

Finally, we may wish to when the closing price was above $125:

```
for i in findall(ta["Close"] .> 125)
  ts   = ta0["Close"].timestamp[i]
  vals = ta0["Close"].values[i]
  println(ts, ": ", vals)
end
```

```
2000-03-01: 130.31
2000-03-03: 128.0
2000-03-06: 125.69
2000-03-10: 125.75
2000-03-21: 134.94
2000-03-22: 144.19
```

Distributions

`Distributions.jl` is a package which covers a wide variety of probability distributions and associated functions, and also provides facilities to create other distributions.

- Moments (mean, variance, skewness, and kurtosis), entropy, and other properties
- Probability density/mass functions (`pdf`), and their logarithm (`logpdf`)
- Moment generating functions, and characteristic functions
- Sampling from population, or from a distribution
- Maximum likelihood estimation
- Posterior w.r.t. conjugate prior, and **Maximum-a-Posteriori (MAP)** estimation

As an example, let's look at Poisson distribution.

This models the occurrence of discrete events, such as goals in a football match or number of children in a family. It is completely described by a single parameter l and the probability that a variate takes a particular value k is given by:

Poisson(k; l) = *Pr(X = k)* = *l^k * exp(-l) / factorial(k)*

Since it is *well-known* that the average family comprises 2.2 children, we can produce the appropriate distribution function as:

```
using Distributions;
Poisson(2.2);   # => Distributions.Poisson(l = 2.2 )
```

The Poisson distribution has mean and variance equal to l, so:

```
mean(Poisson(2.2));     # =>   2.2
std(Poisson(2.2));      # =>   1.4832
median(Poisson(2.2));   # =>   2.0


for i = 0:5
  pf = pdf(Poisson(2.2), i)
  cf = cdf(Poisson(2.2), i)
  @printf "%d : %7.4f %7.4f\n"  i  pf  cf
end


0 :   0.1108   0.1108
1 :   0.2438   0.1106
2 :   0.2681   0.6227
3 :   0.1966   0.8194
4 :   0.1082   0.9275
5 :   0.0476   0.9751


rand(Poisson(2.2),15)
15-element Array{Int64,1}:  [ 4 0 2 3 2 2 3 3 4 2 0 2 1 5 1 ]


fit(Poisson, rand(Poisson(2.2),1000))
Distributions.Poisson( lambda=2.262 )
```

Kernel density

Kernel density estimation (KDE) is a non-parametric way to estimate the probability density function of a random variable. KDE is a fundamental data smoothing problem where inferences about the population are made based on a finite data sample.

Kernel density overcomes the problem inherent with frequency histograms, that of selection of bins size. KDE may show substructures such as two (or more) maxima, which would not be apparent in a histogram.

Consider the GCSE written and coursework marks available from RDatasets:

```
using RDatasets, KernelDensity


mlmf = dataset("mlmRev", "Gcsemv");


df = mlmf[complete_cases(mlmf[[:Written, :Course]]), :];
dc = array(df[:Course]);  kdc = kde(dc);
dw = array(df[:Written]); kdw = kde(dw);
```

In order to generate summary statistics, we need to eliminate any items that have a NaN value by indexing against the logical arrays created by !isnan(dw) and !isnan(dc):

```
i.e  ssw = summarystats(dw[!isnan(dw)])
and  ssc = summarystats(dc[!isnan(dc)])
```

```
Summary Stats:
Written     Course
```

	Written	Course
Mean:	46.50	73.38
Minimum:	0.60	9.25
1st Quartile:	38.00	62.90
Median:	46.00	75.90
3rd Quartile:	56.00	86.10
Maximum:	90.00	100.00

We can display the kernel densities of the course work and written work as follows:

```
using Winston


kdc = kde(dc); kdw = kde(dw)
plot(kdc.x, kdc.density, "r--", kdw.x, kdw.density, "b;")
```

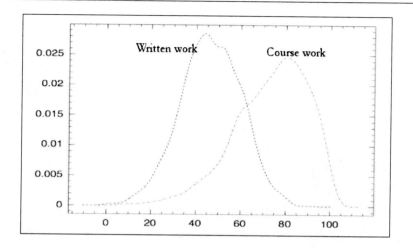

Hypothesis testing

A hypothesis test is a method of statistical inference on a dataset. A result is called significant if it has been predicted as unlikely to have occurred by chance, according to a pre-determined threshold probability termed the significance level.

Julia implements a wide range of hypothesis testing via the HypothesisTests.jl package that is well documented at https://readthedocs.org/.

We will look at GCSE scores that are subset by schools using the groupby() function, and we will look at schools that have at least 40 students:

```
for subdf in groupby(df, :School)
  (size(subdf)[1] > 40) &&
  @printf "%10s : %8.4f %8.4f\n" subdf[:School][1]
mean(subdf[:Written])  mean(subdf[:Course])
end
22520 :    35.4482    57.4580
60457 :    53.4773    85.9568
68107 :    44.9107    74.6750
68125 :    47.1556    77.5322
68137 :    28.2807    62.5373
68411 :    40.4615    59.4369
68809 :    42.7705    71.1115
```

We will create `DataFrames` for the schools `68107` and `68411` that have similar written scores but different ones for course work:

```
using HypothesisTests
df68107 = mlmf[mlmf[:School] .== "68107", :];
df68107 =
  df68107[complete_cases(df68107[[:Written, :Course]]), :];

df68411 = mlmf[mlmf[:School] .== "68411", :];
df68411 =
  df68411[complete_cases(df68411[[:Written, :Course]]), :];
```

We can test the hypothesis that the two distributions have same means with differing variances:

```
UnequalVarianceTTest(
  float(df68107[:Written]), float64(df68411[:Written]) )
```

```
Two sample t-test (unequal variance)
------------------------------------
Population details:
   parameter of interest:   Mean difference
   value under h_0:         0
   point estimate:          4.4492
   95% confidence interval: (-0.1837, 9.0821)

Test summary:
   outcome with 95% confidence: fail to reject h_0
   two-sided p-value:        0.05963 (not significant)

Details:
   number of observations:  [56,65]
   t-statistic:             1.9032531870995715
   degrees of freedom:      109.74148002018097
   empirical standard error: 2.337668920946911
```

Upon running the test we fail to reject the null hypothesis at the 95% significance level (note the double negative).

This means that the result could occur at least one in twenty times even if the values were taken at random from the same population dataset.

Now if we apply the same test to the coursework, we get the following:

```
UnequalVarianceTTest(
    float(df68107[:Course]), float64(df68411[:Course]) )



Two sample t-test (unequal variance)
------------------------------------
Population details:
    parameter of interest:   Mean difference
    value under h_0:         0
    point estimate:          15.2381
    95% confidence interval: (10.6255, 19.8506)

Test summary:
    outcome with 95% confidence: reject h_0
    two-sided p-value:    1.6304e-9 (extremely significant)

Details:
    number of observations:   [56,65]
    t-statistic:              6.5420
    degrees of freedom:       118.1318
    empirical standard error: 2.3293
```

GLM

A **generalized linear model (GLM)** is a flexible extension of ordinary linear regression that allows response variables that have error distribution models other than a normal distribution.

GLM generalizes linear regression by allowing the linear model to be related to the response variable via a link function, and by allowing the magnitude of the variance of each measurement to be a function of its predicted value.

In Julia, the GLM package uses distributions to provide the link functionality.

Fitting may be by maximum likelihood or via a Bayesian method such as MCMC methods.

GLM has many methods for fitting; names are chosen to be similar to those in R:

- `coef`: Extract the estimates of the coefficients in the model
- `deviance`: Measure of the model fit, weighted residual sum of squares for lm's
- `df_residual`: Degrees of freedom for residuals, when meaningful
- `glm`: Fit a generalized linear model (an alias for `fit(GeneralizedLinearModel, ...)`)
- `lm`: Fit a linear model (an alias for `fit(LinearModel, ...)`)
- `stderr`: Standard errors of the coefficients
- `vcov`: Estimated variance-covariance matrix of the coefficient estimates
- `predict`: Obtain predicted values of the dependent variable from the fitted model

To fit a GLM operates with `DataFrames` and uses:

```
glm(formula, data, family, link)
```

In the preceding command: `glm()` is a shortform for `fit(GeneralizedLinearModel, ...)`.

- Formula is expressed in terms of the column symbols from the `DataFrame` data
- Data may contain `NA` values, any rows with `NA` values are ignored
- Family is chosen from `Binomial()`, `Gamma()`, `Normal()`, or `Poisson()`
- Link may be as `LogitLink()`, `InverseLink()`, `IdentityLink()`, `LogLink()`

Links are related to specific families, for example `LogitLink()` is a valid link for the `Binomial()` family.

We will just look at the `lm()` fit, a linear model, which is also a short form, this time for `fit(LinearModel, ...)` and apply this to the GSCE data (by school) from the previous section.

We will need to sample each dataset and sort the sample. Then, we will construct a `DataFrame` of corresponding low `<->` high pairs and see how the distribution of marks compares by looking at both written and course work marks.

The two schools we that will look at are 68411 and 68107 that have similar written marks but different ones for coursework:

```
using GLM;
dw68411s =  sort(sample(df68411[:Written],50));
dw68107s =  sort(sample(df68107[:Written],50));
dc68411s =  sort(sample(df68411[:Course],50));
dc68107s =  sort(sample(df68107[:Course],50));


cor(dw68107s, dw68411s); # => 0.9894
cor(dc68107s, dc68411s); # => 0.8926
```

We can see that the correlation scores for both are good, for the given 50 samples, especially so for the written ones.

So constructing a couple of data frames:

```
dw = DataFrame(float64(dw68107s), float64(dw68411s));
names!(dw, [symbol("s68107"), symbol("s68411")]);
dc = DataFrame(float64(dc68107s), float64(dc68411s));
names!(dc, [symbol("s68107"), symbol("s68411")]);
```

I have renamed the column names to reflect the id of each school.

The model we are going to fit, for both the written (dw) and coursework (dc) dataframes, is a linear one as:

```
lm1 = fit(LinearModel, s68107 ~ s68411, dw)
DataFrameRegressionModel{LinearModel{DensePredQR{Float64}},Float64}:


Coefficients:
             Estimate Std.Error   t value  Pr(>|t|)
(Intercept)   0.12675  0.980441  0.129279   0.8977
s68411        1.15335 0.0244878   47.0988   <1e-41


i.e.  s68107  ~   0.12675  +  1.15335 * s68411
```

The fit has a low intercept and also a unity gradient reflecting the closeness of the two samples from the schools 68107 and 68411 for written scores.

Turning to the course work:

```
lm1 = fit(LinearModel, s68107 ~ s68411, dc)
DataFrameRegressionModel{LinearModel{DensePredQR{Float64}},Float64}:

Coefficients:
            Estimate Std.Error t value Pr(>|t|)
(Intercept)  28.0251   2.75815 10.1608    <1e-12
s68411      0.741007 0.0447073 16.5746    <1e-20


i.e.    s68107  ~    28.0251  +  0.741007 * s68411
```

Here, the intercept is around 28 because of much higher marks for course work from s68107 to s6841. The gradient correspondingly lowers, implying that the low-end scores in s68107 are much higher than the high-end ones at s68411.

Summary

In this chapter, we looked at the terminal I/O in Julia, and also accessed text-based and binary disk files. We discussed how to access and work with data stored in a structured manner in files such as CSV, XML, and HDF5 and then introduced the important topic of data arrays and data frames.

We then continued with a review of some statistical methods applied to data frames available from the RDatasets package, including elementary hypothesis testing and general linear methods.

Statistics has been a particular success within the Julia community and the extremely productive group JuliaStats is an excellent reference for this work, with its own web pages at https://github.com/JuliaStats and a Google Groups forum **julia-stats**. Also, many of the projects are using https://readthedocs.org/ to provide quite extensive documentation. For example, the guidance on the basic statistics can be found at http://statsbasejl.readthedocs.org.

In the next chapter, we will look at application of Julia to scientific problems. A dissatisfaction with existing programming languages, such as MATLAB and its clones, arguably formed the initial raison d'etre for the development of Julia and as we will see, it remains especially strong in this area too.

6
Scientific Programming

Julia was initially designed as a language directed to find solutions to the problems arising from science and mathematics. The current scripting languages then, and to some extent now, were slow especially when dealing with 'looping' code (devectorized) that is normally the algorithmic approach that the analyst will take in his/her blocked pseudo-coding.

This leads to the 'two-language' approach where analysis is made using the scripting language, whereas code needs to be compiled into a second language, usually C, in order to achieve enterprise performance.

Julia compiles its sources to the appropriate machine code using just-in-time compilation from LLVM and so achieves execution times comparable with those of C and Fortran.

It is natural that the applications of Julia in the fields of scientific programming are many and varied and in a single chapter I can do no more than point the reader to some of the more elemental examples. However, in a fashion similar to **JuliaStats** in statistics, a number of community groupings have been formed and these will be noted as we go along.

The Julia base (standard library) contains most of Python modules NumPy and some of SciPy. In addition, Julia has a great wealth of packages for scientific programming, both specialist and general purpose.

Among the packages, are those that support finance, astronomy, bioinformatics, machine learning plus many others. The general purpose packages may be native implementations of low-level data structures or wrappers around open source libraries. Worthy of note in the latter category is the interface to the GNU Scientific Library (GSL.jl).

In this chapter, I am going to concentrate on a few areas between the specialist and general purpose. It is not an exhaustive list, so I encourage you to review the pkg. julialang.org web pages as the number and breadth of Julia packages is growing rapidly. Please be aware that because of the nature of the subject matter of this chapter, one or two of the topics covered may prove to be little more challenging than other areas of the book to the non-mathematical minded readers.

Linear algebra

Linear algebra is the branch of mathematics concerning vector spaces and linear mappings between such spaces. It includes the study of lines, planes, and subspaces, but is also concerned with properties common to all vector spaces.

In Julia, basic linear algebra is built into the standard library. Much of this is achieved using the **Basic Linear Algebra System (OpenBLAS)** and **Linear Algebra PACKage (LAPACK)** libraries that ship as shared libraries in binary distros or are built when installing the system from source.

We will begin our study by looking at sets of linear equations and the application of matrix methods to their solutions.

Simultaneous equations

A set of n equations in n unknown quantities will have a unique solution, provided that one of the equations is not a multiple of another. In the latter case, the system is term degenerate since effectively we only have n-1 equations.

Clearly n is a positive number, with n >= 2, since n = 1 is trivial.

The solution of such equations is obtained by matrix methods with which many of the readers will be familiar. Consider the case of the following:

```
 x  - 2y  +  2z  =  5
 x  -  y  +  2z  =  7
-x  +  y  +   z  =  5
```

In matrix notation, we write this as: Av = b, where v is the [x y z] vector of unknowns, A is a matrix of coefficients, and b is a vector of constants on the right-hand side. So setting up A and b as:

```
julia> A = [1 -2  2; 1 -1  2; -1  1  1];
3x3 Array{Int64,2}:

julia> b = [5, 7, 5];
3-element Array{Int64,1};
```

We first note that the matrix A has a non-zero determinate, which implies that the system is not degenerate and will have a solution:

```
det(A) ; # => 3
```

In fact, the solution is derived by multiplying each side of the equation Av = b by the inverse of A giving: v = inv(A)*b, since inv(A)*A is the identity matrix I. This is such a common operation that it is also defined as the matrix division operation A\b:

```
julia> v = A\b ; # or inv(A)*b
3-element Array{Float64,1}:
  1.0
  2.0
  4.0
```

Note that both v and b are (column) vectors present in order to satisfy matrix multiplication rules.

However, the transpose of v will be a matrix consisting of a single row:

```
julia> transpose(v); # usually written as: v'
1x3 Array{Float64,2}:
  1.0   2.0   4.0
```

Consider an over-determined system, that is, three equations in two unknowns:

```
A1 = A[:, 2:3] ; #   A1 ==> [-2 2; -1 2; 1  1];
```

Effectively, this is the same system of equations but just in y and z. Matrix division produces a solution, but by minimizing the least squares residuals of y and z:

```
julia> (A1\b)'   # output the transpose for brevity
1x2 Array{Float64,2}:
1.27586   3.93103
```

The alternative is an under-determined system comprising just the first two equations:

```
A2 = A[1:2,:]; b2 = b[1:2];
```

Now, there is an infinite set of solutions obtained by specifying one variable and solving for the other two. In this case, the minimum norm of the solutions is returned as:

```
julia> (A2\b2)'
1x2 Array{Float64,2}:
  1.8 2.0 3.6
```

Decompositions

In this section, we are going to consider the process of factorizing a matrix into a product of a number of other matrices. This is termed as matrix decomposition and proves useful in a number of classes of problems.

The \ function hides how the problem is actually solved. Depending on the dimensions of the matrix A, different methods are chosen to solve the problem.

An intermediate step in the solution is to calculate a factorization of the A matrix. This is a way of expressing A as a product of triangular, unitary, and permutation matrices.

Julia defines an {Factorization} abstract type and several composite subtypes for actually storing factorizations. This can be thought of as a representation of the A matrix.

When the matrix is square, it is possible to factorize it into a pair of upper and lower diagonal matrices (U, L) together with a P permutation matrix such that A = PLU:

```
julia>Alu = lufact(A);
# => LU{Float64,Array{Float64,2}}(3x3 Array{Float64,2}
```

The components of the factorization can be accessed using the symbols :P, :L, and :U:

```
julia> Alu[:U]
3x3 Array{Float64,2}:
  1.0  -2.0  2.0
  0.0   1.0  0.0
  0.0   0.0  3.0
```

Moreover, we can compute the solution from the components as:

```
julia> Alu[:U]\(Alu[:L]\Alu[:P]'*b)
3-element Array{Float64,1}:
  1.0
  2.0
  4.0
```

This computation is encapsulated in the \ operator from LU factorizations, so can be simply written as: Alu\b.

In the case where the system is over specified, a LU factorization is not appropriate as the matrix is tall, that is, has more rows than columns; here we can use QR factorization:

```julia
julia> A1 = A[:,2:3]
julia> Aqr = qrfact(A1)
QRCompactWY{Float64}(3x2 Array{Float64,2}:
  2.44949    -2.04124
  0.224745   -2.19848
 -0.224745    0.579973,2x2 Triangular{Float64,Array{Float64,2},:U,false}:
  1.8165    -0.256629
  0.0        1.49659 )
```

The \ operator has a method for the QR and the least squares problem can be solved as:

```julia
julia> Aqr\b
2-element Array{Float64,1}:
 1.27586
 3.93103
```

It is worth noting that while it is possible to call specific factorization methods explicitly (such as `lufact`), Julia as a `factorize(A)` function that will compute a convenient factorization, including LU, Cholesky, Bunch-Kaufman, and Triangular, based upon the type of the input matrix.

Also, there are the ! versions of functions such as `lufact!()` and `factorize!()` that will compute in place to conserve memory requirements.

Eigenvalues and eigenvectors

An eigenvector or characteristic vector of a A square matrix is a non-zero v vector that, when the matrix multiplies v, gives the same result as when some scalar multiplies v. The scalar multiplier is usually denoted by λ.

That is: Av = λv and λ is called the eigenvalue or characteristic value of A corresponding to v.

Considering our set of three equations, this will yield three [eigvecs] eigenvectors and the corresponding [eigvals] eigenvalues:

```julia
A = [1 -2  2; 1 -1  2; -1  1  1];
eigvals(A)
3-element Array{Complex{Float64},1}:
 -0.287372+1.35im
```

```
-0.287372-1.35im
 1.57474+0.0im


V = eigvecs(A)
3x3 Array{Complex{Float64},2}:
   0.783249+0.0im          0.783249-0.0im         0.237883+0.0im
   0.493483-0.303862im     0.493483+0.303862im    0.651777+0.0im
  -0.0106833+0.22483im    -0.0106833-0.22483im     0.720138+0.0im
```

The eigenvectors are the columns of the V matrix.

To confirm, let's compute the difference of (Av - λv) for the first vector:

```
julia> A*V[:,1] - λ[1]*V[:,1]
3-element Array{Complex{Float64},1}:
 -2.22045e-16+2.22045e-16im
  1.11022e-16+0.0im
  2.77556e-16-1.38778e-16im
```

That is, all the real and imaginary parts are of the e-16 order, so this is in effect a zero matrix of complex numbers.

Why do we wish to compute eigenvectors?

- They make understanding linear transformations easy, as they are the directions along which a linear transformation acts simply by "stretching/compressing" and/or "flipping". Eigenvalues give the factors by which this compression occurs.

- They provide another way to affect matrix factorization using singular value decomposition using svdfact().

- They are useful in the study of chained matrices, such as the cat and mouse example we saw earlier.

- They arise in a number of studies of a variety of dynamic systems.

We will finish this section by considering a dynamic system given by:

```
x' = ax + by
y' = cx + dy
```

Here, x' and y' are the derivatives of x and y with respect to time and a, b, c, and d are constants.

This kind of system was first used to describe the growth of population of two species that affect one another and are termed the Lotka-Volterra equations.

We may consider that species x is a predator of species y.

1. The more of x, the lesser of y will be around to reproduce.
2. But if there is less of y then there is less food for x, so lesser of x will reproduce.
3. Then if lesser of x are around, this takes pressure off y, which increases in numbers.
4. But then there is more food for x, so x increases.

It also arises when you have certain physical phenomena, such a particle in a moving fluid where the velocity vector depends on the position along the fluid.

Solving this system directly is complicated and we will return to it in the section on differential equations. However, suppose that we could do a transform of variables so that instead of working with x and y, you could work with p and q that depend linearly on x and y.

That is, $p = \alpha x + \beta y$ and $w = \gamma x + \delta y$, for some constants α, β, γ, and δ.

The system is transformed into something as follows:

$$p' = \kappa p \ \ and \ \ q' = \lambda q$$

That is, you can "decouple" the system, so that now you are dealing with two independent functions.

Then solving this problem becomes rather easy: `p = Aexp(Kt) and q = Bexp(λt)`.

Then, you can use the formulas for z and w to find expressions for x and y. This results precisely to finding two linearly independent eigenvectors for the `[a c; b d]` matrix.

p and q correspond to the eigenvectors and to the eigenvalues.

So by taking an expression that "mixes" x and y, and "decoupling" it into one that acts independently on two different functions, the problem becomes a lot easier.

This can be reduced to a generalized eigenvalue problem by clever use of algebra at the cost of solving a larger system. The orthogonality of the eigenvectors provides a decoupling of the differential equations, so that the system can be represented as linear summation of the eigenvectors. The eigenvalue problem of complex structures is often solved using finite element analysis, but it neatly generalizes the solution to scalar-valued vibration problems.

Special matrices

The structure of matrices is very important in linear algebra. In Julia, these structures are made explicit through composite types such as `Diagonal`, `Triangular`, `Symmetric`, `Hermitian`, `Tridiagonal`, and `SymTridiagonal`.

Specialized methods are written for the special matrix types to take advantage of their structure.

So, `diag(A)` is the diagonal vector of the `A` but `Diagonal(diag(A))` is a special matrix:

```
julia> Diagonal(diag(A))
3x3 Diagonal{Int64}:
  1   0   0
  0  -1   0
  0   0   1
```

A symmetric eigenproblem

Whether or not Julia is able to detect if a matrix is symmetric/Hermitian, it can have a big influence on how fast an eigenvalue problem is solved. Sometimes it is known that a matrix is symmetric or Hermitian, but due to floating point errors this is not detected by the `eigvals` function.

In following example, `B1` and `B2` are almost identical, if Julia is not told that `B2` is symmetric, the elapsed time for the computation is very different:

```
n = 2000;
B = randn(n,n);
B1 = B + B';
B2 = copy(B1);
B2[1,2] += 1eps();
B2[2,1] += 2eps();
issym(B1)' # => true
issym(B2)' # => false
```

The `B1` matrix is symmetric whereas `B2` is not because of the small error added to cells `(1,2)` and `(2,1)`.

Calculating the eigenvectors of `B1` and `B2` and timing the operation gives:

```
@time eigvals(B1);
elapsed time: 1.543577865 seconds (37825492 bytes allocated)

@time eigvals(B2);
elapsed time: 8.015794532 seconds (33142128 bytes allocated)
```

However, if we symmetrize B2 and rerun the calculation:

```
@time eigvals(Symmetric(B2));
elapsed time: 1.503028261 seconds (33247616 bytes allocated)
```

Signal processing

Signal processing is the art of analyzing and manipulating signals arising in many fields of engineering. It deals with operations on or analysis of analog as well as digitized signals, representing time-varying, or spatially-varying physical quantities.

Julia has the functionality for processing signals built into the standard library along with a growing set of packages and the speed of Julia makes it especially well-suited to such analysis.

We can differentiate between 1D signals, such as audio signals, ECG, variations in pressure and temperature and so on, and 2D resulting in imagery from video and satellite data streams. In this section, I will mainly focus on the former but the techniques carry over in a straightforward fashion to the 2D cases.

Frequency analysis

A signal is simply a measurable quantity that varies in time and/or space. The key insight of signal processing is that a signal in time can be represented by a linear combination of sinusoids at different frequencies.

There exists an operation called the Fourier transform, which takes a x(t) function of time that is called the time-domain signal and computes the weights of its sinusoidal components. These weights are represented as a X(f) function of frequency called the frequency-domain signal.

The Fourier transform takes a continuous function and produces another continuous function as a function of the frequencies of which it is composed. In digital signal processing, since we operate on signals in discrete time, we use the **discrete Fourier transform (DFT)**.

This takes a set of N samples in time and produces weights at N different frequencies. Julia's signal processing library, like most common signal processing software packages, computes DFTs by using a class of algorithms known as **fast Fourier transforms (FFT)**.

Filtering and smoothing

We will construct a signal of three sinusoids with frequencies of 500 Hz and multiples such as 1000 Hz, 1500 Hz, and so on, using the following code:

```
using Winston
fq = 500.0;
N = 512;
T = 6 / fq;
td = linspace(0, T, N);
x1 = sin(2pi * fq * td);
x2 = cos(8pi * fq * td);
x3 = cos(16pi * fq * td);
x = x1 + 0.4*x2 + 0.2*x3
plot(td, x)
```

Now use the `rfft` function (the real FFT function), since our input signal is composed entirely of real numbers -- as opposed to complex numbers. This allows us to optimize by only computing the weights for frequencies from `1` to `N/2+1`.

The higher frequencies are simply a mirror image of the lower ones, so they do not contain any extra information. We will need to use the absolute magnitude (modulus) of the output of `rfft` because the outputs are complex numbers. Right now, we only care about the magnitude, and not the phase of the frequency domain signal.

```
X = rfft(x);
sr = N / T;
fd = linspace(0, sr / 2, int(N / 2) + 1);
plot(fd, abs(X)[1:N/8])
```

This transforms the time domain representation of the signal (amplitude versus time) into one in the frequency domain (magnitude versus frequency).

The following figure shows the two representations:

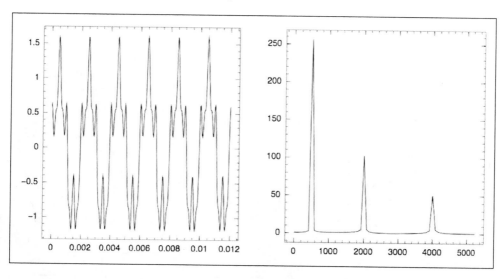

Now we can add some high frequency noise to the signal using:

```
ns = 0.1*randn(length(x));
xn = x + ns;
```

Then use a convolution procedure in the time domain to attempt to remove it. In essence, this is a moving average smoothing technique.

We define a 16-element window and use a uniform distribution, although it might be sensible to use a Gaussian or parabolic one that would weigh the nearest neighbors more appropriately.

```
M = 16;
xm = ones(Float64, M) / M;
plot(xm)
```

It is important that the sum of the weights is 1.

The Julia standard library has a built-in convolution function and applying xm to xn:

```
xf = conv(xn, xm);
t = [0:length(xf) - 1] / sr
plot(t, xf, "-", t, x, ";" )
```

The following figure shows the noisy signal together with the filtered one:

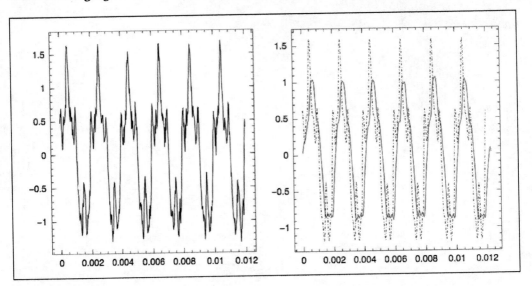

The main carrier wave is recovered and the noise eliminated, but given the size of the window chosen the convolution has a drastic effect on the higher frequency components.

Digital signal filters

Moving average filters (convolution) work well for removing noise, if the frequency of the noise is much higher than the principal components of a signal.

A common requirement in RF communications is to retain parts of the signal but to filter out the others. The simplest filter of this sort is a low-pass filter. This is a filter that allows sinusoids below a critical frequency to go through unchanged, while attenuating the signals above the critical frequency. Clearly, this is a case where the processing is done in the frequency domain.

Filters can also be constructed to retain sinusoids above the critical frequency (high pass), or within a specific frequency range (medium band).

Julia provides a set of signal processing packages as the DSP group and we will apply some of the routines to filter out the noise on the signal we created in the previous section:

```
using DSP
responsetype = Lowpass(0.2)
```

```
prototype = Elliptic(4, 0.5, 30)
tf = convert(TFFilter, digitalfilter(responsetype, prototype))
numerator_coefs   = coefb(tf)
denominator_coefs = coefa(tf)
```

This constructs a fourth order elliptic low-pass filter with normalized cut-off frequency 0.2, 0.5 dB of passband ripple, and 30 dB attenuation in the stopband. Then the coefficients of the numerator and denominator of the transfer function will be:

```
responsetype = Bandpass(10, 40; fs=1000)
prototype = Butterworth(4)
xb = filt(digitalfilter(responsetype, prototype), x);
plot(xb)
```

This code filters the data in the x signal, sampled at 1000 Hz, with a fourth order Butterworth bandpass filter between 10 and 40 Hz. The resultant signal is displayed as follows:

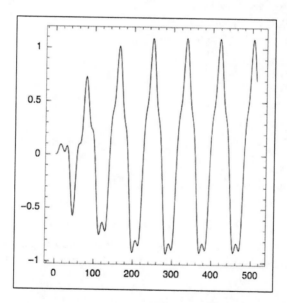

While being cleaner than convolution, this still affects the high frequencies. Also, while the band pass filter is infinite in extent, the one constructed is truncated and this means that the initial portion of the signal is modulated.

Image processing

Frequency-based methods can be applied to 2D signals, such as those from video and satellite data streams. High frequency noise in imagery is termed "speckle".

Essentially, due to the orthogonality of the FFT, processing involves applying a series of row-wise and column-wise FFTs independently of each other.

The DSP package has routines to deal with both 1D and 2D cases. Also, the convolution techniques we looked at in the section on *Frequency analysis* are often employed in enhancing or transforming images and we will finish by looking at a simple example using a 3x3 convolution kernel.

The kernel needs to be zero-summed, otherwise histogram range of the image is altered. We will look at the lena image that is provided as a 512x512 PGM image:

```
img = open("lena.pgm");
magic = chomp(readline(img));
params = chomp(readline(img));
while ismatch(r"^\s*#", params)
  params = chomp(readline(img));
end
pm = split(params);
if length(pm) < 3
  params *= " " * chomp(readline(img));
end
wd = int(pm[1]);
ht = int(pm[2]);

data = uint8(readbytes(img,wd*ht));
data = reshape(data,wd,ht);
close(img);
```

The preceding code reads the PGM image and stores the imagery as a byte array in data, reshaping it to be wd by ht. Now we define the two 3x3 Gx and Gy kernels as:

```
Gx = [1 2 1; 0 0 0; -1 -2 -1];
Gy = [1 0 -1; 2 0 -2; 1 0 -1];
```

The following loops over blocks of the original image applying Gx and Gy, constructs the modulus of each convolution, and outputs the transformed image as dout, again as a PGM image. We need to be a little careful that the imagery is still preserved as a byte array:

```
dout = copy(data);
for i = 2:wd-1
```

```
    for j = 2:ht-1
      temp = data[i-1:i+1, j-1:j+1];
      x = sum(Gx.*temp)
      y = sum(Gy.*temp)
      p = int(sqrt(x*x + y*y))
      dout[i,j] = (p < 256) ? uint8(p) : 0xff
    end
end
out = open("lenaX.pgm","w");
println(out,magic);
println(out,params);
write(out,dout);
close(out);
```

The result is shown in the following figure:

Differential equations

Differential equations are those that have terms that involve the rates of change of variates as well as the variates themselves. They arise naturally in a number of fields, notably dynamics. When the changes are with respect to one dependent variable, most often the systems are called ordinary differential equations. If more than a single dependent variable is involved, then they are termed partial differential equations.

Julia has a number of packages that aid the calculation of differentials of functions and to solve systems of differential equations. We will look at a few aspects of these in the next section.

The solution of ordinary differential equations

Julia supports the solution of ordinary differential equations through a couple of packages such as ODE and Sundials. ODE consists of routines written solely in Julia whereas Sundials is a wrapper package around a shared library.

We will look at the ODE package first.

ODE exports a set of adaptive solvers; adaptive meaning that the step size of the algorithm changes algorithmically to reduce the error estimate below a certain threshold.

The calls take the `odeXY` form, where `X` is the order of the solver and `Y` is the error control:

- `ode23`: 2nd order adaptive solver with 3rd order error control
- `ode45`: 4th order adaptive solver with 5th order error control
- `ode78`: 7th order adaptive solver with 8th order error control

To solve the explicit ODE defined as a vectorize set of the `dy/dt = F(t,y)` equations, all routines of which have the same basic form, we use: `(tout, yout) = odeXY(F, y0, tspan)`.

As an example, I will look at this as a linear three-species food chain model where the lowest-level x prey is preyed upon by a mid-level y species, which in turn is preyed upon by a top level z predator. This is an extension of the Lotka-Volterra system from two to three-species.

Some examples might be three-species ecosystems, such as mouse-snake-owl, vegetation-rabbits-foxes, and worm-sparrow-falcon.

```
x' =   a*x - b*x*y
y' = -c*y + d*x*y - e*y*z
z' = -f*z + g*y*z   #for a,b,c,d,e,f g > 0
```

In the preceding equations, a, b, c, d are in the 2-species Lotka-Volterra equations, e represents the effect of predation on species y by species z, f represents the natural death rate of the predator z in the absence of prey, and g represents the efficiency and propagation rate of the predator z in the presence of prey.

This translates to the following set of linear equations:

```
x[1] =   p[1]*x[1] - p[2]*x[1]*x[2]
x[2] = -p[3]*x[2] + p[4]*x[1]*x[2] - p[5]*x[2]*x[3]
x[3] = -p[6]*x[3] + p[7]*x[2]*x[3]
```

It is slightly over-specified, since one of the parameters can be removed by rescaling the timescale. We define the F function as follows:

```
function F(t,x,p)
  d1 =  p[1]*x[1]  - p[2]*x[1]*x[2]
  d2 = -p[3]*x[2]  + p[4]*x[1]*x[2]  - p[5]*x[2]*x[3]
  d3 = -p[6]*x[3]  + p[7]*x[2]*x[3]
  [d1, d2, d3]
end
```

This takes the time range, vectors of the independent variables and coefficients, and returns a vector of the derivative estimates:

```
p = ones(7);        # Choose all parameters as 1.0
x0 = [0.5, 1.0, 2.0];  # Setup the initial conditions
tspan = [0.0:0.1:10.0];  # and the time range
```

Solve the equations by calling the `ode23` routine. This returns a matrix of solutions in a columnar order that we can extract and display with the `using Winston` function:

```
(t,x) = ODE.ode23((t,x) -> F(t,x,pp), x0, tspan);

n = length(t);
y1 = zeros(n); [y1[i] = x[i][1] for i = 1:n];
y2 = zeros(n); [y2[i] = x[i][2] for i = 1:n];
y3 = zeros(n); [y3[i] = x[i][3] for i = 1:n];

using Winston
plot(t,y1,"b.",t,y2,"g-.",t,y3,"r--")
```

The output is shown as the LH graph of the figure as follows:

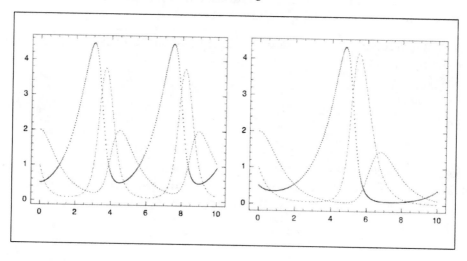

This model assumes the z species does not directly *eat* x. That might not be true, for example, for the mouse-snake-owl ecosystem, so in this case we would add an additional term:

```
x' = a*x - b*x*y - h*xz
```

Redoing the model as:

```
d1 =  p[1]*x[1] - p[2]*x[1]*x[2] - p[8]*x[1]*x[3]
pp = ones(7);
pp[5] = pp[8] = 0.5;  # Split rate so that p5 + p8 = 1
```

Apparently, the peak populations of the three species are little altered by the extra term but the periodicity is almost doubled. This is shown in the preceding RH graph.

Non-linear ordinary differential equations

Non-linear ODEs differ from their linear counterparts in a number of ways. They may contain functions, such as sine, log, and so on, of the independent variable and/or higher powers of the dependent variable and its derivatives.

A classic example is the double pendulum that comprises of one pendulum with another pendulum attached to its end. It is a simple physical system that exhibits rich dynamic behavior with strong sensitivity to initial conditions that under some instances can result in producing chaotic behaviors.

The example we are going to look at is somewhat simpler, a non-linear system arising from chemistry.

We will consider the temporal development of a chemical reaction. The reaction will generate heat by the $e^{-E/RT}$ Arrhenius function and lose heat at the boundary proportional to the $(T - T_0)$ temperature gradient.

Assuming the reaction is gaseous, then we can ignore heat transfer across the vessel. So the change in temperature will be given by:

$$\frac{dT}{dt} = Ae^{-E/RT} + B(T - T_0)$$

It is possible to write $e^{-E/RT} \sim e^{-E/RT0} (T - T_0)$, which means at the low temperature, behavior is proportional to the exponential value of the temperature difference.

In addition, we will assume that the source of the heat (that is, the reactant 1) is limited. So the first term will now be a second differential equation in `1n`, where n is the order of the reaction usually 1 or 2.

Although the ODE package is capable of handling non-linear systems, I will look at a solution that utilizes the alternative Sundials package.

Sundials is a wrapper around a C library and the package provides:

- **CVODES**: For integration and sensitivity analysis of ODEs. CVODES treats stiff and non-stiff ODE systems such as `y' = f(t,y,p),y(t0) = y0(p)` where p is a set of parameters.
- **IDAS**: For integration and sensitivity analysis of DAEs. IDAS treats DAE systems of the form `F(t,y,y',p) = 0,y(t0) = y0(p),y'(t0) = y0'(p)`.
- **KINSOL**: For solution of nonlinear algebraic systems. KINSOL treats nonlinear systems of the form `F(u) = 0`.

Tom Shorts' `Sim.jl` is a Julia package to support equation-based modeling for simulations, but this is outside the scope of this book. See the repository on GitHub for more details (`https://github.com/tshort/Sims.jl`).

By redefining the time scales, it is possible to simplify the equations and write the equations in terms of temperature difference x1 and reactant concentration x2 as:

```
x1 = x2^n * exp(x1) - a*x1
x2 = -b*x2^n * exp(x1)
```

Here, a and b are parameters and initial concentrations of `x1 = 0` and `x2 = 1`.

This can be solved as:

```
using Sundials
function exoterm(t, x, dx; n=1, a=1, b=1)
  p = x[2]^n * exp(x[1])
  dx[1] = p - a*x[1]
  dx[2] = -b*p
  return(dx)
end;


t = linspace(0.0,5.0,1001);
fexo(t,x,dx) = exotherm(t, x, dx, a=0.6, b=0.1);
x1 = Sundials.cvode(fexo, [0.0, 1.0], t);
```

Executing this for a in [0.9, 1.2. 1.5, 1.8] and keeping b = 0.1 gives four solutions, which are shown in the LH panel of the following figure:

```
using Winston
plot(t,x1[:,1],t,x2[:,1],t,x3[:,1],t,x4[:,1]))
```

The solutions are stable for a = 1.8, but starts to increase for lower values of a and are only pulled back by depletion of the fuel.

If we start solving this for a simple case without any fuel depletion: x1 = exp(x1) - a*x1.

This is only stable for values of a greater than exp(1):

```
using Roots
f(x) = exp(x) - a*x
for a = 2.8:-0.02:2.72
  @printf "%f : %f\n" a fzero(f,1)
end
2.80 : 0.775942
2.78 : 0.802795
2.76 : 0.835471
2.74 : 0.879091
2.72 : 0.964871
```

So simplifying the exotherm function to that of a single variable with the heat loss a parameter and re-running for a in [2.6, 2.8, 3.0, 3.2] produces the set of solutions shown in the RH panel in the following figure:

```
function exotherm2(t, x, dx; a=1)
  dx[1] = exp(x[1]) - a*x[1]
  return dx
end;

fexo2(t,x,dx) = exotherm2(t, x, dx, a=2.6);
x1 = Sundials.cvode(fexo2, [0.0, 1.0], t);
''''
```

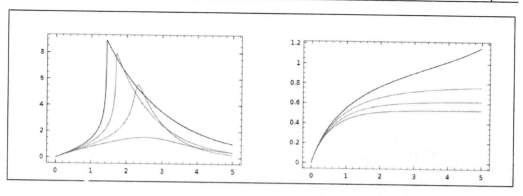

Partial differential equations

At the time of writing, solving differential equations in more than a single variable was not well supported in Julia as in the ODE case. Some work has been done on finite element analysis, but there is little in the way of any packages providing general purpose PDE solvers.

Consider the temporal development of temperature in the standard diffusion equation with a non-linear (heating) source.

The full equation in three spatial dimensions can be written as:

$$\frac{\partial u}{\partial t} = \frac{\partial^2 u}{\partial x^2} + \frac{\partial^2 u}{\partial y^2} + \frac{\partial^2 u}{\partial z^2} + \Theta(u)$$

The internal heating term can once again be considered as exponential for low temperature differences, but we are now considering the case where there is conduction across the medium.

This can be solved by a recurrence relation and for simplicity we will consider time plus just a single spatial dimension, but the extension to three dimensions is straightforward.

To get the reaction started, we will assume a hotspot at the centre and segment the spatial dimension into 2n+1 intervals of δx.

The $\Theta(u)$ heating term may be parameterized by two constants p1 and p2 and the equation written as:

```
u[i] = u[i-1] - (1-2r)*u[i] + u[i+1] + p1*exp(p2*u[i])
```

With u[1] = u[2n+1] = 0 and initial condition u[n] = 10, where $r = \delta t / \delta x^* \delta x$ and boundary conditions u[0] - u[1] = u[2n] - u[2n+1] = p3.

In Julia, this can be written as:

```
p = [0.001, 0,01, 0.1 ];
r = 0.01;
n = 100;
t = linspace(1,2n+1,2n+1);
u = zeros(2n+1);
u[n] = 10;          # Hot spot in centre
w = zeros(5,2n + 1);

for k1 = 1:5
  for j = 1:15000
    v = copy(u);
    v[1]     =  p[3]*(v[1]  - v[2]);
    v[2n+1] =  p[3]*(v[2n] - v[2n+1]);
    for i = 2:2n
      u[i] = v[i] + r*(v[i-1] - 2*v[i] + v[i+1]) +
      p[1]*(exp(p[2]*v[i]) - 1);
    end
  end
  [w[k1,k2] = u[k2] for k2 = 1:2n+1];
  (k1 == 1) ? plot(w[k1,:]) : plot(w[k1,:])
end
```

If p[1] = p[2] = p[3], then there is no internal heating term and the solution is one for the regular diffusion equation.

This is shown in the LH panel of the following figure, whereas the RH panel is the parameterized solution as shown previously:

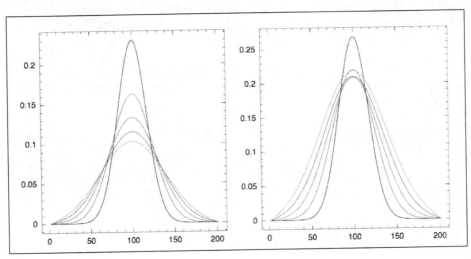

It is clear that temperature within the body has begun to rise since the heat loss at the boundaries is insufficient to dissipate the internal heating and in the absence of fuel depletion, the body will ignite.

Optimization problems

Mathematical optimization problems arise in the field of linear programming, machine learning, resource allocation, production planning, and so on.

One well-known allocation problem is that of the travelling salesman who has to make a series of calls, and wishes to compute the optimal route between calls. The problem is not tractable but clearly can be solved exhaustively. However by clustering and tree pruning, the number of tests can be markedly reduced.

The generalized aim is to formulate as the minimization of some $f(x)$ function for all values of x over a certain interval, subject to a set of $gi(x)$ .restrictions

The problems of local maxima are also included by redefining the domain of x. It is possible to identify three cases:

- No solution exists.

- Only a single minimum (or maximum) exists.

- In this case, the problem is said to be convex and is relatively insensitive to the choice of starting value for x.

- The function $f(x)$ having multiple extreminals.

- For this, the solution returned will depend particularly on the initial value of x.

Approaches to solving mathematical optimization may be purely algebraic or involve the use of derivatives. The former is typically exhaustive with some pruning, the latter is quicker utilizing hill climbing type algorithms.

Optimization is supported in Julia by a community group JuliaOpt and we will briefly introduce three packages: `JuMP`, `Optim`, and `NLopt`.

JuMP

Mathematical programming problems are supported in Python and MATLAB with packages such as PuLP, CVX, YALMIP; there are also commercial offerings such as AMPL, and GAMS. In general, the objective of the algorithms is not immediately apparent from the code.

The aim of the JuMP package is to create coding that provides a natural translation of the mathematics of the problem, preferably by loosely coupling the specific method of solution from the data. This is achieved by extensive generation of boilerplate code using macros and the application of specialized solvers for linear, conic, and semidefinite problems.

JuMP utilizes a MathProgBase secondary package whose function is to interface to solvers such as Gurobi, Clp, Mosek, and Ipopt, all of which are defined in Julia in packages such as Gurobi.jl, and so on.

The backend solvers are often commercial offerings, although in some cases academic licenses exist.

A simple example is to maximize the 5x + 3y function subject to the constraint that:

```
3x + 5y < 7
using JuMP
m = Model()
@defVar(m, 0 <= x <= 5 );
@defVar(m, 0 <= y <= 10 );
@setObjective(m, Max, 5x + 3y );
@addConstraint(m, 2x + 5y <= 7.0 );
```

The use of the @defVar, @setObjective, and @addConstraint define the starting domain form (x, y), function (objective), and constraints in a clear manner:

```
status = solve(m);   # => :Optimal
@printf "Function value of %5.2f at (%4.2f,%4.2f)\n"
  getObjectiveValue(m) getValue(x) getValue(y)
Functional value of 15.60 at (3.00, 0.20)
```

Calling solve() produces the result (when possible). The solver used is default for the case of problem (in this case Clp) and this has to be available.

It is possible to call Model() with specific solvers such as Model(solver=GurobiSolver()) that will execute as long as the solver specified is appropriate to the problem type.

The solution to the travelling salesman problem is given in the JuMP (GitHub) source. However, this requires the Gurobi solver, so as an alternative we will look at a solution to the **knapsack** problem.

This is a problem in combinatorial optimization; given a set of items, each with a mass and a value, determine the number of each item to include in a collection so that the total weight is less than or equal to a given limit, and the total value is as large as possible. It derives its name from the problem faced by someone who is constrained by a fixed-size knapsack, and must fill it with the most valuable items.

The knapsack problem has been studied for more than a century, with early works dating as far back as 1897, and nowadays often arises in resource allocation where there are financial constraints. It is studied in fields such as combinatorics, computer science, complexity theory, cryptography, and applied mathematics.

```
using JuMP
N = 6;
m = Model();   # Use default solver
@defVar(m, x[1:N], Bin);   # Define array variable to hold results
profit  = [ 5, 3, 2, 7, 4, 4 ];   # Profit vector of size N
weight = [ 2, 8, 4, 2, 5, 6 ];     # Weights vector of size

capacity = 12;
@setObjective(m, Max, dot(profit, x));
@addConstraint(m, dot(weight, x) <= capacity);
```

The objective is to maximize profit by a choice of values in the x vector, subject to the constraint that any sack can only carry weights up to a total of maxcap:

```
status = solve(m);     # Solve problem using MIP solver
@printf "Value of the objective is %.1f" getObjectiveValue(m);

println("Solution is:")
for i = 1:N
  print("x[$i] = ", getValue(x[i]));
  println(", p[$i]/w[$i] = ", profit[i]/weight[i]);
end


Value of the objective is 16.0
x[1] = 1.0, p[1]/w[1] = 2.5
x[2] = 0.0, p[2]/w[2] = 0.375
x[3] = 0.0, p[3]/w[3] = 0.5
x[4] = 1.0, p[4]/w[4] = 3.5
x[5] = 1.0, p[5]/w[5] = 0.8
x[6] = 0.0, p[6]/w[6] = 0.667
```

Optim

Optim is a native package, with which calculations are coded in Julia without the need for separate solvers, or third-party libraries.

The main call is to the optimize() function that requires at least a function definition and vectors the starting values. Optionally, a value for the solution method can be supplied with one of the following:

- :bfgs
- :cg
- :gradient_descent
- :momentum_gradient_descent
- :l_bfgs
- :nelder_mead
- :newton
- :simulated_annealing

It is also possible to aid optimization by additionally providing functions based on the first (gradient) and second (hessian) partial derivatives.

The value returned is a data structure with 15 elements, whose symbols may be displayed using the names() function

The values for the optimization process are set by default, but these can be overwritten:

- xtol: Threshold tolerance in x (1e-32)
- ftol: Threshold tolerance in f (1e-32)
- grtol: Gradient tolerance (1e-8)
- iterations: Maximum number of iterations (1000)
- store_trace: Stores algorithm's state (false)
- show_trace: Outputs algorithm's state (false)

The Rosenbrock function is a non-convex function used as a performance test problem for optimization algorithms. The global minimum is inside a long, narrow, parabolic-shaped flat valley. To find the valley is trivial, however, to converge to the global minimum is difficult.

The function is defined by: f(x, y) = (a-x)^2 + b(y-x^2)^2.

It has a global minimum at (x, y)=(a, a^2), where f(x, y) = 0.

Usually the (a,b) parameters are chosen as (1, 100).

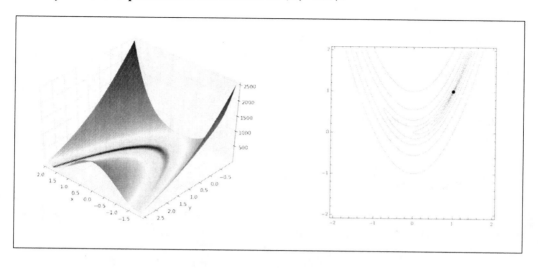

We can define the Rosenbrock function and solve the problem using Optim starting at (0.0,0.0) as:

```
function rb(x::Vector)
    return (1.0 - x[1])^2 + 100.0 * (x[2] - x[1]^2)^2;
end
```

```
using Optim
opt1 = optimize(rb, [0.0, 0.0]);
```

```
Results of Optimization Algorithm
 * Algorithm: Nelder-Mead
 * Starting Point: [0.0, 0.0]
 * Minimum: [1.000005438687492,1.0000079372595394]
 * Value of Function at Minimum: 0.000000
 * Iterations: 60
 * Convergence: true
   * |x - x'| < NaN: false
   * |f(x) - f(x')| / |f(x)| < 1.0e-08: true
   * |g(x)| < NaN: false
   * Exceeded Maximum Number of Iterations: false
 * Objective Function Calls: 115
 * Gradient Call: 0
```

The minimum value took 115 iterations. This can be changed markedly by supplying gradient and Hessian functions:

```
function rb_grad(x::Vector, sv::Vector)
  sv[1] = -2.0*(1.0 - x[1]) - 400.0*(x[2] - x[1]^2) * x[1];
  sv[2] = 200.0*(x[2] - x[1]^2);
end

function rb_hess(x::Vector, sm::Matrix)
  sm[1, 1] = 2.0 - 400.0*x[2] + 1200.0*x[1]^2;
  sm[1, 2] = -400.0*x[1];
  sm[2, 1] = -400.0*x[1];
  sm[2, 2] = 200.0;
end
```

In the preceding code:

$$gradient = \left[\frac{\partial f}{\partial x} \quad \frac{\partial f}{\partial y} \right] \quad hessian = \begin{bmatrix} \dfrac{\partial^2 f}{\partial x} & \dfrac{\partial^2 f}{\partial x \partial y} \\ \dfrac{\partial^2 f}{\partial x \partial y} & \dfrac{\partial^2 f}{\partial y} \end{bmatrix}$$

Re-running the optimization produces:

```
optimize(rb, rg_grad, rb_hess, [0.0,0.0], method=:newton, show_trace=true);
```

Inter	Function value	Gradient norm
0	1.000000e+00	2.000000e+00
1	8.431140e-01	1.588830e+00
2	6.586412e-01	4.959487e+00
.	. . . .	. . . .
.	. . . .	. . . .
12	3.784204e-13	2.087334e-05
13	5.639268e-24	5.214740e-11

```
Results of Optimization Algorithm
 * Algorithm: Newton's Method
 * Starting Point: [0.0,0.0]
 * Minimum: [0.9999999999979515,0.9999999999960232]
 * Value of Function at Minimum: 0.000000
 * Iterations: 13
 * Convergence: true
   * |x - x'| < 1.0e-32: false
```

```
    * |f(x) - f(x')| / |f(x)| < 1.0e-08: false
    * |g(x)| < 1.0e-08: true
    * Exceeded Maximum Number of Iterations: false
 * Objective Function Calls: 54
 * Gradient Call: 54
```

This converges to the same ~ (1.0, 1.0) solution, but now in just 13 iterations.

NLopt

NLopt is a free/open source library for nonlinear optimization problems with or without gradient information, and can be built from source from http://ab-initio.mit.edu/nlopt, although binaries exist for Windows. The manual on NLopt is also available from the MIT site.

This provides a common interface for many different optimization algorithms, including:

- Both global and local optimization
- Algorithms using function values only (derivative-free) and also algorithms exploiting user-supplied gradients
- Algorithms for unconstrained optimization, bound-constrained optimization, and general nonlinear inequality/equality constraints

The interface in Julia (NLopt.jl) can utilize the NLopt library directly with calls via its API, or alternatively by using the generic MathProgBase interface.

The NLopt API defines a structure of the nlopt_opt type, and this is encapsulated in the Julia package by the Opt type, which is normally created by the Opt (algor, ndims) constructor for a given type of the algor algorithm, and number of the ndims optimization parameters.

Algorithms are specified by symbols such as :LD_MMA, :NL_COBYLA, :PRAXIS, and so on, the full list is given at https://github.com/JuliaOpt/NLopt.jl. In this case:

- The objective function is either min_objective!(opt, n) or max_objective!(opt).
- The form of the function is f(x:Vector, grad::Vector). A zero length vector can be passed for grad, otherwise it should be equivalent to the partial derivative of f with respect to xi.
- Constraints are specified by lower_bounds!(opt, lb) or upper_bounds(opt,rb), where lb and rb. An unbounded dimension may be specified as +/- Inf.

- It is also possible to specify non-linear constraints using `inequality_constraint()` or `equality_constraint()`.

Consider a non-linearly constrained minimization problem:

Minimise `sqrt(x2)`, subject to `x2 > 0, x2 > (a1*x1 + b1)^3`, and `x2 > (a2*x1 + b2)^3` for parameters `a1=2, b1=0, a2=-1, b2=1`.

The feasible region defined by these constraints is shown as follows:

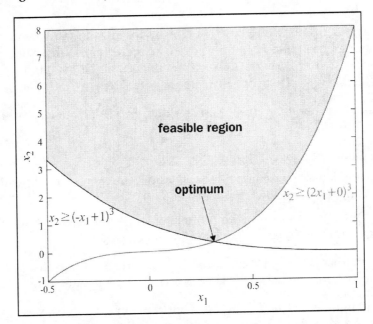

x2 is constrained to lie above the maximum of the two cubic functions and the optimum point is located at their intersection `(1/3, 8/27)`.

The value of the objective at this point is `sqrt(x2)    => sqrt{8//27} ~ 0.5443`.

The solution in Julia is:

```
using NLopt
count = 0;
function myfunc(x::Vector, grad::Vector)
  if length(grad) > 0
    grad[1] = 0
    grad[2] = 0.5/sqrt(x[2])
  end
  global count;
```

```
   count::Int += 1;
   sqrt(x[2]);
end
function mycons(x::Vector, grad::Vector, a, b)
   if length(grad) > 0
     grad[1] = 3*a * (a*x[1] + b)^2
     grad[2] = -1
   end
   (a*x[1] + b)^3 - x[2]
end
```

The routine checks the `grad` vector for non-zero length, in which case the derivatives with respect to x1 and x2 are returned:

```
opt = Opt(:LD_MMA, 2);
lower_bounds!(opt, [-Inf, 0.]);
xtol_rel!(opt,1e-4);
min_objective!(opt, myfunc);
```

`xtol_rel()` specifies a tolerance condition for the optimization and the constraints are defined as follows:

```
inequality_constraint!(opt, (x,g) -> mycons(x,g,2,0), 1e-8);
inequality_constraint!(opt, (x,g) -> mycons(x,g,-1,1), 1e-8);
```

Finally, the `optimize()` function is called with a starting estimate and returns the function value, a vector of the optimal point, and a return code.

Possible successful values of the return code are:

```
:SUCCESS, :XTOL_REACHED, :STOP_VALUE_REACHED, :FTOL_REACHED
```

This does not necessarily indicate that the algorithm has produced definitive results.

Failure-style return values indicate that the algorithm did not run, and include:

```
:FAILURE, :INVALID_ARGS, :OUT_OF_MEMORY
```

So running the minimization gives:

```
(minf,minx,ret) = optimize(opt, [1.2, 5.6]);
@printf "Ans => %6.3f at (%6.3f,%6.3f)" minf minx[1] minx[2];

Ans # => 0.5433 at (0.333, 0.296)
```

Using with the MathProgBase interface

As noted, NLopt implements the `MathProgBase` interface for non-linear optimization, so it can be used interchangeably with JuMP.

The NLopt solver is named `NLoptSolver` and the solution for the preceding problem is:

```
using JuMP
using NLopt
m = Model(solver=NLoptSolver(algorithm=:LD_MMA));

a1 = 2;  b1 = 0;
a2 = -1; b2 = 1;

@defVar(m, x1);
@defVar(m, x2 >= 0);
@setNLObjective(m, Min, sqrt(x2));
@addNLConstraint(m, x2 >= (a1*x1+b1)^3);
@addNLConstraint(m, x2 >= (a2*x1+b2)^3);

setValue(x1, 1.2);
setValue(x2, 5.6);
status = solve(m);
@printf "Ans => %6.4f at (%5.3f,%5.3f)\n"
getObjectiveValue(m) getValue(x1) getValue(x2);

Ans # => 0.5433 at (0.333,0.296)
```

This indicates the power of the macro definitions in decoupling the problem definition from the actual details of the coding.

The call requires an algorithm parameter to be specified. There are a number of other parameters that are can be default, unless provided explicitly.

Stochastic problems

Problems encountered so far are completely determined by the models, and will produce the same solutions repeatedly. Some models have terms that occur randomly, and these are called stochastics.

We have already seen one example earlier, that of the price a volatile stock. While the price increases roughly which the underlying price of money, fluctuations were considered to exist on a day-to-day process sampled from a Gaussian process.

Time series analysis is often used to reduce the effect of such fluctuations and reveal the underlying trends, but there are certain systems where the stochastics are paramount. Typical examples are models of queueing systems that might occur in service at banks, or checkouts in supermarkets. I will discuss a particular case of the bank teller later in this section.

Stochastic simulations

Simulations are often dealt with using a framework that attempts to hide the details of the coding as part of the model definition. This has similarities with the approach we saw with the JuMP package in optimization problems.

The approach is not a new one, in fact it was introduced for simulation problems by IBM with GPSS in 1961; modern day inheritors are jDisco and SimPy.

SimJulia

The SimJulia package is similar to the Python-based SimPy module, although as it is a native implementation, neither a wrapper nor requires the use of PyCall.

SimJulia is both a discrete event and a continuous time process simulation framework. A process is implemented as a type containing a Task (co-routine).and the produce() function is used to schedule future events providing a pointer to the Task object.

In discrete event models, the time is advanced in steps and individual events fire according to their schedules/triggers. For continuous events, the change is per-step and computed according to derivative as well as variable values.

Clearly, being able to handle discrete events is a prerequisite for stochastic simulations, but the ability to handle continuous events is a useful addition.

SimJulia implements the following process intrinsics:

- sleep: The current process is deactivated and can be reactivated by another process
- hold: The process is busy for a certain amount of time, during this period an interruption can force the control back to the process
- wait and queue: A process can wait or queue for some signals to be fired by another process
- waituntil: A process can wait for a general system to be satisfied

- **request** and **release**: A resource, a discrete congestion point to which processes may have to queue up, can be requested and when it is finished, be released
- **put** and **get**: A level (continuous) and a store (discrete) model congestion point that can produce or consume continuous/discrete "material"
- **observe**: A monitor enables the observation of a single variable of interest and can return a data summary during or at the end of a simulation run

Many of the examples provided in the Julia package are direct analogues of these in the Python module. The classic example is that of a queue for service in a bank, post office, or grocery shop and we will illustrate the use of SimJulia with such a model.

Bank teller example

Consider example of modeling a bank service with the following assumptions:

- Customers wait in a single queue arriving at random intervals
- There are a number of resources (bank tellers) who service the next customer in the queue
- Customers may decide to wait or leave depending on the length of the queue

All three may involve stochastic variates and these will need to be generated from a probability distribution, or will be based on actual empirical measurement.

Distributions will clearly not be Gaussian, since we cannot have negative waiting and service times. Arrivals may differ in a city situation where there is a peak around lunchtimes and a 'rush' towards closing.

Service times may also be long tailed as some transactions may be more complex than the 'norm', and require considerably more resources.

We will be interested in determining the mean time to serve customers and may be interested in the effects of increasing the number of tellers to match demand, but also balance against the need to minimise the idle time of tellers.

The principle aim of such a simulation would be to decide whether it is desirable to increase the resource (tellers) to meet demand; with the obvious trade-off between the cost of the extra tellers balanced against the extra revenue generated.

We will need the `Distributions` package to provide density functions to sample against, as we have noted that uniform or normal distributions are inappropriate. We will assume in this example that the arrival times and service times follow an exponential (Poisson) distribution, although in a real simulation we noted that the modeling of these would need to be more exact. Also, we will assume if the queue length is more than a given maximum, the customer does not wait.

First, we need a function to represent the entire customer experience from arriving, through being served, to leaving, and output the relevant time steps and waiting times:

```
using SimJulia
using Distributions

function visit(customer::Process,
   time_in_bank::Float64,
   counter::Resource,
   max_in_queue::Int)
   arrive = now(customer);
   @printf("%8.4f %s: Here I am\n", arrive, customer);
   if length(counter.wait_queue) < max_in_queue
     request(customer, counter);
     wait = now(customer) - arrive;
     push!(wait_times, wait);
     @printf("%8.4f %s: Waited %6.3f\n",
     now(customer), customer, wait);
     hold(customer, time_in_bank)

     release(customer, counter);
     @printf("%8.4f %s: Finished\n", now(customer), customer)
   else
     @printf("%8.4f %s: Waiting\n", now(customer), customer)
   end
end
```

Next, we need to be able to create a number of customer processes and define the following function to do this:

```
function generate(source::Process, number::Int,
mean_time_between_arrivals::Float64,
mean_time_in_bank::Float64,
counter::Resource,
max_in_queue::Int)
  d_tba = Exponential(mean_time_of_arrivals);
  d_tib = Exponential(mean_time_in_bank);
  for i = 1:number
```

```
    c = Process(simulation(source),
    @sprintf("Customer%02d", i));
    tib = rand(d_tib);
    activate(c, now(source), visit, tib,
    counter, max_in_queue);
    tba = rand(d_tba);
    hold(source, tba);
  end
end

function number_in_system(counter::Resource)
  length(counter.active_set) + length(counter.wait_queue);
end
```

As mentioned earlier, both arrivals and service (time in bank) times are Poisson processes, and so are solely parameterized by the distribution means. Processes are activated or held depending on whether resource is available and the number in the bank at any onetime is simply the number of customers being served and the number waiting.

We need to set some limits for the time the bank is open, the maximal queue length, and also values for the means that parameterize the exponential distributions.

Finally, we need to set the random number seed, activate the initial processes, and run the simulation:

```
# Set simulation data
max_number = 20;
max_time =  300.0;
max_queue = 1;
mean_arrival_time = 5.0;
mean_service_time = 8.0;
number_of_tellers = 2;
seed = randomize();  # Use function defined early or pick # a value to
make run reproducible

global wait_times = Array(Float64,1);

# Model/Experiment
srand(seed);
sim = Simulation(uint(16));
k = Resource(sim, "Counter", uint(1), false);
s = Process(sim, "Source");
activate(s, 0.0, generate,
            max_number, mean_arrival_time,
            mean_service_time, k, max_queue);
```

The bank is open for 5 hours, or until 20 customers have been served. Customers arrive on an average every 5 minutes and it takes around 8 minutes to be served:

```
run(sim, max_time);
@printf "Average waiting time is %5.3f\n" mean(wait_times);
```

```
 0.0000 Customer01: Arrives
 0.0000 Customer01: Waited  0.000
 3.1863 Customer01: Finished
 9.9273 Customer02: Arrives
 9.9273 Customer02: Waited  0.000
10.9117 Customer03: Arrives
19.0337 Customer02: Finished
19.0337 Customer03: Waited  8.122
21.2591 Customer04: Arrives
26.3771 Customer05: Arrives
26.6146 Customer03: Finished
26.6146 Customer04: Waited  5.355
29.2442 Customer04: Finished
29.2442 Customer05: Waited  2.867
32.1817 Customer05: Finished
35.8994 Customer06: Arrives
35.8994 Customer06: Waited  0.000
. . . . . . . . . . . . . . . . . . . . . . . . . . . . . . . .
. . . . . . . . . . . . . . . . . . . . . . . . . . . . . . . .

Average waiting time is 8.762
```

Bayesian methods and Markov processes

To end this sortie to some of the aspects of scientific methods in Julia, we will look at another framework that is used in investigation problems arising in Bayesian analysis.

Some of these problems are difficult to vectorize, so Julia has a distinct advantage over alternative data science languages since de-vectorize programs run as quick or even more quickly than the vectorized ones.

Bayesian analysis is a form of statistic inference and at the heart of the analysis is the Bayes' Rule, which tells us how to do inference about hypotheses from data.

A model describes data that we can observe from a system. If we use probability theory to express all forms of uncertainty and noise associated with our model, then inverse probability (that is, Bayes rule) allows us to infer unknown quantities, adapt our models, make predictions, and learn from data.

Bayesian inference is about the quantification and propagation of uncertainty defined via a probability, in light of observations of the system. This is fundamentally different from classical inference that tends to be concerned with parameter estimation.

Monte Carlo Markov Chains

The aspect of Bayesian methods with which we will be concerned is **Monte Carlo Markov Chain (MCMC)**.

The MCMC procedure enables you to carry out analysis on a wide range of complex Bayesian statistical models. It uses algorithms to draw samples from an arbitrary posterior distribution, which is defined by the prior distributions for the parameters and the likelihood function for the specified data.

The algorithms are also called samplers and many exist, notable among these are the Gibbs sampler and the Metropolis-Hastings algorithm. Gibbs sampling has given rise to frameworks specifically utilizing the methods such as **Bayesian inference Using Gibbs Sampling (BUGS)** and **Just Another Gibbs Sampler (JAGS)**.

MCMC algorithms generate a Markov chain of samples, each of which is correlated with nearby samples. Care must be taken that if independent samples are desired, they can be obtained typically by thinning the resulting chain of samples by only taking every *nth* value. In addition, samples from the beginning of the chain may not accurately represent the desired distribution, so may need to be discarded (burn-in period).

MCMC frameworks

One popular approach for the frameworks is currently based on the **Stan**. Stan is available on Linux, OS X, and Windows and has a command line interface. It is also ported to Python, R, MATLAB, and Julia.

It compiles its models using its own compiler (`stanc`) via C++ to an executable in order to produce sensible execution times. The interface from Julia (`Stan.jl`) builds the model seamlessly, and then runs the executable to dump the results of the simulation. Then, it uses a second package, the `Mamba` (`.jl`) package, to display and diagnose the results.

`Mamba` is a native Julia package that is a comprehensive toolset for the implementation and inference using MCMC sampling.

It provides a framework for:

- The specification of hierarchical models through stated relationships between data, parameters, and statistical distributions
- The block-updating of parameters with samplers provided, defined by the user, or available from other packages
- The execution of sampling schemes
- Posterior inference

The `Mamba` package is designed for general Bayesian model fitting via MCMC. Like OpenBUGS and JAGS, it supports a wide range of model and distributional specifications, and provides a syntax for model specification but differing from those. However like PyMC, Mamba provides a unified environment in which all interactions with the software are made through a single, interpreted language.

Any operator, function, type, or package can be used for model specification and custom distributions and samplers can be written in Julia to extend the package. This is of great benefit when compared to OpenBUGS and JAGS, where extensions can involve `tR` wrappers used to call the programs, their DSLs, and the underlying implementations in C++.

A comprehensive treatment of Mamba is given at `mambajl.readthedocs.org`. To illustrate the use of the package, let's look at an example drawn from OpenBUGS concerning a log-linear model for binary data via the Solomon-Wynne experiment on dogs.

A dog is put in a compartment, the lights are turned out, and a barrier is raised. 10 seconds later an electric stimulus is applied. The results are recorded as a success (`Y = 1`) if the dog jumps the barrier before the stimulus occurs, or failure (`Y = 0`) otherwise.

Thirty dogs were each subjected to 25 such trials. A plausible model is to suppose that a dog learns from previous trials, with the probability of success depending on the number of previous shocks and the number of previous avoidances. Lindley thus uses the following model:

$$pj = \left(A \wedge xj \right) * \left(B \wedge j - xj \right)$$

The preceding model is for the probability of a shock (failure) at the `j`, trial, where `x j` = number of success (avoidances) before trial `j` and `j - x j` is the number of previous failures (shocks).

This is equivalent to a log linear model:

$$\log\ pj = \alpha\alpha xj + \beta\left(j - xj\right)$$

We have included the data from the trails in the dogs.wsv file and we wish to test the feasibility of the model by obtaining estimates for α and β, and determining how close this fits to the actual results.

So we can read in the experimental results and setup into a dogs array as follows:

```
using Mamba
dogs = (Symbol => Any) [:Y => int(readdlm("dogs.wsv")) ];
dogs[:Dogs]  = size(dogs[:Y], 1);
dogs[:Trials] = size(dogs[:Y], 2);
dogs[:xa]  = mapslices(cumsum, dogs[:Y], 2);
dogs[:xs]  = mapslices(x -> [1:25] - x, dogs[:xa], 2);
dogs[:y]  = 1 - dogs[:Y][:, 2:25];
```

The data goes into the Y component and we need to create further components for the number (sizes) of dogs and trials, and slice and dice the data in order to create the following stochastic model:

```
model = Model(
  y = Stochastic(2,
    @modelexpr(Dogs, Trials, alpha, xa, beta, xs,
    Distribution[
      begin
        p = exp(alpha * xa[i,j] + beta * xs[i,j])
        Bernoulli(p)
      end
      for i in 1:Dogs, j in 1:Trials-1]), false),

  alpha = Stochastic(:(Truncated(Flat(), -Inf, -1e-5))),
  A = Logical(@modelexpr(alpha, exp(alpha))),

  beta = Stochastic(:(Truncated(Flat(), -Inf, -1e-5))),
  B = Logical(@modelexpr(beta, exp(beta))) );

inits = [
  [:y => dogs[:y], :alpha => -1, :beta => -1],
  [:y => dogs[:y], :alpha => -2, :beta => -2]
];
```

Choosing model expressions for α and setting initial values to start off the runs, we can perform the simulation as:

```
scheme = [Slice([:alpha, :beta], [1.0, 1.0])];
setsamplers!(model, scheme);
sim =
    mcmc(model,dogs,inits,10000,burnin=2500,thin=2,chains=2);
```

This is over 2 chains and has a long burn-in of 25 percent of the iterations; every other result (`thin = 2`) is used. So over two chains and for `10000` iterations, this will produce 3,750 results per chain:

```
## MCMC Simulation of 10000 Iterations x 2 Chains...
Chain 1:    0% [0:07:47 of 0:07:48 remaining]
Chain 1:   10% [0:00:47 of 0:00:53 remaining]
.................................................. .

.................................................. .
Chain 1: 100% [0:00:00 of 0:00:50 remaining]

Chain 2:    0% [0:00:17 of 0:00:17 remaining]
Chain 2:   10% [0:00:43 of 0:00:48 remaining]
.................................................. .

.................................................. .
Chain 2: 100% [0:00:00 of 0:00:49 remaining]


describe(sim)

Iterations = 2502:10000
Thinning interval = 2
Chains = 1,2
Samples per chain = 3750

Empirical Posterior Estimates:
5x6 Array{Any,2}:
```

""	"Mean"	"SD"	"Naive SE"	"MCSE"	"ESS"
"A"	0.782932	0.0191798	0.000221469	0.000323638	5132.34
"B"	0.924379	0.0109682	0.000126649	0.000164441	5776.37
"alpha"	-0.24501	0.0245322	0.000283274	0.000413172	5142.05
"beta"	-0.0787042	0.0118855	0.000137241	0.000178353	5771.19

```
Quantiles:
5x6 Array{Any,2}:
```

""	"2.5%"	"25.0%"	"50.0%"	"75.0%"	"97.5%"
"A"	0.745209	0.769936	0.783456	0.796246	0.819994

"B"	0.901388	0.917295	0.924706	0.932047	0.944471
"alpha"	-0.29409	-0.261448	-0.24404	-0.227847	-0.198458
"beta"	-0.103819	-0.086326	-0.0782797	-0.0703723	-0.0571298

`Mamba` also links very well with the `Gadfly` package to a graphic visualization of the fit:

```
Using Gadfly
P = plot(sim)
draw(p, filename="dog.svg");
```

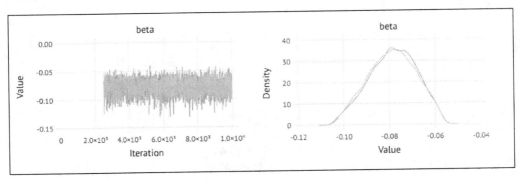

Summary

This chapter has covered a diverse range of topics arising from the discipline of scientific computing.

We began by looking at classical linear algebra problems, the solutions of which are provided by routines from within the Julia base system. For the remaining sections, we turned to a variety of packages and applied them to examples from signal processing, optimization, and the solution of ordinary and partial differential equations.

Finally, we turned to an area in which the use of Julia is particularly well suited, the solution of non-vectorized problems such as those arising from stochastic processes modeled by Monte Carlo methods.

In the next chapter, we will look in greater detail at the question of production of graphics and data visualization and will see that Julia's various approaches are especially rich and diverse.

7
Graphics

It has been often noted that Julia has no built-in graphics command. This means that it is not possible to create some datasets and issue a plot command without first installing and loading a package.

One reason for this is that Julia needs to build from source a variety of different operating systems and any libraries that are shipped, such as OpenBLAS and LibUV, must as be in source form and not interfere with the building process.

Graphics engines have a variety of different backends such as Gtk, Qt; and, whereas specialist packages may be restricted in their OS support, the overall Julia system may not.

At first, the inclusion of built-in graphics was seen as a long term goal and one that would be added in future releases. However with an emphasis on package compilation and rapid loading, this does not seem as pressing as it originally did. I will return to this topic at the end of this chapter.

One additional point to notice is that the Julia method of importing symbols into its main namespace via the `using` command means that most graphics packages, which tend to have functions such as `plot()` and `display()`, do not produce a name clash. Of course, it is possible to use `import` and fully qualify any function call. Normally we will be working with a single package.

To tackle Julia's approach to graphics, I will classify the approaches in three main sections:

- Basic graphics
- Graphic engines
- Web graphics

The classification is far from perfect, but by basic graphics I mean where the bulk of the work is done in Julia coding, albeit utilizing calls to low-level libraries. Graphic engines rely on third-party support such as Gnuplot or Python's matplotlib and the final category utilizes web browsers and HTML.

Basic graphics in Julia

We have already encountered some graphics in the previous chapters of this book, both text plots and two-dimensional graphics using modules such as `ASCIIPlots` and `Winston`. In this section, we are going to look a little further into these and similar packages.

Text plotting

In *Chapter 1*, *The Julia Environment*, we had seen some simple graphics using the ASCII plots package.

This has largely been replaced with a second package, the `TextPlots` package. While it does not provide sophisticated visualization, it is worth a look as it is very lightweight and loads quickly, being independent of any graphic libraries or drivers.

The basic call uses a function of a single variable together with an optional range of values for that variable.

The range can be specified in the `x0:x1` form or as separate arguments `(,,,.x0,x1)`. If no range is provided, then a default of `-10:10` is used.

It is possible to define more than one function, but the display can be confusing.

Consider the following damped sinusoid in the `0:3π` range, which we pass as an anonymous function:

```
Julia> using TextPlots
julia> plot(x->x*sin(3x)*exp(-0.3x),0,3pi)
```

The resulting plot is shown in the following figure:

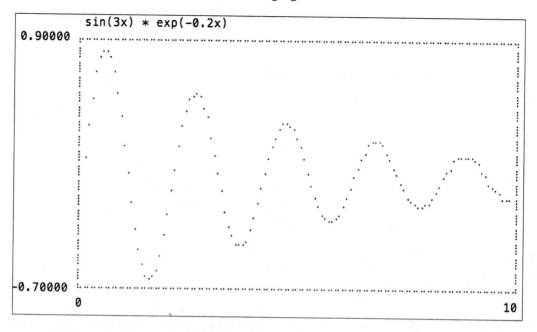

The routine computes the bounding box for the generated points suitably scaled up, and provides a default title equivalent to the function definition. The limits for evaluating the function can be passed separately, as shown previously, or as a range. If the limits are not provided, the default `-10:10` is used.

Normally, the plot displays a title, labels, and a border, but all can be switched off by setting the appropriate optional parameters to `false`.

In order to control the size of the displayed text, the number of rows and columns and also a value for columns can be specified explicitly.

It is possible to define more than one function, but within the context of a text plot, the result can be often confusing.

However, passing arrays of values rather than a function definition creates a quite acceptable scatter diagram.

The following code generates a simple random walk (with drift) by generating some random numbers and displaying the cumulative sum:

```julia
julia> using TextPlots
julia> t = linspace(0,1,400);
Julia> x = 0.3*sqrt(t) + 10*randn(400);
julia> plot(t, cumsum(x), title=false)
```

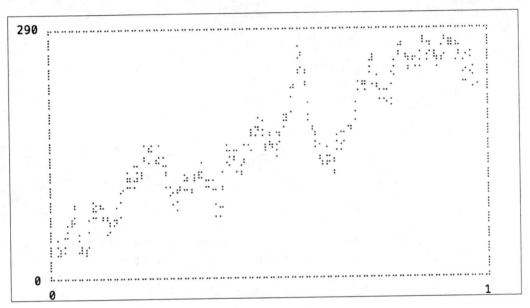

Cairo

Cairo is a 2D graphics library with support for multiple output devices and Cairo.jl is a pretty faithful correspondence to the C API.

This is the next level up from the base graphics as it implements a device context to the display system and works with X Window (Linux), OS X, and Windows. Additionally, Cairo can create disk files in PostScript, PDF, and SVG formats.

Cairo.jl is used by the Winston package and I find it is convenient to add it separately before installing Winston. The package addition script for Cairo will also install the required base software for the appropriate operating system and if this installation runs smoothly the higher level graphics should encounter no problems.

The examples provided in the Julia package correspond to those on the cairographics.org website and the documentation there on the C API is useful too.

The following is an example to draw a line (stroke) through four points:

1. First we create a `cr` context and add a 512x128 rectangle with a gray background:

```
using Cairo
c   = CairoRGBSurface(512, 128);
cr = CairoContext(c);
save(cr);
set_source_rgb(cr, 0.8, 0.8, 0.8);      # light gray
rectangle(cr, 0.0, 0.0, 512.0, 128.0); # background
fill(cr);
restore(cr);
save(cr);
```

2. Next, we define the points and draw the line through the points:

```
x0=51.2;   y0=64.0;
x1=204.8;  y1=115.4;
x2=307.2;  y2=12.8;
x3=460.8;  y3=64.0;
move_to (cr, x0, y0);
curve_to (cr, x1, y1, x2, y2, x3, y3);
set_line_width (cr, 10.0);
stroke (cr);
restore(cr);
```

3. Finally, we can add some text and write the resulting graphics to disk:

```
move_to(cr, 12.0, 12.0);
set_source_rgb (cr, 0, 0, 0);
show_text(cr,"Figure 7-2")
write_to_png(c,"fig7-2.png");
```

The result is shown in the following figure:

Winston

`Winston` is a 2D package and resembles the built-in graphics available within MATLAB.

The majority of the plots produced in the earlier chapters have made use of `Winston`, but there are a number of features that we have not yet covered.

The typical usage we have already seen is via the `plot()` function:

```
using Winston
t = linspace(0,4pi,1000);
f(x::Array) = 10x.*exp(-0.3x).*sin(3x);
g(x::Array) = 0.03x.*(2pi - x).*(4pi - x);
h(x::Array) = 1./(1 + x.^2);
y1 = f(t); y2 = g(t); y3 = h(t)
plot(t,y1,"b--")
```

Alternatively, use `fplot()` and define the function directly that produces the same graph as shown in the following:

```
fplot(x->10*x.*exp(-0.3*x).*sin(3*x), [0,4pi],"b—")
```

In addition, there is a `plothist()` function that can take the result of the `histo()` function.

The following code generates a set of normally distributed numbers and displays the frequency histogram for 100 intervals:

```
a = randn(10000)
ha = hist(a,100)
plothist(ha)
```

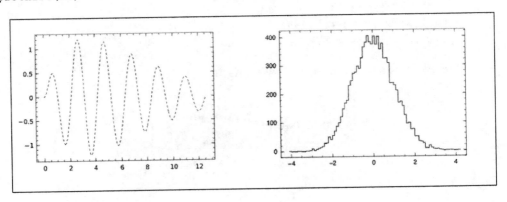

When we need to plot multiple curves on a single graph, we have seen that this can be done using a single statement:

```
plot(t, y1, "r-", t, y2, "b-")
```

Alternatively, this can done with separate statements in a couple of ways:

```
plot(t, y1, "r-")
oplot(t, y2, "b-")
plot(t, y1, "r-")
hold()
plot(t, y2, "b-")
```

This is particularly useful as calls such as `fplot()` do not take multiple arguments.

In addition to plotting linear scales, it is possible to plot logarithmic ones using the `loglog()`, `semilogx()`, and `semilogy()` functions:

```
semilogx(t,y1)
title("log(t) vs 10x * exp(-0.3x) * sin(3x)")
semilogy(y2,y3)
title("0.03*(2\\pi - x)*(4\\pi - x)  vs  log(1 /( 1 + x*x))")
```

The two plots are shown in the following figure:

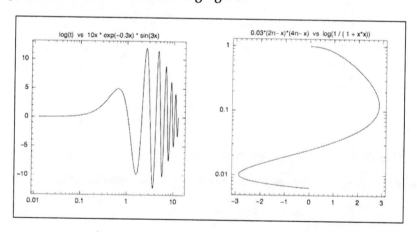

Notice the use of the \\ syntax in the title statements to create non-ASCII characters using the LaTeX conventions for the symbols.

The calls to routines such as `plot()` are convenience functions to write to the current plotting frame, the ID of which can be retrieved by a call to `gcf()`.

Working explicitly with framed plots can offer additional functionality as the following redrawing of two functions `f()` and `g()`, defined previously shows:

```
p = FramedPlot( title="Frequency vs Time",
                          ylabel="\\Theta",
                          xlabel="\\Tau");


add(p,FillBetween(t,y1,t,y2));
add(p,Curve(t,y1,color="red"));
add(p,Curve(t,y2,color="blue"));
display(p)
```

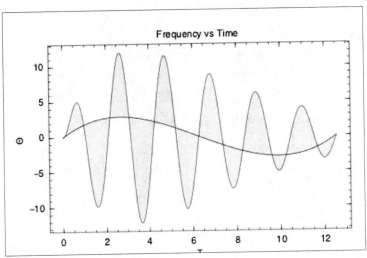

Finally, let's look at a more complex example using a framed plot:

```
p = FramedPlot(aspect_ratio=1,xrange=(0,100),yrange=(0,100));

n = 21;

x = linspace(0, 100, n);


# Create a set of random variates

yA = 40 .+ 10*randn(n);

yB = x   .+ 5*randn(n);
```

```
# Set labels and symbol styles
a = Points(x, yA, kind="circle");
setattr(a,label="a points");
b = Points(x, yB);
setattr(b,label="b points");
style(b, kind="filled circle");


# Plot a line which 'fits' through the yB points
# and add a legend in the top LHS part of the graph
s = Slope(1, (0,0), kind="dotted");
setattr(s, label="slope");
lg = Legend(.1, .9, {a,b,s});
add(p, s, a, b, lg);
display(p)
```

The setattr() routine is a general routine for setting attributes to Winston objects. In fact, calls to title(), xlabel(), and ylabel() are also convenience calls to set the appropriate attributes of the current plotting window.

As we can see, it is possible to attach a label attribute to an object and use that as part of the legend in conjunction with the objects style (kind).

The resulting graph is shown in the following figure:

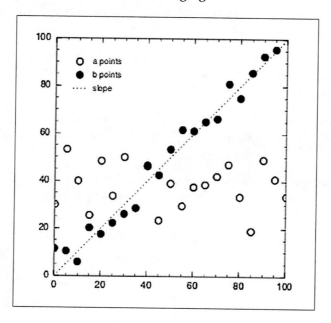

In addition to displaying plot, it is possible to save it to file using `savefig()`.

The type of image saved is determined by the file extension and there are a couple of options, such as `width` and `height` (in pixels), that will rescale the plot to the desired dimensions.

Data visualization

Visualization is the presentation of data in a variety of graphical and pictorial formats. The reader will be familiar with examples such as pie and bar charts. Visualizations help us see things that are not immediately obvious, even when data volumes are very large patterns can be spotted quickly and easily.

Interactivity is one of the useful features of successful visualizations, providing the ability to zoom, filter, segment, and sort data.

In this section, we will look at the extremely powerful `Gadfly` Julia package.

Gadfly

`Gadfly` is a large and complex package, and provides great flexibility in the range and breadth of the visualizations possible in Julia. It is equivalent to the `ggplot2` R module and similarly is based on the *The Grammar of Graphics* seminal work by Leland Wilkinson.

The package was written by Daniel Jones, and the source on GitHub contains numerous examples of visual displays together with the accompanying code.

An entire text could be devoted just to `Gadfly`, so I can only point out some of the main features here and encourage the reader interested in print standard graphics in Julia to refer to the online website at `gadflyjl.org`.

The standard call is to the `plot()` function that creates a graph on the display device via a browser either directly or under the control of IJulia, if that is being used as an IDE.

It is possible to assign the result of `plot()` to a variable and invoke this using `display()`. In this way, output can be written to files including: SVG, SVGJS/D3, PDF, and PNG:

```
dd  =  plot(x =  rand(10),  y = rand(10));
draw(SVG("random-pts.svg",  15cm, 12cm)  , dd);
```

Notice that if writing to a backend, the display size is provided and this can be specified in units of cm or inch.

Gadfly works well with C libraries of cairo, pango, and fontconfig installed.

It will produce SVG and SVGJS graphics, but for PNG, PS (PostScript), and PDF cairo is required. Also, complex text layouts are more accurate when pango and fontconfig are available.

The plot () call can operate on three different data sources:

- Dataframes
- Functions and expressions
- Arrays and collections

Unless specified, the type of graph produced is a scatter diagram.

The ability to work directly with data frames is especially useful.

To illustrate this, let's look at the GCSE result set we investigated in *Chapter 5, Working with Data*. Recall that this is available as part of the RDatasets suite of source data. So we begin by creating a dataframe as previously:

```
using Gadfly, RDatasets, DataFrames;
set_default_plot_size(20cm, 12cm);
mlmf = dataset("mlmRev","Gcsemv")
df = mlmf[complete_cases(mlmf), :]
```

After extracting the data, we need to operate with values that do not have any NA values. So we use the complete_cases() function to create a subset of the original data.

```
names(df)
5-element Array{Symbol,1}: ;
 # => [ :School,   :Student, :Gender,   :Written, :Course ]
```

If we wish to view the data values for the exam and course work results and at the same time differentiate between boys and girls, this can be displayed by:

```
plot(df, x="Course", y="Written", color="Gender")
```

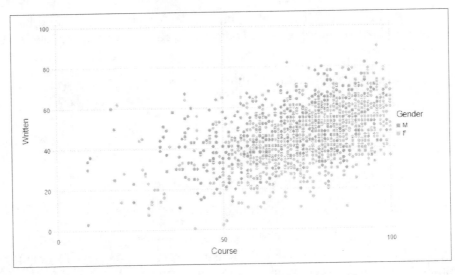

Notice that `Gadfly` produces the legend for the gender categorization automatically.

For an example of a function type invocation, here is one from the GitHub sources that shows what can be produced in a single call:

```
plot((x,y) -> x*exp(-(x-int(x))^2-y^2), -8., 8, -2., 2)
```

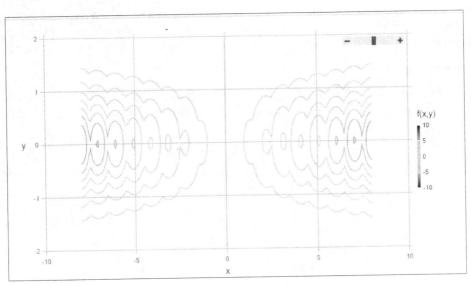

Looking at the third type invocation, let's plot two arrays of data but as line graphs rather than on a scatter diagram.

Gadfly produces multiline plots using the layer() routine and uses the concept of themes to overwrite the color schemes.

Here is a plot of 100 samples of a uniform variate (in red) together with a normal variate (in blue), both centered on zero and with unit variance:

```
x = [1:100;];

y1 = 1 - 2*rand(100);

y2 = randn(100);

plot(
  layer(x=x,y=y1,Geom.line,Theme(default_color=color("red"))),
  layer(x=x,y=y2,Geom.line,Theme(default_color=color("blue")))
)
```

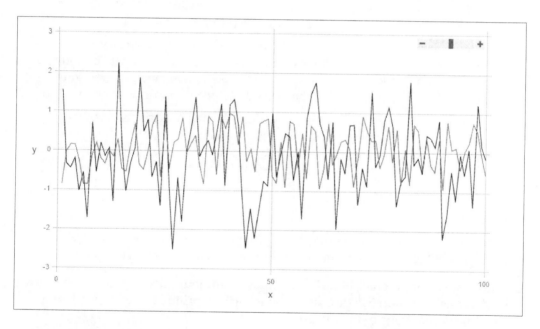

To summarize, in the spirit of the *Grammar of Graphics* seminal work, the basic form of the plot instruction is:

```
plot(data-source, element1, element2, …; mappings )
```

In the preceding plot instruction, the data-source is a dataframe, function, or array: the elements are the various options such as themes, scales, plot markers, labels, titles, and guides that you need to adjust to fine-tune the plot: and the mappings are the symbols and assignments that link to the data.

Plot elements in Gadfly are categorized as statistics, scales, geometries, and guides and are bound to data aesthetics as follows:

- **Statistics**: These are functions that take as input one or more aesthetics, operate on these values, then output to one or more aesthetics. For example, drawing of boxplots typically uses the boxplot statistic (Stat.boxplot) that takes as input the x and y aesthetic and outputs the middle, upper and lower hinge, and upper and lower fence aesthetics.

- **Scales**: Similar to statistics, apply a transformation to the original data, typically mapping one aesthetic to the same aesthetic, while retaining the original value. The Scale.x_log10 aesthetic maps the x aesthetic back to the x aesthetic after applying a log10 transformation, but keeps track of the original value so that data points are properly identified.

- **Geometries**: These are responsible for actually doing the drawing. A geometry takes as input one or more aesthetic, and uses data bound to these aesthetics to draw things. The Geom.point geometry draws points using the x and y aesthetics, the Geom.line geometry draws lines, and so on.

- **Guides**: These are similar to geometries. The major distinction is that geometries always draw within the rectangular plot frame, while guides have some special layout considerations such as themes, scales, plot markers, labels, titles, and guides that you need to adjust to fine tune the plot.

Compose

Compose is a declarative vector graphics system that is also authored by Daniel Jones as part of the Gadfly system, but which can be used in its own right.

Unlike most vector graphics libraries, Compose is thoroughly declarative. Graphics are defined using a tree structure, assembling various primitives, and then letting the module decide how to draw them.

The primitives can be classified as: context, form, and property, and the assembly operation is achieved via the compose() function:

- context: An internal node
- form: A leaf node that defines some geometry, like a line or a polygon

- `property`: A leaf node that modifies how its parent's subtree is drawn, such as fill color, font family, or line width

- `compose(a, b)`: This returns a new tree rooted at a and with b attached as a child

A typical invocation has a distinctly LISP-like feel.

The following code creates three filled shapes. The default context has a `cornflowerblue` fill color (the default is `black`), and the subcontexts define bounding boxes and call the `circle()`, `rectangle()`, and `polygon()` functions within those boxes.

Possible values for the fill color are given in the `Color.jl` module. Note that the default is a filled shape, but specifying `fill(nothing)` will produce a non-filled shape:

```
shapes = compose(context(), fill("cornflowerblue"),
        (context( 0.1, 0.1, 0.15, 0.1 ),  circle()),
        (context( 0.35, 0.06, 0.2, 0.18 ),
        rectangle(), fill("red")),
        (context( 0.6, 0.05, 0.2, 0.2), fill("magenta3"),
        polygon([(1, 1), (0.3, 1), (0.5, 0)]) ));
img = SVG("shapes.svg", 10cm, 8.66cm)
draw(img,shapes)
```

For a full discussion of drawing with Compose, the reader is directed to the package's website at `http://composejl.org/`.

The site provides an example of building a complex drawing based on the **Sierpinski** gasket, which is a fractal and attractive fixed set with the overall shape of an equilateral triangle subdivided recursively into smaller equilateral triangles.

```
using Compose
function sierpinski(n)
  if n == 0
    compose(context(), polygon([(1,1), (0,1), (1/2, 0)]));
  else
    t = sierpinski(n - 1);
    compose( context(), (context( 1/4, 0, 1/2, 1/2), t),
                        (context( 0, 1/2, 1/2, 1/2), t),
                        (context( 1/2, 1/2, 1/2, 1/2), t));
  end
end
```

The triangle is composed using the `polygon()` function and built up recursively.

The following figure shows the result of three separate invocations for `n = 1,3,5`:

```
cx1 = compose(sierpinski(1), linewidth(0.2mm),
    fill(nothing), stroke("black"));
img = SVG("sierp1.svg", 10cm, 8.66cm); draw(img,cx1)

cx3 = compose(sierpinski(3), linewidth(0.2mm),
    fill(nothing), stroke("black"));
img = SVG("sierp3.svg", 10cm, 8.66cm); draw(img,cx3)

cx5 = compose(sierpinski(5), linewidth(0.2mm),
    fill(nothing), stroke("black"));
img = SVG("sierp5.svg", 10cm, 8.66cm); draw(img,cx5)
```

Graphic engines

Native graphics are constructed by developing the plots in Julia and using wrapper calls to libraries such as `cairo`, `pango`, and `tk`.

In this section, we will consider creating graphics by means of an external tasks (programs) rather than shared libraries. Clearly, this means that the program must be installed on the specific computer and not all operating systems are equivalent with respect to the various packages on offer.

PyPlot

`PyPlot` is a part of the work of Steven Johnson of MIT, which arose from the previous development of the `PyCall` module. Together with `Winston` and `Gadfly`, it is the third part in the Julia graphics triumvirate.

It provides an interface to the matplotlib plotting library from Python and in particular to `matplotlib.pyplot`. The API of matplotlib can be used as the basis for a comprehensive reference source to the various function calls: `matplotlib.org/api`.

Therefore in order to use `PyPlot`, the installation of Python and matplotlib is necessary. If this is successful, it will work either by creating an independent window (via Python) or embedding in a Jupyter workbook.

 I found that the easiest way to install both Python and matplotlib is using the Anaconda distribution from `Continuum.io`. This works on all three common platforms Windows, OS X, and Linux.

After the installation, it is important to update the distribution with the `conda` command. This command is also used for installing any additional Python modules that are not present in the standard distro. If Python is already present on the system, it is important that the execution search path is set up so that the Anaconda version is found first.

`PyPlot` makes direct calls to the API by passing data arrays to Python with very little overhead, so the production of the graphics is extremely swift.

As an example, I have picked one from the early PyPlot documentation that of a sinusoidally modulated sinusoid. The flowing code creates the code, displays it (via a native Python window), and also writes the disk as an SVG file:

```
using PyPlot
x = linspace(0,2pi,1000)
y = sin(3*x + 4*cos(2*x));
plot(x, y, color="red", linewidth=2.0, linestyle="--");
title("A sinusoidally modulated sinusoid");
savefig("sinusoid.svg");
```

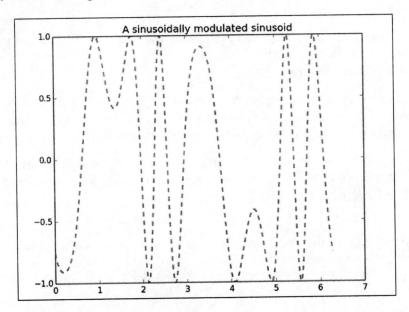

The PyPlot package also imports functions from Matplotlib's mplot3d toolkit.

Unlike matplotlib, however, you can create 3D plots directly without first creating an Axes3d object, simply by calling bar3D, contour3D, contourf3D, plot3D, plot_surface, plot_trisurf, plot_wireframe, or scatter3D.

`PyPlot` also exports the MATLAB-like synonyms such as `surf` for `plot_surface` and `mesh` for `plot_wireframe`. The following is a simple 3D surface; this time displayed in an IJulia notebook:

```
y = linspace(0,3π,250)
surf(y, y, y .* sin(y) .* cos(y)' .* exp(-0.4y))
```

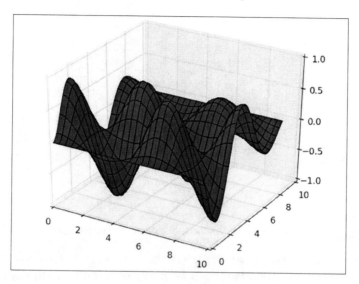

As a final example, let's create a more substantial display with axes, titles, and annotations using the XKCD comic mode.

The module includes an `xkcd()` call to switch to this mode:

```
xkcd()
fig = figure(figsize=(10,5))
ax = axes()
p = plot(x,sin(3x + cos(5x)))
ax[:set_xlim]([0.0,6])
annotate("A little\nsketchy",xy=[0.98,.001],
arrowprops=["arrowstyle"=>"->"],xytext=[1.3,-0.3])
xticks([])
yticks([])
xlabel("TIME")
ylabel("PRODUCTIVITY")
```

```
title("An xkcd-style plot in Julia")
ax[:spines]["top"][:set_color]("none")
ax[:spines]["right"][:set_color]("none")
```

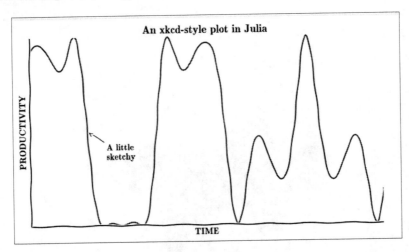

Note that plots in IJulia are sent to the notebook by default as PNG images.

Optionally, you can tell PyPlot to display plots in the browser as SVG images by calling PyPlot.svg(true) that has the advantage of being resolution independent.

Regardless of whether PyPlot uses SVG for browser display, you can export a plot to SVG at any time using the matplotlib savefig() routine.

Gaston

Gaston was written by Miguel Bazdresch and is one of the earliest packages providing graphics in Julia. Although virtually untouched recently, it remains a flexible plotting package.

Gaston uses the gnuplot GNU utility program that is easily installed on Linux and also on OS X via XQuartz. On Windows there is a *sourceforge* project, but using it with Gaston is a little clunky.

With the rise of graphics via PyPlot, it has fallen somewhat out of favor but nevertheless is interesting when working on Linux and also architecturally. The package employs a messaging system to send commands from Julia to gnuplot, so all features of the latter are potentially available.

To use the system, it is necessary to set the terminal type with the `set_terminal()` routine. The default is **wxt** and is not universally available. On OS X, an alternative was **aqua** but this has been omitted since version 10.7; although it can still be added separately.

An alternative is **X11** that is a little less sophisticated than either wxt or aqua.

The terminal type can also be set to various backend file types such as SVG, PDF, and PNG. The main work is done via three levels of components such as `gaston_hilvl` (high), `gaston_midlvl` (middle) and `gaston_lowlvl` (low) plus some auxiliary functions:

- **High**: This contains the sources for the callable routines such as plot, histogram, surf, and so on
- **Middle**: This contains an additional set of calls including the `llplot()` routine that is the workhorse of the system
- **Low**: This comprises just a single `gnuplot_send` call that writes the actual messages through a TCP socket (pipe) to do the actual work
- **Aux**: This is a set of additional routines to start up `gnuplot`, open a TCP pipe, validate and set the terminal type, and so on

Not all routines are exported, so it is useful to set a variable to `Gaston` (viz Python-style) and call the routines with reference to it. The package contains a useful `gaston_demo()` set of 20 different plots, two of which are reproduced as follows:

```
using Gaston
g = Gaston;
set_terminal("x11");
c = g.CurveConf();
c.legend = "Random";
c.plotstyle = "errorbars";
y = exp(-(1:.1:4.9));
ylow = y - 0.05*rand(40);
yhigh = y + 0.05*rand(40);
g.addcoords(1:40,y,c);
g.adderror(0.1*rand(40));
a = g.AxesConf();
a.title = "Error bars (ydelta)";
g.addconf(a);
g.llplot();
```

This code adds some random error bars to an exponentially decreasing function and displays the resultant graph.

The type curve is configured by a call to the `CurveConf()` routine that sets a legend and the style of plot. Axes are set up using `AxesConf()` and a title is defined. Finally, `llplot()` is called to create the display:

 Note, as mentioned before, the use of the `g = Gaston` assignment and reference to routines via `g`, as not all functions are exported by the `Gaston` package.

```
using Gaston
g = Gaston;
set_terminal("x11");
c = g.CurveConf();
c.plotstyle = "pm3d";
x = -15:0.33:15;
y = -15:0.33:15;
Z = g.meshgrid(x, y, (x,y) ->
                        sin(sqrt(x .* x+y .* y)) / sqrt(x .* x+y
.* y));
g.addcoords(x,y,Z,c);
a = g.AxesConf();
a.title = "3D: Sombrero";
g.addconf(a);
g.llplot()
```

This second example illustrates the ability of `Gaston` to produce 3D plots. This is the Sombrero plot that is created as a $sin(\phi)/\phi$ style curve, defined as an anonymous function and used in the `meshgrid()` routine.

The two resulting plots are shown in the following figure:

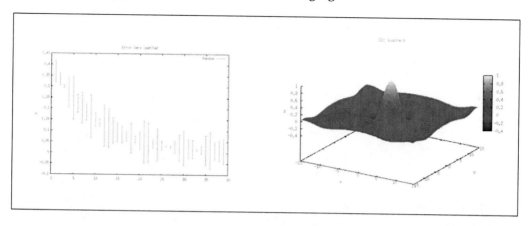

PGF plots

In contrast to `Gaston`, this is a relatively new package that uses the `pgfplots` LaTeX routines to produce plots. It integrates well with IJulia to output SVG images to the notebook.

The user supplies axis labels, legend entries, and the plot coordinates for one or more plots. `PGFPlots` applies axis scaling, computes any logarithms, and axis ticks, and draws the plots.

The TEX library supports line, scatter, bar, area, histogram, mesh, and surface plots, but at the time of writing not all of these have been implemented in the Julia package.

As with all graphic engine type packages, certain additional executables need to be present in order for `PGFPlots` to work.

These are:

- `Pdf2svg`: This is required by `TikzPictures`
- `Pgfplots`: This is installed using a LaTeX package manager such as `texlive` or `MiKTeX`
- `GNUPlot`: This is required in order to plot contours

The package operates by generating messages (as similar to `Gaston`) that are LaTeX strings, which need to be passed to the `TitzPictures` package to produce the SVG output.

Additionally, in order to use `TitzPictures`, `lualatex` must be installed. Note that both, the `texlive` and `MiKTeX` distributions, include `lualatex`.

This following example generates multiple curves on the same axis and assigns their legend entries (in LaTeX format):

```
using PGFPlots;
p = Axis( [ Plots.Linear(x->sin(3x)*exp(-0.3x), (0,8),
    legendentry = L"$\sin(3x)*exp(-0.3x)$"),
        Plots.Linear(x->sqrt(x)/(1+x^2), (0,8),
        legendentry = L"$\sqrt{2x}/(1+x^2)$") ]);
save("linear-plots.svg", p);
```

`Plots.Linear` is just one type of plotting style available in the `Plots` module.

It is very easy to make histograms with another type of style, the `Plots.Histogram` style:

```
fq  =  randn(10000);
p = Axis(Plots.Histogram(fp, bins=100), ymin=0)
save("histogram-plot.svg", p);
```

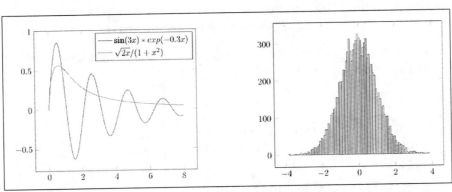

The `Plots` library also contains the Image and Contour styles, examples demonstrating their use can be found on the website: `http://pgfplots.sourceforge.net`

Furthermore, the reader is directed to the documentation on `tikz` and `pgfplots` that can provide more information about all the styles that are supported, the associated arguments, and possible values.

Using the Web

All operating systems are able to display web pages and modern standards of HTML5 and CSS3 including drawing capabilities. The addition of JavaScript client-side libraries, such as jQuery and D3, provides straightforward means to add interactive and drag and drop functionality.

These are available to some extent in the `Gadfly` package. This was classified as a native package even though it required additional of libraries such as `cairo`, `pango`, and `tk` because these were accessed by means of wrapper functions using `ccall()`.

In this section, we will explore a couple of approaches that use HTML graphics directly. The first runs on the workstation and the other is a different approach using an online system.

Bokeh

`Bokeh` is a Python interactive visualization library that utilizes web browsers for presentation.

The Julia package is written in native code. It is independent of the original Python module but works in the same fashion. The basic operation consists of creating HTML code and writing it to disk. This is then passed to the (default) browser.

The current implementation is relatively sparse when compared to the Python implementation, but is still very capable of producing basic line graphs.

All parameter values are defaulted using global parameter, but the packet includes a set of routines to change these.

The HTML output is sent to a `bokeh_plot.html` file (temporary) that will be overwritten using the `plotfile()` function.

`Bokeh` will also work well with IJulia notebooks. In this case, it is necessary to call the `setupnotebook()` function that writes a CSS style sheet and set of JavaScript routines to the file.

The following code creates a plot of the two test functions that we defined when considering the `PGFPlots` package and this is run under IJulia:

```
using Bokeh

setupnotebook()


x = linspace(0,3pi)
f1(x) = sin(3x).*exp(-0.3x)
```

```
f2(x) = sqrt(x)./(1 + x.^2)
y = [f1(x) f2(x)]
title("Two test functions")
plot(x, y, "r;|b--")
```

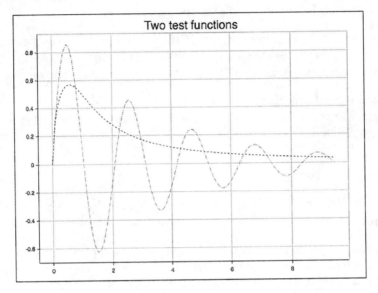

The default title is changed using the `title()` function and displayed by a call to `plot()`.

In order to create a multicurve display, we pass an array of function definitions. Also, with `plot()` the array of **abscissa** (x) values is optional. We wish to specify a range of values, but when not provided this defaults to `1:500`; the upper limit for this range can be changed using a `counteval()` routine.

The type of line drawn utilizes the set of glyphs we met in `Winston`. In order to specify multiple glyphs as a single string, use the | character as a separator.

Plotly

`Plotly` is a data analysis and graphing web application that is able to create precise and beautiful charts. It is based on D3 and as such incorporates a high degree of interaction such as hover text, panning, and zoom controls, as well as real-time data streaming options.

Originally, access to `Plotly` was via a REST API to the website `http://plot.ly` but a variety of programming languages now can access the API including Julia.

The `Plotly.jl` package is not listed (as yet) in the standard packages repository, so needs to be added using a `Pkg.clone()` statement:

```
Pkg.clone(https://github.com/plotly/Plotly-Julia)
```

To use `Plotly`, you will need to sign up for an account via `http://plot.ly` providing a unique username and e-mail address. On registration, an API key will be generated and emailed to you together with a confirmation link.

All plots are stored under this account and can be viewed and managed online as well as embedded in web pages.

So all coding require a call to the `signin()` routine:

```
using Plotly
Plotly.signin("myuserid", "abc32def7g")
```

On successful execution, the routine returns a `PlotlyAccount` data object and an online graph is created under that account by formulating and executing a response function. The response function posts the data to `Plot.ly` that creates the plot and generates a URL for it as a reply.

The following is a script to display some log-log plots. The data is passed as an array of arrays (allowing for multiple curves) and a layout array is constructed to set the axis to logarithmic.

Additionally, we need to pass a name under which the plot is to be stored and indicate that, if the script is rerun the plot can be overwritten:

```
trace1 = [
  "x" => [0, 1, 2, 3, 4, 5, 6, 7, 8],
  "y" => [8, 7, 6, 5, 4, 3, 2, 1, 0],
  "type" => "scatter"
];
trace2 = [
  "x" => [0, 1, 2, 3, 4, 5, 6, 7, 8],
  "y" => [0, 1, 2, 3, 4, 5, 6, 7, 8],
  "type" => "scatter"
];
data = [trace1, trace2];
layout = [
  "xaxis" => ["type" => "log", "autorange" => true],
```

```
    "yaxis" => ["type" => "log", "autorange" => true]
];
response = Plotly.plot(data,
    ["layout" => layout,
    "filename" => "plotly-log-axes",
    "fileopt" => "overwrite"]);
plot_url = response["url"]
```

A value for `plot_url`, such as `http://plot.ly/~myuserid/17`, indicates that it is stored with ID 17 under the `myuser` ID account.

Logging on the `Plot.ly` site, you will see the plot stored as `plotly-log-axes`.

The site contains a wide variety of code examples that can be downloaded as templates for your graphics; moreover, they are tailored with your specific username and password.

As a second example, here is a contour plot of some sinusoids with a randomly generated component:

```
N = 100;
x = linspace(-2*pi, 2*pi, N);
y = linspace(-2*pi, 2*pi, N);
z = rand(N, N);
for i = 1:N, j = 1:N
    r2 = (x[i]^2 + y[j]^2);
    z[i,j] = sin(x[i]) * cos(y[j]) * sin(r2)/log(r2+1);
end
data = [ [ "z" => z,"x" => x,"y" => y,"type" => "contour"] ];
response = Plotly.plot(data,
    ["filename" => "simple-contour",
    "fileopt" => "overwrite"]);
plot_url = response["url"];
Plotly.openurl(plot_url)   # Display the plot via its URL
```

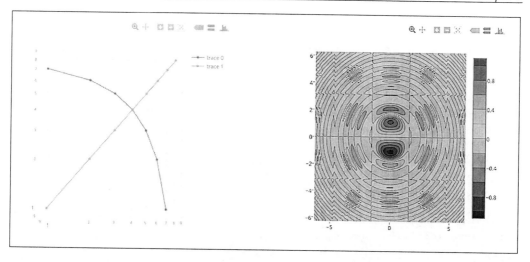

Once generated, it is possible online to switch from `public` to `edit` mode.

In edit mode, you can add/modify a main and the axis titles, show a legend, and apply one of the `Plotly` themes.

There is also the ability to export the plots in PNG, PDF, SVG, and EPS formats.

Raster graphics

Most of the types of displays we have been considering so far are termed vector graphics. These are defined in terms of points, curves, and shapes such as circles, rectangles, and polygons.

Working with images and colormaps is often referred to as raster graphics.

Since low-level packages eventually translate vector plots to rasters, these packages are capable of working with images directly.

So far in this book we have been working with simple netbpm format images, but in practice we will wish to operate with the more common formats such as PNG, GIF, and JPEGs.

So in this final section, we'll turn our attention to a brief overview of some of the ways you can manipulate images in Julia.

Cairo (revisited)

The `Cairo` package is a low-level package that we met earlier in the *Basic graphics in Julia* section and used it to create a curve between four points.

In the following example, we will create the graphics context from an `RGBSurface` method as before and fill the background with a light grey, but now we will load an image and clip it:

```
using Cairo
c = CairoRGBSurface(256,256);        # Canvas is 256x256
cr = CairoContext(c);
save(cr);
set_source_rgb(cr,0.8,0.8,0.8);      # light gray
rectangle(cr,0.0,0.0,256.0,256.0); # background
fill(cr);
restore(cr);
save(cr);
```

Next we create an arc of half the canvas dimensions and with length 2π, so in fact this is a complete circle. Calling `clip()` creates a window on the canvas:

```
arc (cr, 128.0, 128.0, 76.8, 0, 2*pi);
clip (cr);
new_path (cr);
```

All that now remains is to read the image from disk, and if necessary scale it to the 256x256 window size:

```
image = read_from_png ("towerbridge.png");
w = image.width;
h = image.height;
scale(cr, 256.0/w, 256.0/h);
set_source_surface (cr, image, 0, 0);
paint (cr);
write_to_png(c,"towerbridge-cropped.png");
```

The original and the resulting cropped images are shown as follows:

Winston (revisited)

Winston uses Cairo to create its displays and at present has some limited raster support via a couple of functions: colormap() to load RGB colormaps and imagesc() to display am image from a matrix of pixel values.

Winston defines one rainbow-style Jet colormap, but it is also capable of loading any maps defined in the Color package or indeed any maps created by the user:

```
using Winston, Color
x = linspace(0.,4π,1000);
y = linspace(0.,4π,1000);
z1 = 100*(x.^0.5).*exp(-0.1y)';
colormap("jet", 10);
imagesc(z1);
z2 = sin(x).*cos(y)'
colormap("rdbu");
imagesc(z2);
```

Here are a couple of images created on [0: 4π, 0: 4π] using both the Jet and **RdBu (from Red to Blue)** colormaps:

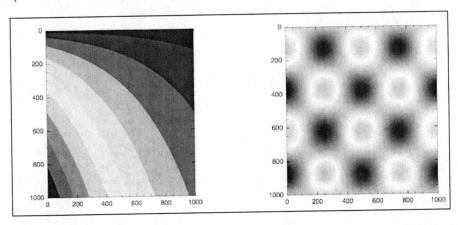

Images and ImageView

The set of packages from Tim Holy provides the most comprehensive support for manipulating images in Julia.

The main package, the `Images.jl` package, uses the utility programs that form part of the ImageMagick suite. As such, Images falls in the same class of packages as `PyPlot` and `Gaston`, since it requires the presence of some specific third-party support.

The ImageMagick program needs to be on the executable path and installation of the `Images` package will attempt to install them whenever this is necessary.

There is a second package, the `ImageView.jl package`, that can be used to display an imagery to screen. When using IJulia, this is not needed as the workbook provides all that is required to display the imagery.

There is an additional package, the `TestImages.jl` package, that functions a little as `RDatasets` does in the statistics world. This is a set of common images that can be used in developing and testing Julia routines. The images are somewhat large and are not stored on GitHub, rather the installation and build process of `TestImages` will retrieve them and store them locally.

An image can be loaded with a statement of the form:

```
using TestImages;
img = testimage("earth_apollo17");
```

The image format is one of PNG, TIFF, or JPG and the extension can be supplied or omitted according to preference.

Images can also be loaded from local files or via the Internet using the `imread()` routine. Note that a few other packages define overlapping functions or types -- `PyPlot` defines `imread` and `Winston` defines `Image`.

When using both `Images` and these packages, you can always specify and fully qualify the call by using `Images.imread("earth_apollo17")`.

```
using Images, ImageView
img = imread("lena.png");
```

This code reads the grayscale image of Lena Söderberg, which we worked with earlier, from disk in PNG format. It could be loaded from the test images as `lena_grey_512`, this time as a TIFF.

Once loaded, the representation in Julia is completely equivalent for either a PNG or TIFF image

```
julia> names(img)
2-element Array{Symbol,1}:
 :data
 :properties
```

An image has two named symbols `:data` and `:properties`.

```
julia> img.properties
Dict{ASCIIString,Any} with 4 entries:
  "suppress"         => Set{Any}({"imagedescription"})
  "imagedescription" => ""
  "spatialorder"     => ASCIIString["x","y"]
  "pixelspacing"     => [1,1]
```

In this image, the `"spatialorder"` property has value `["x", "y"]`.

This indicates that the image data is in *horizontal-major* order, meaning that a pixel at the (x, y) spatial location would be addressed as `img[x,y]` rather than `img[y,x]`.

`["y", "x"]` would indicate *vertical-major*.

```
typeof(img.data); # => Array{Gray{UfixedBase{Uint8,8}},2}
size(img.data);   # => (512,512)
```

The `type` indicates it is a grayscale image. An alternative when working with color images is an array of the `RGB{UfixedBase{Uint8,8}}` data values.

The size array can be used to determine the dimensions of the image data:

```
w = size(img.data)[1]; w0 = w/2;
h = size(img.data)[2]; h0 = h/2;
```

The actual data can be extracted by either using `convert()` or referencing the `img.data` or `data(img)`:

```
imA = convert(Array, img);
julia> summary(imA)
"512x512 Array{Gray{UfixedBase{Uint8,8}},2}"
imB = reinterpret(Uint8, img.data);
```

This is the raw data as a byte array.

For RGB images, it will be a $512 \times 512 \times 3$ array.

Individual pixel values can be referenced by indexing and also by using slice ranges:

```
data(img)[w0,h0];
data(img)[w0-16:w0+15, h0-16:h0+15]
```

To illustrate some image processing techniques, let's define a 5x5 convolution kernel and redo the edge detect filtering on the `Lena` that we first demonstrated in the previous chapter:

```
kern = [ 0  0 -1  0  0
         0 -1 -4 -1  0
        -1 -4 24 -4 -1
-1 -4 -1  0
0 -1  0  0 ];
# => 5x5 Array{Int64,2}
imgf = imfilter(img, kern)
Gray Image with:
  data: 512x512 Array{Gray{Float64},2}
  properties:
    imagedescription: <suppressed>
    spatialorder:  x y
    pixelspacing:  1 1
```

The original image of Lena together with the result of applying the convolution kernel is shown as follows:

Summary

This chapter has presented the wide variety of graphics options available to the Julia programmer.

In addition to the more popular packages, such as `Winston`, `Gadfly`, and `PyPlot`, we identified others such as `Gaston`, `Bokeh`, and `PGFPlots`. Although, they may be less familiar, but they offer additional approaches in the production of graphical and pictorial displays.

Also, we looked at how the `Plotly` system can be utilized in Julia to generate, manipulate, and store data visualizations online.

Finally, we discussed the means by which raster graphics and imagery can be processed and displayed.

In the next chapter, we will return to the subject of accessing data by looking at the various ways with which we can interact with SQL and NoSQL databases in Julia.

8
Databases

In *Chapter5, Working with Data*, we looked at working with data that is stored in disk files, looked at plain text files, and also datasets that take the form of R datafiles and HDF5.

In this chapter, we will consider data residing in databases but will exclude the "big data" data repository as networking and remote working is the theme of the next chapter.

There are a number of databases of various hues, and as it will not be possible to deal with all that Julia currently embraces, we will to pick one specific example for each category as they arise.

It is not the intention of this chapter to delve into the working of the various databases or to set up any complex queries, nor to go in depth into any of the available packages in Julia. All we can achieve in this section is to look at the connection and interfacing techniques of a few common examples.

A basic view of databases

In this section, we are going to cover a little bit of groundwork to work with databases. It's a large topic, and many texts are devoted to specific databases and also to accessing databases in general.

It is assumed that the reader has knowledge of these, but here we will briefly introduce some of the concepts that are necessary for the topics in the remaining sections of this chapter.

Packages are being developed and modified at an ever increasing rate, so I urge the reader to review the availability for access to a specific flavor of database, which may not be available at the time of writing, with reference to the standard Julia package list at `http://pkg.julialang.org` and also by searching at `http://github.com`.

The red pill or the blue pill?

A few years ago discussing databases was simple. One talked of relational databases such as Oracle, MySQL, and SQL Server and that was pretty much it. There were some exceptions such as databases involved in **Lightweight Directory Access Protocol (LDAP)** and some configuration databases based on XML, but the whole world was relational. Even products that were not relational, such as Microsoft Access, tried to present a relational face to the user.

We usually use the term relational and SQL database interchangeably, although the latter more correctly refers to the method of querying the database than to its architecture.

What changed was the explosion of large databases from sources such as Google, Facebook, and Twitter, which could not be accommodated by scaling up the existing SQL databases of the time, and indeed such databases still cannot. Google produced a "white" paper proposing its **BigTable** solution to deal with large data flows, and the classification of NoSQL databases was born.

Basically, relational databases consist of a set of tables, normally linked with a main (termed primary) key and related to each other by a set of common fields via a schema. A schema is a kind of blueprint that defines what the tables consist of and how they are to be joined together. A common analogy is a set of sheets in an Excel file, readers familiar with Excel will recognize this parallel example.

NoSQL data stores are often deemed to be schemaless. This means it is possible to add different datasets with some fields not being present and other ones occurring. The latter is a particular difficulty with relational databases, as the schema has to be amended and the database rebuilt. Data stores conventionally comprising of text fall into this category, as different instances of text frequency throw up varying metadata and textual structures.

There are, of course, some databases that are termed NoSQL, but nevertheless have quite a rigorous schema and SQL-like (if not actual conventional SQL) query languages. These usually fall into the classification of columnar databases and I will discuss these briefly later in the chapter.

Possibly the biggest difference between SQL and NoSQL databases is the way they scale to support increasing demand. To support more concurrent usage, SQL databases scale vertically whereas NoSQL ones can be scaled horizontally, that is, distributed over several machines, which in the era of *Big Data* is responsible for their new-found popularity.

Interfacing to databases

Database access is usually via a separate task called a **database management system (DBMS)** that manages simultaneous requests to the underlying data. Querying data records presents no problems, but adding, modifying, and deleting records impose "locking" restrictions on the operations.

There is a class of simple databases that are termed "file-based" and aimed at a single user. A well-known example of this is SQLite and we will discuss the Julia support package for this in the next section.

With SQL databases one other function of the DBMS is to impose consistency and ensure that updates are transactional safe. This is known by the acronym **ACID (atomicity, consistency, isolation and durability)**. This means that the same query will produce the same results and that a transaction such as transferring money will not result in the funds disappearing and not reaching the intended recipient.

Although it may seem that all databases should operate in this manner, the results returned by querying search engines, for example, do not always need to produce the same result set. So we often hear that NoSQL data stores are governed by the **CAP** rule, that is **Consistency, Availability, and Partition Tolerance**. We are speaking of data stores spread over a number of physical servers, and the rule is that to achieve consistency we need to sacrifice 24/7 availability or partition tolerance; this is sometimes called the *two out of three* rule.

In considering how we might interface with a particular database system we can (roughly) identify four mechanisms:

1. A DBMS will be bundled as a set of query and maintenance utilities that communicate with the running database via a shared library. This is exposed to the user as a set of routines in an application program interface (API). The utilities will often be written in C and Java, but scripts can also be written in Python, Perl, and of course Julia. In fact Julia with its zero-overhead `ccall()` routine is ideal for this form of operation, and we will term the packages that use this as their principal mode of interface as wrapper packages. Often there is a virtual one-to-one correspondence between the Julia package routines and those in the underlying API. The main task of the package is to mimic the data structures that the API uses to accept requests and return results.

2. A second common method of accessing a database is via an intermediate abstract layer, which itself communicates with the database API via a driver that is specific for each individual database. If a driver is available, then the coding is the same regardless of the database that is being accessed. The first such system was **Open Database Connectivity** (**ODBC**) developed by Microsoft in the 1990s. This was an early package and remains one of the principal means of working with databases in Julia. There are couple of other intermediate layers: **Java Database Connectivity** (**JDBC**) and **Database Interface** (**DBI**). The former naturally arises from Java and necessitates a compatible JNDI driver, whereas the latter was introduced in Perl and uses DBD drivers that have to be written for each individual database and in each separate programming language. All three mechanisms are available in Julia, although ODBC is the most common.

3. When we considered graphics in the previous chapter, one mode of operation was to abrogate the responsibility of producing the plots to Python via `matplotlib` using the `JavaPlot` package. The same approach can be utilized for any case where there is a Python module for a specific database system, of which there are many. Routines in the Python module are called using the `PyCall` package, which will handle the interchange of datatypes between Julia and Python.

4. The mode access is by sending messages to the database, to be interpreted and acted on by the DBMS. This is typified by usage over the Internet using HTTP requests, typically `GET` or `POST`. The most common form of messaging protocols are called **Representational State Transfer** (**RESTful**), although in practice it is possible to use similar protocols, such as SOAP or XMLRPC. Certain database APIs may expose a shared library and also a REST-type API. The REST one is clearly an advantage when accessing remote servers, and the ubiquitous provision of HTTP support in all operating systems makes this attractive, especially in situations where firewall restrictions are in place.

Other considerations

In the remainder of this chapter, I'll endeavor to cover all the preceding means of access to database systems looking at, in most cases, a specific example using a Julia package.

There is one class of systems that is outside the scope of this chapter and this is where the dataset essentially comprises a set of separate text documents organized as a directory structure (folders and file), which can be implemented either as a physical (real) or logical directory structure. Such a system is less common, but EMC's Documentum system may be seen as an example of this type.

Also, we will not be dealing in detail with XML-based database systems, as we discussed the general principles when we looked at working with files in *Chapter 5, Working with Data*, and the reader is encouraged to re-read that chapter if dealing with XML data.

In terms of the mechanism for storing XML data, these are sometimes held individually as part of a directory structure as records in a document data store, such as MongoDB, or alternatively as **Character Large Objects** (**CLOBS**) in a relational database, such as Oracle.

What we need to be concerned with is the speed of retrieval for queries. Exhaustive searches on large datasets would lead to unacceptable performance penalties, so we look at the underlying database to provide the necessary metadata and indexing, regardless of the means by which the data is stored.

One example that links these together is BaseX, which is an open source, lightweight, high performance, and scalable XML Database engine and incorporates XPath/ XQuery processing. There is a REST API and several language implementations, although there is not yet one that is implemented in Julia. However, Python does have one such module: the `PyCall` module, mentioned previously and this can be employed here when working with BaseX.

Relational databases

As we have said, the primary difference between relational and non-relational databases is the way data is stored. Relational data is tabular by nature, and hence stored in tables with rows and columns. Tables can be related to one another and cooperate in data storage as well as swift retrieval.

Data storage in relational databases aims for higher normalization -- breaking up the data into smallest logical tables (related) to prevent duplication and gain tighter space utilization.

While normalization of data leads to cleaner data management, it often adds a little complexity, especially to data management where a single operation may have to span numerous related tables.

Since relational databases are on a single server and partition tolerance is not an option, in terms of the CAP classification they are consistent and accessible.

Building and loading

Before looking at some of the approaches to handling relational data in Julia, I'm going to create a simple script that generates a SQL load file.

The dataset comprises a set of "quotes", of which there are numerous examples online. We will find this data useful in the next chapter, so we will create a database here.

There are only three (text) fields separated by tabs and separate records per line, for example:

```
category <TAB> author <TAB>  quote
```

Some examples are:

```
Classics,  Aristophanes  You can't teach a crab to walk straight.
Words of Wisdom  Voltaire  Common sense is not so common.
```

For the script (etj.jl), the possible choices for the command line will be:

```
[julia]  etl.jl indata.tsv  [loader.sql]
```

The second choice is:

```
[julia]  etl.jl [ -o loader.sql] [-d '\t'] indata.dat
```

The [] designates an optional argument, and I've made the Julia command optional as (under OS X and Linux) the script can be marked as executable using the **shebang** convention (see following section).

The second format is more flexible as it is possible to specify the field separator rather than assuming it is a tab.

We wish to create a table for the quotes and another for the categories. This is not totally normalized as there may be duplication in authors but this denormalization saves a table join.

The downside is that we can extract quotes by category more easily than by author, which will require definition of a foreign index (with corresponding DB maintenance penalty) or an exhaustive search.

The following SQL file (build.sql) will create the two tables we require:

```
create table categories (
    id integer not null,
    catname varchar(40) not null,
    primary key(id)
);
```

```
create table quotes (
   id        integer not null,
   cid       integer not null,
   author    varchar(100),
   quoname   varchar(250) not null,
   primary key(id)
  );
```

The simpler case of our command line script can be implemented as:

```
#! /usr/local/bin/julia
# Check on the number of arguments, print usage unless 1 or 2.
nargs = length(ARGS);
if nargs == 0 || nargs > 2
  println("usage: etl.jl infile [outfile]");
  exit();
end
# Assign first argument to input file
# If second argument this is the output file otherwise STDOUT
infile = ARGS[1];
if nargs == 2
  outfile = ARGS[2];
  try
    outf = open(outfile,"w");
  catch
    error("Can't create output file: ", outfile);
  end
else
  outf = STDOUT;
end
```

In the case of the more complex command line, Julia has a ArgParse package. This has similarities with the Python argparse module, but some important differences too.

In building the load file, we need to handle single quotes (') that are used for text delimiters. The usual convention is to double them up (''), but some loaders also accept escaped backslashing (\').

For a short data file, we can use `readdlm()` to read all the data with a single call. If the file is very large, it may be more appropriate to read records and process the data on a line-by-line basis.

```
# One liner to double up single quotes
escticks(s) = replace(s,"'","''");
# Read all file into a matrix, first dimension is number of lines
qq = readdlm(infile, '\t');
n = size(qq)[1];
```

Because we are going to create a separate table for categories, we will keep track of these in a hash (dictionary) using sequentially generated IDs and output the hash as a table later.

```
# Going to store all categories in a dictionary
j = 0;
cats = Dict{String,Int64}();


# Main loop to load up the quotes table
for i = 1:n
  cat = qq[i,1];
  if haskey(cats,cat)
    jd = cats[cat];
  else
    j = j + 1; jd = j;
    cats[cat] = jd;
  end
  sql = "insert into quotes values($i,$jd,";
  if (length(qq[i,2]) > 0)
    sql *= string("'", escticks(qq[i,2]), "',");
  else
    sql *= string("null,");
  end
  sql *= string("'", escticks(qq[i,3]), "');");
  write(outf,"$sql\n");
end
```

After creating the quotes table, we create the second one for the categories:

```
# Now dump the categories
for cat = keys(cats)
  jd = cats[cat];
  write(outf,"insert into categories values($jd,'$cat');\n");
end
close(outf);  # Will have no effect if outf = STDOUT
```

This produces an intermediate SQL load file that can be used with the most standard loaders that can output to STDOUT and piped into the loader. Indeed if the input file argument was also optional, it could be part of a Unix command chain.

The merits of using this approach is that it can be used to load any relational database with a SQL interface, and also it is easy to debug if the syntax is incorrect or we have failed to accommodate some particular aspect of the data (UTF-8, dealing with special characters, and so on.)

On the downside, we have to drop out of Julia to complete the load process. However, we can deal with this by either spawning the (specific) database load command line as a task or inserting the entries in the database on a line-by-line basis via the particular Julia DB package we are using.

Native interfaces

By a native interface, I am referring to the paradigm under which a package makes calls to an underlying shared library API.

As an example, we are going to look at the case of SQLite, which is a simple DBMS-less style system. It will be built from source and a wide variety of precompiled binaries, all of which are obtainable from the main website at www.sqlite.org, along with installation instructions, which in some cases, is little more than unzipping the download file.

As a dataset, we are going to work with the "queries" tables for which we created a build and load file in the previous section.

To start SQLite, assuming it is on the execution path, we type: sqlite3 [dbfile].

If the database file (dbfile) does not exist, it will be created, otherwise SQLite will open the file. If no filename is given, SQLite will work with an in-memory database that can be later saved to disk.

SQLite has a number of options that can be listed by typing sqlite3 -help. The SQLite interpreter accepts direct SQL commands terminated by a ;.

In addition to this, instructions to SQLite can be applied using a special set of commands prefixed by a dot (`.`), all these can all be listed with the `.help` command.

Usually these commands can be abbreviated to the short forms so long as it is unique. For example `.read` can be shortened to `.re`. Note that command is case sensitive and must be written in lowercase.

So we can use the following sequence of instructions to create a database from our quotes `build`/`load` scripts:

```
/home/malcolm> sqlite3
sqlite> .read  build.sql
sqlite> .read  load.sql
sqlite> .save  quotes.db
sqlite> .ex
```

On OS X or Linux, we can also pipe the build scripts and use the loader script as:

```
cat build.sql  |  sqlite3 quotes.db

julia etl.jl indata.tsv  |  sqlite3 quotes.db
```

Now let's turn our attention to the `SQLite.jl` Julia package and run some queries. If we wish to list the quotes and their particular category, we need to join the two tables together based on the category ID.

We can connect to our quotes database by calling the `SQLiteDB()` routine that returns a database handle. The following query returns the number of quotes in the database:

```
using SQLite
db = SQLiteDB("quotes.db")
res = query(db,"select count(*) from quotes");
size(res)
res[1][1]; # => 36
```

This is returned as a `ResultSet` type, which can be thought of as an {Any} matrix with each row corresponding to a result and each column to the queried fields.

In the case of a simple count, there is just one row with a single column.

If we return a count of all the query table entries:

```
res = query(db,"select * from quotes");
size(res); # => (36,4)

res[21,4]; # =>   35
```

This query will return all the quotes from the database:

```
sql =  "select q.quoname, q.author, c.catname from quotes q ";
sql *= "join categories c on q.cid = c.id limit 5";
res = query(db,sql);
```

This query finds all the quotes of `Oscar Wilde`:

```
sql =  "select q.quoname from quotes q ";
sql *= " where q.author = 'Oscar Wilde'";
res = query(db,sql);


nq = size(res)[1];  # Number of records returned
for i = 1:nq
  println(res[i,1]);
end;
```

```
I am not at all cynical, I have merely got experience, which is very much
the same thing.
To love oneself is the beginning of a lifelong romance.
We are all in the gutter, but some of us are looking at the stars.
London society is full of women of the very highest birth who have, of
their own free choice, remained thirty-five for years.
```

There are a number of other functions in the package. One of the most important is the `execute()` statement that is used to run non-query (DML/DDL) statements.

It is possible to create a SQLite statement, which is a combination of the connection handle and the SQL string, as `stmt = SQLiteStmt(db, sql)`. So executing a statement can take the form:

```
execute(stmt)    or    execute(db, sql)
```

Statements are useful when using placeholders and passing parameterized values.

Passing values can be achieved either by using the `bind()` function of an optional argument of array values.

Database tables can be set up using a single statement using an array of data values, passing the column names and column types:

```
create( db::SQLiteDB,name::String,table::AbstractMatrix,
   colnames=String[],coltypes=DataType[]; temp::Bool=false)
```

The final optional argument is a flag to indicate that the table is temporary and will be deleted when closed.

The package also provides an `append()` function to add data to an existing table:

```
append(db::SQLiteDB,name::String,table::AbstractMatrix)
```

This takes the values in the table and appends (by repeated inserts) to the SQLite table name. No column checking is done to ensure correct types, so care should be taken as SQLite is "typeless" since it allows items of any type to be stored in columns.

SQLite provides syntax for calling the REGEXP function from inside the WHERE clauses.

Unfortunately, however, SQLite does not provide a default implementation of the REGEXP function, so `SQLite.jl` creates one automatically when you open a database.

For example, selecting the quotes from Oscar Wilde we could use:

```
query(db, "SELECT quoname FROM quotes
                WHERE author REGEXP 'e(?=Oscar)'")
```

ODBC

The stock way of handling SQL databases in Julia is based on the use of the ODBC layer. As mentioned earlier, this approach has been in operation for many years and imposes certain performance penalties but on the plus side there is a vast wealth of ODBC drivers available.

To use ODBC requires the installation of a specific driver and setting up of a connection string by use of an administration interface. For Windows, this comes as standard and is found by use of the control panel: system and security -- administration tools group.

With Unix and OS X, there are two administration managers available: unixODBC and iODBC. The former is more standard in approach that sets up the drivers by means of editing configuration files, while the latter is more GUI-based. I tend to use iODBC when working on OS X and unixODBC on Linux, but both work and it is largely a matter of choice.

unixODBC does have a separate GUI wrapper based on Qt, but I have found it as easy to use the command utility.

To look at some more sophisticated queries than in the previous section, I am going to introduce the Chinook database (`https://chinookdatabase.codeplex.com`). This is an open source equivalent to the Northwinds dataset that accompanies Microsoft Office.

Chinook comes with load files for SQLite, MySQL, Postgres, Oracle, and many others.

The data model represents a digital media store, including tables for artists, albums, media tracks, invoices, and customers.

The media-related data was created using real data from an iTunes library, although naturally customer and employee information was manually created using fictitious names, addresses, emails, and so on. Information regarding sales was auto-generated randomly.

The schema is shown in the following figure:

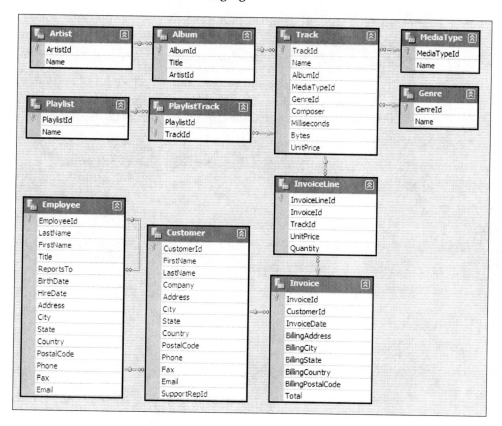

In the Chinook schema, there are two *almost* separate subsystems:

- **Artist / Album / Track / Playlist,** and so on
- **Employee / Customer / Invoice**

These are linked together via the **InvoiceLine (TrackId)** table to the **Track** table.

Notice that the schema is not totally normalized as the **InvoiceLine** table can also be joined to **PlaylistTrack** bypassing the **Track** table.

I am going to look at using Chinook with the popular database MySQL; an ODBC driver can be obtained from the development site at `http://dev.mysql.com`.

It is worth noting that since the purchase of MySQL by Oracle, the original team now produces an alternate database MariaDB (v5) that is a direct drop in for MySQL. The MariaDB driver can also be obtained from `https://downloads.mariadb.org/driver-odbc/`.

Maria v10 is an additional product that promises other features such as columnar access and is well worth a look-see.

The following queries have been run under Ubuntu 12.10, using unixODBC and the MySQL 5.6 driver. For installation and setup of the connection string, the reader is referred to the web page at `http://www.unixodbc.org/odbcinst.html`.

Both unixODBC and iODBC require two configuration files, odbcinst.ini and odbc.ini, the first specifies the drivers and the other the data sources. These can be placed in the /etc directory, which requires admin privileges, or as hidden files (.odbcinst.ini and .odbc.ini).

So to interface with the Chinook database using a MySQL ODBC driver my configuration files look like the following:

```
cat /etc/odbcinst.ini
[MySQL]
Description=MySQL ODBC Driver
Driver=/usr/lib/odbc/libmyodbc5a.so
Setup=/usr/lib/odbc/libmyodbc5S.so


cat odbc.ini
[Chinook]
Description=Chinook Database
Driver=MySQL
```

```
Server=127.0.0.1

Database=Chinook

Port=3306

Socket=/var/run/mysqld/mysqld.sock
```

There is also a Qt-based utility to manage the configuration files, if they are system wide, that is, in /etc, this needs to be run in Linux as `root`:

```
sudo ODBCManageDataSourcesQ4
```

Getting the configuration files for the drivers and data sources correct can be a little tricky at first, so it is possible to use the `odbcinst` utility to check them and also to connect with `isql`, and run some queries:

```
odbcinst -q -d; # =>   [MYSQL]
odbcinst -q -s; # =>   [Chinook]


isql -v Chinook malcolm mypasswd
```

Assuming you can connect with `isql`, then using it in Julia is straightforward:

```
conn = ODBC.connect("Chinook",usr="malcolm",pwd="mypasswd")
res = ODBC.query("select count(*) from Customers", conn)
println("Number of customers: $(res[:K][1])")
Number of customers:   59
```

Note that at present the connection handle, if present, comes after the query, although the documentation suggests the reverse. If in doubt, use `methods(query)` to check.

To demonstrate some more complex queries, let's join the `Customers` and `Invoice` tables by the customer ID, and by running a `group by` query select the customers who are the highest spenders, that is, spending more the $45:

```
sql = "select a.LastName, a.FirstName,";
sql *= " count(b.InvoiceId) as Invs, sum(b.Total) as Amt";
sql *= " from Customer a";
sql *= " join Invoice b on a.CustomerId = b.CustomerId";
sql *= " group by a.LastName having Amt >= 45.00";
sql *= " order by Amt desc;";


res = ODBC.query(sql);
```

```
for i in 1:size(res)[1]
   LastName  = res[:LastName][i]
   FirstName = res[:FirstName][i]
   Invs      = res[:Invs][i]
   Amt       = res[:Amt][i]
   @printf "%10s %10s %4d %10.2f\n" LastName FirstName Invs Amt
end
```

```
Holy        Helena      7     49.62
Cunningham  Richard     7     47.62
Rojas       Luis        7     46.62
O'Reilly    Hugh        7     45.62
Kovacs      Ladislav    7     45.62
```

Next, we will select the tracks purchased by `Richard Cunningham`.

This comprises a set of joins on tables as follows:

```
sql = "select a.LastName, a.FirstName, d.Name as TrackName";
sql *= " from Customer a";
sql *= " join Invoice b on a.CustomerId = b.CustomerId";
sql *= " join InvoiceLine c on b.InvoiceId = c.InvoiceId";
sql *= " join Track d on c.TrackId = d.TrackId";
sql *= " where a.LastName = 'Cunningham' limit 5;";


res = ODBC.query(sql);


for i in 1:size(res)[1]
   LastName  = res[:LastName][i]
   FirstName = res[:FirstName][i]
   TrackName = res[:TrackName][i]
   @printf "%15s %15s %15s\n" LastName FirstName TrackName
end
```

```
Cunningham      Richard       Radio Free Europe
Cunningham      Richard       Perfect Circle
Cunningham      Richard       Drowning Man
Cunningham      Richard       Two Hearts Beat as One
Cunningham      Richard       Surrender
```

Other interfacing techniques

ODBC remains largely universal today, with drivers available for most platforms and databases. It is not uncommon to find ODBC drivers for database engines that are meant to be embedded, such as SQLite, and also for non-databases such as CSV files and Excel spreadsheets; also, recently there are ODBC drivers for NoSQL data stores such as MongoDB.

There are a number of alternate approaches in Julia to use ODBC that I will explore now.

DBI

The DBI method of working with databases is very close to my heart as a self-confessed Perl monger, since the mid-1990s. DBI/DBD was introduced by Tim Bunce with Perl 5 to replace a mishmash of techniques that existed at the time.

The Julia DBI.jl package (see https://github.com/JuliaDB/DBI.jl) offers the same promise, that of an abstract layer of calls to which specific DBD (drivers) need to conform.

At the time of writing this, there are only three examples of Julia DBD drivers.

SQLite

The DBD driver for SQLite is available in the DBDSQLite.jl package. (see https://github.com/JuliaDB/DBDSQLite.jl).

It is used by importing SQLite and it is worth noticing the SQLite.jl native module, earlier with the SQLiteDB namespace, in order to distinguish with this driver. Since I have looked at accessing the sqlite files using the native package previously, the reader is referred to the online documentation for the alternative use of the DBD driver.

MySQL

A DBD driver for MySQL was provided at the same time as the DBI package (see https://github.com/johnmyleswhite/MySQL.jl). It has (currently) a couple of severe restrictions that makes it impractical at present:

- It looks for shared libraries of the dylib type, which only makes it usable on the OS X operating system

- It does not implement the select statements and record sets, so can't be used to query the database

It is worth checking the current status of the driver, since when fully functional it is a more convenient approach to work with MySQL than via an ODBC middle layer. I will illustrate an alternate approach in the next section.

Nevertheless, it is possible to do some database ETL scripts to create and manipulate tables, grant access privileges and to insert, amend and delete records. If we consider the `etl.jl` file and script developed earlier, it was necessary to run the SQL output file through the `mysql` utility in order to insert the records; this could be written in Julia as:

```
# Skipping the argument processing
# Assuming that the input file is quotes.tsv
# and using the test database

Using DBI
Using MySQL


escticks(s) = replace(s,"'","''");
qq = readdlm("quotes.tsv",'\t');
n = size(qq)[1];
conn = connect(MySQL5,"localhost","malcolm","mypasswd","test");


# We can create the categories table and quotes tables:
sql  = "create table categories ";
sql *= "(id integer primary key, ";
sql *= "catname varchar(40) not null");
execute(prepare(conn,sql);
if (errcode(conn) > 0)
   error("Can't build categories table")
end;


# Note: Similar code for building the quotes table ...


j = 0;
cats = Dict{String,Int64}();


# Main loop to load up the quotes table
for i = 1:n
```

```
  cat = qq[i,1];
  if haskey(cats,cat)
    jd = cats[cat];
  else
    j = j + 1; jd = j;
    cats[cat] = jd;
  end
  sql = "insert into quotes values($i,$jd,";
  if (length(qq[i,2]) > 0)
    sql *= string("'", escticks(qq[i,2]), "',");
  else
    sql *= string("null,");
  end
  sql *= string("'", escticks(qq[i,3]), "');");
  stmt = prepare(conn,sql); execute(stmt);
  if errcode(conn) > 0 error(errstring(conn); end;
end


# Now dump the categories
for cat = keys(cats)
  jd = cats[cat];
  sql = "insert into categories values($jd,'$cat')";
  stmt = prepare(conn,sql); execute(stmt);
  if errcode(conn) > 0 error(errstring(conn); end;
end;
disconnect(conn);
```

PostgreSQL

`PostgreSQL.jl` (see `https://github.com/iamed2/PostgreSQL.jl`) is a Julia package that obeys the `DBI.jl` protocol and works on multiple platforms using `libpq`, (the C PostgreSQL API) which is included as part of the Postgres installation.

I have been an advocate of PostgreSQL for a long time, as it contained transactions, stored procedures, and triggers, long before these were added to MySQL. With the dichotomy between commercial and community editions of MySQL, it is becoming more popular of late.

We can load the `Chinook_PostgreSql.sql` Chinook data in to a running system using the `createdb` and `psql` utility from the command line as follows:

```
createdb Chinook
psql -d Chinook -a -f Chinook_PostgresSql.sql
```

```
using DBI, PostgreSQL
connect(Postgres) do conn
  stmt = prepare(conn,"SELECT * FROM \"MediaType\"");
  res = execute(stmt);
  for row in res
    @printf "ID: %2d, Media: %s\n" row[1] row[2]
  end
  finish(stmt);
end
```

```
ID:  1, Media: MPEG audio file
ID:  2, Media: Protected AAC audio file
ID:  3, Media: Protected MPEG-4 video file
ID:  4, Media: Purchased AAC audio file
ID:  5, Media: AAC audio file
```

A couple of points to note here:

- The Chinook dataset follows the Northwind-style, that is, it uses capitalized and CamelCased identifiers. These are all converted (by default) to lowercase, so it is necessary to encase them in quotes and in Julia to escape the quotes using a backslash.

- Executing the SELECT query returns a `PostgresResultHandle`, which is a pointer to an in-memory data structure with a set of results, each of which is an `Any {}` array.

PyCall

We have seen previously that Python can be used for plotting via the `PyPlot` package that interfaces with `matplotlib`. In fact, the ability to easily call Python modules is a very powerful feature in Julia and we can use this as an alternative method to connect to databases.

Any database that can be manipulated by Python is also available to Julia. In particular, since the DBD driver for MySQL is not fully DBT compliant, let's look at this approach to run some queries.

Our current MySQL setup already has the Chinook dataset loaded, we will execute a query to list the Genre table.

In Python, we will first need to download the MySQL Connector module.

For Anaconda, this needs to use the source (independent) distribution rather than a binary package, and the installation is performed using the setup.py file.

The query (in Python) to list the Genre table would be:

```
import mysql.connector as mc
cnx = mc.connect(user="malcolm", password="mypasswd")
csr = cnx.cursor()
qry = "SELECT * FROM Chinook.Genre"
csr.execute(qry)
for vals in csr:
    print(vals)


(1, u'Rock')
(2, u'Jazz')
(3, u'Metal')
(4, u'Alternative & Punk')
(5, u'Rock And Roll')
...

...

csr.close()
cnx.close()
```

We can execute the same in Julia by using the PyCall module to the mysql. connector module and the form of the coding is remarkably similar:

```
using PyCall
@pyimport mysql.connector as mc

cnx = mc.connect (user="malcolm", password="mypasswd");
csr = cnx[:cursor]()
```

```
query = "SELECT * FROM Chinook.Genre"
csr[:execute](query)


for vals in csr
  id    = vals[1]
  genre = vals[2]
  @printf "ID: %2d,   %s\n" id genre
end
ID:  1,   Rock
ID:  2,   Jazz
ID:  3,   Metal
ID:  4,   Alternative & Punk
ID:  5,   Rock And Roll
...
...
csr[:close]()
cnx[:close]()
```

Note that the form of the call is a little different from the corresponding Python method, since Julia is not object-oriented, the methods for a Python object are constructed as an array of symbols.

For example, the `csr.execute(qry)` Python routine is called in Julia as `csr[:execute](qry)`.

Also, be aware that although Python arrays are zero-based, this is translated to one-based by `PyCall`, so the first value is referenced as `vals[1]`.

JDBC

JDBC is another middle layer that functions similar to ODBC, but most operating systems have Java installed so JDBC offers a different option when connecting to databases. Also, databases may have JDBC connectors but not ODBC ones.

In Julia, using JDBC is achieved via the `JavaCall` module, in a fashion similar to calling methods in any Java classes.

For example, consider the Derby database, which is Java-based and distributed by the Apache projects. The prerequisite JAR files need to be downloaded and available via the `Classpath` Java.

```
CP = $DERBY_HOME/lib/derby.jar:$DERBY_HOME/lib/derbytools.jar
```

Using Derby tools IJ interface and previous SQL build/load files, it is possible to populate the database and then run simple query to count the number of quotes in the database:

```
java -cp $CP org.apache.derby.tools.ij
ij version 10.3
ij> connect 'jdbc:derby:Books; create=true';
ij> help;
ij> run 'build.sql';
ij> run 'qloader.sql';
ij> select count(*) as K from quotes;
K
--
36
```

Now let's look at how to do the same in Julia via `JavaCall` and JDBC:

```
Using JavaCall
jsd = @jimport java.sql.DriverManager;
dbURL = "jdbc:derby:Books1";
conn = nothing;
try
  db = jcall(jsd,"getConnection",JavaObject,(JString,),dbURL);
  jsp = @jimport java.sql.PreparedStatement;
  jsr = @jimport java.sql.ResultSet;
  sql = "select count(*) as K from quotes";
  stmt = jcall(db,"prepareStatement",isp,(JString,),sql);
  res = jcall(stmt,"executeQuery",jsr,());
  k = jcall(res,"getString",JString,(JString,),"K");
catch e
  println(e);
finally
  if conn != nothing
```

```
    jcall(conn,"close",Void,());
  end;
end;
println("\nNumber of quotes in database: $k);
```

```
Number of quotes in database: 36
```

The points to note are the use of the `@jimport` macro used to import the various classes and the `jcall()` function then called to run methods in the classes.

NoSQL datastores

When compared to relational databases, NoSQL databases are more scalable and provide superior performance, and their data model addresses several issues that the relational model is not designed to address when dealing with large volumes of structured, semi-structured, and unstructured data.

To achieve this, requires a wide variety of different database designs developed in response to a rise in the volume of data stored, the frequency in which this data is accessed, and performance and processing needs.

Types of NoSQL databases can be (roughly) classified under the following four headings:

- **Key-value stores**: These are among the simplest NoSQL databases. Every single item in the database is stored as an attribute name (or "key"), together with its value.

- **Document databases**: These pair each key with a complex data structure known as a document, which themselves may can contain many different key-value pairs or key-array pairs, or even nested documents.

- **Wide-column stores**: These are optimized for queries over large datasets, and store columns of data together instead of rows.

- **Graph stores**: These are used to store information about networks using a data model consisting of nodes, with associated parameters, and relations between the nodes.

NoSQL database technologies are especially prevalent in handling big data systems that have a large volume of data and high throughput, and of necessity are distributed over multiple physical servers.

The Julia community has responded with a number of packages to meet several types of NoSQL systems and undoubtedly more will exist when this book comes to print. A useful online reference is at `https://github.com/svaksha/Julia.jl/blob/master/Database.md` and we will explore a few examples in the rest of this chapter.

Key-value systems

Key-values (KV) systems are the earliest of databases, preceding relational ones. The first were known as **ISAM (index sequential access method)** -- and continued in various forms when used in LDAP and **Active Directory (AD)** services, despite the onset of the SQL database era.

Two Julia implementations are for the Redis and memcached datastores, and I'll discuss the former in this section. Redis is very fast as it operates totally in memory and is sometimes referred to as a data cache, although it is configured to write to disk asynchronously after a series of Redis write operations.

It is a very simple database to install. Downloads are available from `redis.io`, both binaries and source code. The source code builds quite easily and runs in the user space, that is, does not need administrator privileges.

Also, it is possible to get a cloud database from `https://redislabs.com/`, which is free for the first 25 MB. Redis Labs runs on Amazon Web Services and offers both Redis and memcached.

Redis uses a simple set of commands to create and retrieve records.

Its main feature is that in addition to simple (basic) string keys, it is possible to create lists, hashes, sets, and sorted sets. Also, string keys may be bit-mapped and has a new data structure the `hyperloglog`.

So Redis has great flexibility in how data can be stored in it.

In Julia, there are two package implementations:

- `Redis.jl`: This is a native mode package that sends messages to the Redis server, this is available via the standard Julia repository at `pkg.julialang.org`

- `Hiredis.jl`: This is a wrapper package around the `hiredis` C API, a shared library dependency, clone it from `https://github.com/markmo/HiRedis.jl`

Here, I will look at the native package.

The connection is made using `RedisConnection`, and simple keys can be stored and retrieved by the `set()` and `get()` functions:

```
using Redis;
conn = RedisConnection()
set (conn,"Hello","World");
keys(conn,  "*")
Hello
println(get(conn,  "Hello"));
World
disconnect(conn);
```

As an example, we will grab the stock market prices using the `Quandl` package, store it in Redis, retrieve them and display graphically.

It is necessary to decide on the form of the key and the type of data structure to use.

The key needs to be a composition that reflects the nature of the data being stored.

`Quandl` returns stocks against four (or less) character code and a set of values such as `Open`, `Close`, `High`, `Low`, `Volume`, plus the `Date`.

For Apple stocks, a choice of key for a closing price may be `APPL~Date~Open` where the ~ is a separator that will not occur in the data.

However, we could use a hash to store `Open`, `Close`, `High`,and `Low` against the `Date`, but to retrieve this data we will need to make multiple queries.

Better would be to use a set of lists for each type of price (and the dates), so we only need a couple of queries to get the data, one for the price and a second for the dates.

The following gets the Apple (`APPL`) and Microsoft (`MSFT`) stocks, stores them in Redis, retrieves them, and displays them using `Winston`:

```
using Quandl, DataFrames, Redis, Winston


qapi_key = "aaaaaaaaaaaaaaaaaaaa"  # Your Quandl key
set_auth_token(qapi_key)


qdf1 = quandl("WIKI/AAPL", format="DataFrame", order="asc");
aapl = convert(Array, qdf1[:Close]);
```

```
scf1 = 1.0/aapl[1];   aapl = scf1 .* aapl;


qdf2 = quandl("WIKI/MSFT", format="DataFrame", order="asc");
msft = convert(Array, qdf2[:Close]);
scf2 = 1.0/msft[1];   msft = scf2 .* msft;


n = [1:length(aapl)];
conn = RedisConnection()
for i = 1:n
  rpush(conn,'APPL~Close',aapl[i])
  rpush(conn,'MSFT~Close',msft[i])
end


t = [1:n];   # Just plot the data not the dates

aapl-data = float32(lrange(conn,"AAPL~Close",0,-1);
msft-data = float32(lrange(conn,"MSFT~Close",0,-1);
plot(t, aapl-data,"b--", t, msft-data, "r.");
```

The resulting plots are shown in the following figure:

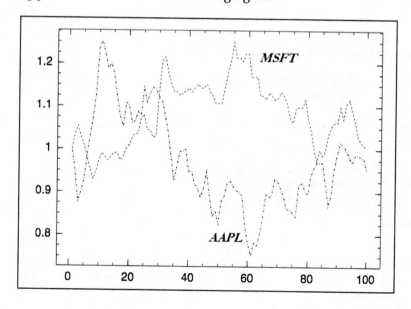

Note the following points:

- The data is retrieved from Quandl as a dataframe
- It is necessary to have an API key to Quandl, this is free on registration
- The key is Stock~Price and is pushed on to the list at the end using RPUSH
- It is possible to return the list in a single call to LRANGE
- Lists in Redis are zero-based and the indexing can be negative, meaning it counts backwards from the end, so the -1 corresponds to the last value

Document datastores

Document-oriented database are designed for storing, retrieving, and managing semi-structured data.

MongoDB is one of the most popular document databases that provides high performance, high availability, and automatic scaling. It is supported by a Julia package that is a wrapper around the C API, and to use this package it is necessary to have the Mongo C drivers installed and available on the library search path.

A record in MongoDB is a document, which is a data structure composed of field and value pairs and documents that are similar to JSON objects. The values of fields may include other documents, arrays, and arrays of documents.

Mongo itself is easy to install, and the server (daemon) process is run via the mongod executable. The location of the database is configurable, but by default is in data that must exist and be writeable.

There is a Mongo shell client program (mongo) that can be used to add and modify records and as a query engine:

```
MongoDB shell version: 2.6.7
> use test
switched to db test
> db.getCollectionNames()
[ "quotes", "system.indexes" ]
> qc = db.quotes
test.quotes
>qc.insert({category:"Words of Wisdom",author:"Hofstadter's Law",quote:"
It always takes longer than you expect, even when you take Hofstadter's
Law into account"})
```

```
>qc.insert({category:"Computing",quote:"Old programmers never die. They
just branch to a new address"})
```

. . . .

. . . .

```
> qc.count()
```

```
35
```

Note that because Mongo is schemaless, in cases where the author is unknown, the field is not specified and also the category is provided in full as a text field and not as an ID.

The Mongo shell can also be used to retrieve records:

```
> qc.find({author:"Oscar Wilde"})
```

```
{"_id" : ObjectId("54db9741d22663335937885d"), "category" : "Books &
Plays", "author" : "Oscar Wilde", "quote" : "The only way to get rid of a
temptation is to yield to it." }
```

Loading Mongo up with all 35 quotes (which are in the file `quotes.js`) we can now use Julia to run some searches:

```
using Mongo, LibBSON
client = MongoClient();  # Defaults to localhost on port 27017
```

```
mc = MongoCollection(client,"test","quotes");
bob = BSONObject({"author" => "Albert Einstein"});
```

The client, database, and collection are combined together with the `MongoCollection()` routine and the query string as a BSON object:

```
println("Quotes by Albert Einstein numbers ", count(mc, bob);
Quotes by Albert Einstein numbers 2
```

To list Einstein's quotes, we must create a cursor to the records and traverse the record set sequentially.

It is a one-way cursor, so the query needs to be rerun to get the records a second time:

```
cur = find(mc,bob); # => MongoCursor(Ptr{Void} @0x00007fadb1806000)
```

```
for obj in cur
  println(obj["category"],": ",obj["quote"])
```

```
end
```

```
Politics: I know not with what weapons World War III will be fought, but
World War IV will be fought with sticks and stones.
```

```
Science: The true sign of intelligence is not knowledge but imagination
```

The Julia package also contains routines to add, modify, and delete documents.

Consider the following three BSON Objects that describe a new quote by Einstein in a "Test" category:

```
bin = BSONObject({"author" => "Albert Einstein","category" =>
"Test", "quote" => "I don't believe that God plays dice."});
bup = BSONObject({"author" => "Albert Einstein","category" =>
"Test", "quote" => "A person who never made a mistake, never
made anything."});
brm = BSONObject({"author" => "Albert Einstein","category" =>
"Test"});
```

Then we can insert a new insert document, modify, and delete it as follows:

```
insert(mc,bin);   # => BSONOID(54e1201c52f2a1f4f8289b61)
count(mc,bob);    # => 3
update(mc,bin,bup); # => true
count(mc,bob);       # => 3
delete(mc,brm); # => true
count(mc,bob);   # => 2
```

By running the find(mc,bob) query, the reader can check the addition and modification of the new quote.

RESTful interfacing

The term REST refers to, which is a software architecture style to create scalable web services. REST has gained widespread acceptance across the Web as a simpler alternative to SOAP and WSDL-based web services.

RESTful systems typically communicate over hypertext transfer protocol with the same HTTP verbs (GET, POST, PUT, DELETE, and so on) used by web browsers to retrieve web pages and send data to remote servers.

With the prevalence of web servers, many systems now feature REST APIs and can return plain text or structured information. A typical example of plain text might be a time-of-day service, but structured information is the more common for complex requests as it contains meta information to identify the various fields.

Historically this was returned as XML, which is still common in SOAP web services, but more popular recently is JSON, since this is more compact and ideal for the Web where bandwidth may be limited. As with XML, which we looked at earlier, the JSON representation can be converted into an equivalent Julia hash array (`Dict`) expression by use of a "parser".

To access them we need a method to mimic the action of the web browser programmatically and to capture the returned response.

We saw earlier that this can be done using a task, such as `wget` or `curl`, with the appropriate command line:

```
rts = run(`wget -q -O- http://amisllp.com /now.php`)
rts = run(`curl  -X  GET  http://amisllp.com/now.php`)
```

These will run the REST web page now, and PHP will return the current (UK) date and time. Either of the tasks will produce the same result:

```
println(rts);
2015-02-18 12:11:56
```

Alternatively in Julia, we can use the `HTTPClient.jl` package that utilizes `LibCURL.jl` to do the heavy lifting or `Requests.jl` that uses to joyent HTTP parser via `HttpParser.jl`.

The following examples use `HTTPClient`, but we will look at the `Request` package in the next chapter.

JSON

In *Chapter 5, Working with Data*, we saw how to parse XML documents, so we now turn our attention to how to handle JSON data.

JavaScript Object Notation (JSON) is a set of markup rules that uses a few special characters, such as { }, [ ], ",:,;, \ , to present data in the `name:value` form. There is no termination tagging (as in XML) and it can handle arrays and other JSON subobjects. For those unfamiliar with JSON, the full specification is given on the official website `http://json.org`.

The following is a simple webservice using `httpbin.org` to return my IP addresses:

```
using HTTPClient.HTTPC, JSON
url = "http://httpbin.org/ip"
uu = HTTPC.get(url);
names(uu)
1x4 Array{Symbol,2}:
 :body  :headers  :http_code  :total_time
```

The `HTTPClient` returns an array that contains both the HTTP header and the HTTP body, as well as the return code (which is usually `200`, denoting `OK`), and the time taken for the request.

Assuming the return status was `OK`, the body is of the most interest. It has a data object comprising a byte (`Uint8`) array, and this needs to be converted to a string and then this can be parsed into JSON.

Parsing creates a `DICT` object that, in our examples, contains the requesting IP address:

```
ubody = bytestring(uu.body.data);
ss = JSON.parse(ubody);
myip = ss["origin"]
@printf "My IP address is %s\n" myip
My IP address is 10.0.141.134
```

For a more detailed example that returns a complex JSON structure, we can query the Google Books API to return data on a book with an ISBN number of `1408855895`:

```
using HTTPClient.HTTPC
using JSON
api = "https://www.googleapis.com/books/v1/volumes"
url = api * "?q=isbn:1408855895"
uu = HTTPC.get(url)
json = JSON.parse(bytestring(uu.body.data));
```

From the returned JSON data structure, we can extract extensive information on the book and I'll leave it to the reader to explore all the data in detail.

Here is the title of the book, the author (there is only one), the publisher, its publication date, and page count:

```
volumeInfo = json["items"][1]["volumeInfo"]
title    = volumeInfo["title"]
author   = volumeInfo["authors"][1]
publisher = volumeInfo["publishedBy"]
pubdate = volumeInfo["publishedDate"]
ppcoount = volumeInfo["pageCount"]
@printf "%s by %s\nPublished by %s (%s), Pages: $d"
          title author pubdate ppcount
```

```
Harry Potter and the Philosopher's Stone by J. K. Rowling
Published by Bloomsbury Childrens (2014-09-01), Pages: 354
```

Web-based databases

Examples of database systems that provide a REST API are:

- **Riak**: This is an alternative key-value datastore, which operates more as a conventional on-disk database than the in-memory Redis system (http://basho.com).

- **CouchDB**: This is an open source system, now part of the Apache project that uses JSON-style documents and a set of key-value pairs for reference (http://couchdb.apache.org/).

- **Neo4j**: This is a prominent example of a graphics database that stores nodes, parameters, and interconnect relationships between nodes in a sparse format rather than as conventional record structures (http://neo4j.com).

In this section, we will look briefly at CouchDB and in the final section at Neo4j.

CouchDB is not to be confused with the commercial product Couchbase, which is similar in operation but is provided as both an Enterprise and Community system.

Apache provides a number of binary downloads for CouchDB for Linux, OS X, and Windows. As it is written in Erlang, building from source is a little more involved but presents no real difficulties.

Starting up the server daemon on the localhost (127.0.0.1) runs the service on the 5984 default port. Querying this confirms that it is up and running:

```
curl http://localhost:5984
{"couchdb":"Welcome",
"uuid":"d9e1f98c96fc513a694936fb60dc96f8",
"version":"1.6.1",
"vendor":{"version":"1.6.11","name":"Homebrew"}}
```

Next, we need to create a database comprising the quotes dataset using either the PUT or POST command and show it exists:

```
curl -X PUT http://localhost:5984/quotes
curl http://localhost:5984/_all_dbs
["_replicator","_users","quotes"]
```

To add records to quotes, we have to specify the content type as a JSON string:

```
curl -H 'Content-Type: application/json' \
-X POST http://127.0.0.1:5984/quotes   \
-d '{category:"Computing",author:"Scott's Law",
"quote":"Adding manpower to a late software project makes it later"})'
```

I'll look at querying CouchDB in Julia after adding all the quotes we used previously when discussing SQLite and Mongo. As with Mongo, anonymous quotes are specified by omitting an author field.

To do this in curl is possible but not very flexible, so CouchDB contains a utility IDE called Futon that can run in the browser using the URL http://127.0.0.1:5984/_utils:

```
using HTTPClient.HTTPC, JSON
cdb = "http://localhost:5984";
dbs = bytestring(get("$cdb/_all_dbs").body.data);
JSON.parse(dbs); # => ["_replicator", "_users", "_quotes"]
```

As with curl, in order to post data to CouchDB, we will need to specify the MIME type and we do this in HTTPClient by setting some request options:

```
qc = cdb * "/quotes";
ropts = RequestOptions(content_type="application/json");
```

So to add a quote to the preceding code, we would use the following:

```
json  =  "{category:\"Computing\",author:\"Scott's Law\",
\"quote\":\"Adding manpower to a late software project makes it
later\"})";
HTTPC.post(qc, json, ropts);
```

To return a list of all documents in the database, we run a command in the form:

```
docs = bytestring(get(qc*"/_all_docs"))
json = JSON.parse(docs.body.data));
```

This returns the number of records, together with an array of records keys:

```
json["total_rows"]; # => 35
json["rows"][24];    # Pick out an specific record
Dict{String,Any} with 3 entries:
   "key"    => "d075d58c26d256c49b965a02cc00b77a"
   "id"     => "d075d58c26d256c49b965a02cc00b77a"
   "value" => ["rev"=>"1-524b4b2c577e2eaff31f4b665cd48055"]
key = json["rows"][24]["key"];
rev = json["rows"][24]["value"]["rev"];
```

To display the full record, we simply do an HTTP GET method against this key:

```
JSON.parse(bytestring(get("$qc/$key").body.data))
Dict{String,Any} with 5 entries:
   "quote"    =>
       "To love oneself is the beginning of a lifelong romance"
   "_rev"     => "1-524b4b2c577e2eaff31f4b665cd48055"
   "author"   => "Oscar Wilde"
   "_id"      => "d075d58c26d256c49b965a02cc00b77a"
   "category" => "Books & Plays"
```

```
The revision field is needed if we want to delete a record. HTTPC.
delete("$qc/$key?rev=$rev");
```

Updating a record is just the process of posting the new data in JSON format to an existing record ID and must use the revision key and also the request options, as now we are executing a POST operation:

```
json  =  "{category:\"Books & Plays\",author:\"Oscar Wilde\",
\"quote\":\"I can resist everything but temptation\"})";
HTTPC.post("$qc/$key", json, ropts);
```

Graphic systems

A graph database is based on graph theory and uses nodes, properties, and relationships to provide index-free adjacency.

One of the most popular graph database is Neo4j. It is open source, implemented in Java and Scala, began in 2003, and has been publicly available since 2007. The source code and issue tracking are available on GitHub.

Neo4j comes in both Community and Enterprise edition and is downloaded from the main website `http://neo4j.com/down`, and being a database on the JVM runs on all operating systems. By default, it is bundled with an interactive, web-based database interface bound to `http://localhost:7474`.

Any language on the JVM can interface with Neo4j directly. In addition, there is a REST API and a group of languages, including Python, Ruby, and NodeJS, that have modules that simplify the use of the API. At present, Julia is not one of these and so it is necessary to interact directly using HTTP commands.

Neo4j comes with some example data that corresponds to some movie information in the form of persons, movie titles, and relationships that connect the two as either actors or directors and properties such as the name of the character portrayed. This can be loaded through the web interface using the Neo4j **Cypher** language via the browser.

One advantage of using the browser is that it provides the output visually in graphic form that can be drilled down to display the underlying data.

However, there is also a `Neo4j-shell` utility program, which is useful in getting familiar with Cypher queries.

So after loading the database with the sample data, we can see the total number of nodes and relationships as follows:

```
neo4j-sh (?)$ start r=node(*) return count(r);
+-----------+
| count(r)  |
+-----------+
| 171       |
+-----------+
neo4j-sh (?)$ start r=rel(*) return count(r);
+-----------+
| count(r)  |
+-----------+
```

```
| 253      |
+----------+
```

Also, we can list some names of people in the database (limiting it to 3):

```
neo4j-sh (?)$MATCH (people:Person) RETURN people.name LIMIT 3;
+----------------------+
| people.name          |
+----------------------+
| "Keanu Reeves"       |
| "Carrie-Anne Moss"   |
| "Laurence Fishburne" |
+----------------------+
```

We can also get a list of co-actors who worked with Tom Hanks (again limiting to 3):

```
neo4j-sh (?)$ MATCH (tom:Person {name:"Tom Hanks"})-
  [:ACTED_IN]->(m)<-[:ACTED_IN]-(coActors)
  RETURN coActors.name LIMIT 5;
+-------------------+
| coActors.name     |
+-------------------+
| "Meg Ryan"        |
| "Greg Kinnear"    |
| "Parker Posey"    |
+-------------------+
```

So let's now look at how to do some queries in Julia using the REST API.

Again we use `curl` and must POST the query from JSON to Neo4j, and specify that the posted data MIME type is JSON.

The translation from the neo4j-shell to Julia is pretty straightforward and the first two queries are:

```
using HTTPClient.HTTPC, JSON;
cypher =  "http://localhost:7474/db/data/cypher";
ropts  = RequestOptions(content_type="application/json");
match = "START r=node(*) RETURN count(r)"
rts = HTTPC.post(cypher,"{\"query\":\"$match\"}",ropts);
json = JSON.parse(string(rts));
json.body.columns; # => [ "count(r)" ];
```

```
json.body.data;      # => [[ 171 ]];


# And using MATCH = "START r=rel(*) RETUrn count(r)"
json.body.columns; # => [ "count(r)" ];
json.body.data;      # => [[ 253 ]];
```

For more complex matches we have:

```
match = "MATCH (people:Person) RETURN people.name LIMIT 3";
json.body.columns; # => [ "people.name" ]
json.body.data
[["Keanu-Reeves"],["Carrie-Ann Moss"],["Laurence Fishburne"]]


match = "MATCH ((tom:Person {name:"Tom Hanks"})-
  [:ACTED_IN]->(m)<-[:ACTED_IN]-(coActors)
  RETURN coActors.name  LIMIT 3";


json.body.columns; # => [ "coActors.name" ]
json.body.data'
[["Meg Ryan"],["Greg Kinnear"],["Parker Posey"]]
```

Summary

This chapter has looked at the means by which Julia interacts with data held in databases and data stores. Until recently, the great majority of databases conformed to the relational model, the so-called SQL database.

However, the rapid explosion in data volumes accompanying the big data revolution has led to the introduction of a range of databases based on other data models. These are normally grouped under the heading NoSQL and are categorized as key-value, document, and graphic databases. With such a large field to cover, we identified some definitive examples in each category.

Julia's approaches are largely specific to each individual case, and the appropriate packages and methods for loading, maintaining, and querying the different types of databases have been presented.

In the next chapter, we will discuss working with various networked systems. We will look at developing Internet servers, working with web sockets, and messaging via e-mail, SMS, and Twitter. Finally, we will explore the use of the cloud services such as those provided by Amazon and Google.

9
Networking

In the previous chapter, we concluded the review of database support by looking at RESTful access. While this can be applicable to data stored in a local environment, it is more often associated with data held on servers accessed over an Internet or Intranet connection.

In this chapter, we will develop methods of working with network connections further, starting with the basic IP sockets and then looking at services that are more commonly associated with the World Wide Web (WWW).

Following this, we will consider the use of messaging services, such as e-mail and Twitter, and conclude with a brief discussion of cloud service such as those offered by Amazon and Google.

Sockets and servers

In this section, we are going to look at a basic cornerstone of network services, the socket, and see how this leads to the creation of familiar operating system tasks such as the web and e-mail servers.

First, we need to introduce the concept of well-known ports.

Well-known ports

The concept of networked services over well-known ports was introduced to Unix by the Berkeley development on the open source operating system in the early 1980s and has formed the bedrock of almost all computing operating systems ever since. The idea is that a particular service is associated with a port number and that network packets are sent tagged with this port number.

For example, originally the file transfer protocol used port 21, SSH port 22 and sendmail port 25. Today other (additional) ports may be used for these services

One port that many readers will be familiar with is 80, this is the one used by web servers to deliver HTTP content.

Security firewalls often block specific traffic on specific IP ports, but in general transmissions on port 80 are allowable.

Ports from 1023 and below are "reserved" and should only be used for the purposes they are intended for, but high port values are available to the general programmer and we saw a few examples for some of the SQL and NoSQL servers in the previous chapter. For instance, the MySQL database commonly uses port 3306, the MongoDB server 28017, and the Redis key-value store 6379.

It is possible to start any of these servers on other ports, but the use is so widespread that the numbers assigned may be considered to be "slightly less well-known".

A network service will be started to run in a loop listening for traffic on a particular port and its purpose is to deal with any requests coming from that port. Usually when a request has been dealt with, the service resumes in a listening state. This operation is usually referred to as a socket to a particular port. A client program sends a request to this socket and in most cases it will establish a connection to facilitate bidirectional communication

It is a primary function of the operating system that it will deny the creation of additional sockets to avoid network clashes occurring that would lead to ambiguities in servicing the requests. However, for services that have to deal with a high volume of requests from different sources, such as web and database servers, it is clearly not practical to have a single resource dealing with each synchronously. So a sophisticated method of a server creating copies of itself, running in parallel, is often the norm.

UDP and TCP sockets in Julia

The IP protocol specifies two types of sockets, unreliable and reliable.

The concept of an unreliable socket may seem at first a little strange but there are some requests, which if not serviced can be merely ignored, are retried. An example of this may be requesting the network time from a time (NNTP) server. The establishment of a reliable socket necessitates a more complex procedure, but most situations require this.

The unreliable sockets are termed as operating via the **User Datagram Protocol (UDP)** and are connectionless. Alternatively, the reliable sockets use the **Transmission Control Protocol (TCP)** and are connection full. The latter are so common that they are often merely referred to as sockets.

Julia supports both UDP and TCP sockets and also named pipes.

The source code is mainly provided in the `socket.jl` and `streams.jl` base modules. These make API calls to the Julia core and rely on the `libuv` Joyent library.

We'll look at an example of a more extensive TCP server in the next section, so let's first spend a little time with an example using UDP:

```
s1 = UdpSocket(); bind(s1,ip"127.0.0.1",8001) # => true
s2 = UdpSocket(); bind(s2,ip"127.0.0.1",8002) # => true
```

This creates two sockets to the localhost on the `8001` and `8002` ports, the operations are asynchronous so then IO does not block.

For a UDP socket the process is termed binding and the IP address of the localhost is defined by the `ip "127.0.0.1"` special string form or alternatively using the `IPv4(127,0,0,1)` function call:

```
using Dates
send(s2,ip"127.0.0.1",8001,string(Dates.now()));
```

This sends the current date and time over the `s2` socket to the `s1` socket, which is bound to the `8001` port:

```
msg = recv(s1);
bytestring(msg);
"2015-03-2015T15:50:40"

close(s2);
close(s1);
```

The message is a byte stream that can be read by the `recv()` function, converted to an ASCII string, and in essence this forms the basis for a simple NNTP time of day server.

A "Looking-Glass World" echo server

In contrast to UDP services, which use the `send()` and `recv()` functions to send and receive messages, TCP services need to establish a duplex channel between server and client and use `connect()`, `listen()`, and `accept()`.

There are several forms for a TCP client connection; a typical one would be a call such as:

```
connect(host::ASCIIString, port::Integer)
```

If only the port is specified, the `localhost` (ip"127.0.0.1") is assumed.

As an alternative to the host string, a predefined `TCPSocket()` method may be passed as the first argument.

Connecting to a socket is simple and if successful, it will return an open status. Then it is possible to send messages to the server over the socket and read the reply since it is a full duplex connection.

Closing the socket will terminate the client and the server response, but normally the server will be written so as to continue listening.

```julia
julia> sock = connect("ljuug.org",80)
TcpSocket(open, 0 bytes waiting)

julia> close(sock);
```

At the base of this functionality is the `getaddrinfo()` routine, which will do the appropriate address resolution:

```julia
julia> getaddrinfo("ljuug.org")
ip"82.165.158.3"
```

Servers operating over TCP sockets use `listen()` and `accept()` to wait for connection. A common example is a simple server that accepts text inputs and simply sends it back to the client process.

The following is my take on a "Through the Looking Glass" version that reverses the text before echoing it back.

We need to munge the returns by stripping them off and reappending at the EOLs.

This is written as a script that uses the `!#` convention to indicate the specify that it must be run via Julia. The `-q` switch is necessary to suppress the Julia opening banner.

The initial part of the script has more complex arguments than with the database ETL example, and so we make use of the `ArgParse` module to simplify the parsing:

```julia
#! /Users/malcolm/bin/julia -q
#
using ArgParse

const ECHO_PORT = 3000
const ECHO_HOST = "localhost"

function parse_commandline()
  s = ArgParseSettings()
  @add_arg_table s begin
```

```
  "--server", "-s"
    help = "hostname of the echo server"
    default = ECHO_HOST
  "--port", "-p"
    help = "port number running the service"
    arg_type = Int
    default = ECHO_PORT
  "--quiet", "-q"
    help = "run quietly, i.e. with no server output"
    action = :store_true
  end
 return parse_args(s)
end


pa = parse_commandline()
```

The server defaults to the `localhost` and will listen on the 3000 port.

Also, it will echo responses to STDOUT. This can be suppressed with −q or −quiet, and it would be possible to provide additional information to log the information to disk file. I'll leave this as an exercise to the reader:

```
ehost = pa["server"]
eport = pa["port"]
vflag = !pa["quiet"]


pp = (ehost == "localhost" ? "" : "$ehost>")
```

After processing the arguments and defaults, we enter the main processing loop.

The server listens on `eport` and loops continuously waiting for connection requests that are accepted, and the processing is run asynchronously using the `@async` macro:

```
if vflag println("Listening on port $eport") end
server = listen(eport)
while true
  conn = accept(server)
  @async begin
    try
      while true
        s0 = readline(conn)
        s1 = chomp(s0)
        if length(chomp(s1)) > 0
          s2 = reverse(s1)
          if s2 == "."
```

```
            println("Done.")
            close(conn)
            exit(0)
          else
            write(conn,string(pp,s2,"\r\n"))
          end
        end
      end
    catch err
      println("Connection lost:  $err")
      exit(1)
    end
  end
end
```

Input is processed line-by-line rather than as a single complete string so that the order of a multiline is preserved. To be certain of the integrity of each line, the trailing returns are stripped by using chomp() and then reappended when writing to the connection.

Empty lines are ignored but a line consisting of a single . will shut down the server.

The server can be started as a background job:

```
./echos.jl &
# Listening on port 3000
```

Testing this is straightforward, open a connection to the port (3000) and create an asynchronous task to wait for any responses sent back over the socket:

```
sock = connect(3000)
TcpSocket(open, 0 bytes waiting)

@async while true
    write(STDOUT,readline(sock))
end
Task (waiting) @0x00007fc81d300560
```

Since this is a "Looking Glass server", it seems appropriate to test this from some poetry from *Thorough the Looking Glass, and What Alice Found There*.

The following reads the first verse of *You are Old Father William* and returns in a manner that Alice would comprehend:

```
fw = readall("/Users/malcolm/Work/Father-William.txt");
println(sock,fw);

,dias nam gnuoy eht ",mailliW rehtaF ,dlo era uoY"
```

```
;etihw yrev emoceb sah riah ruoy dnA"
,daeh ruoy no dnats yltnassecni uoy tey dnA
"?thgir si ti ,ega ruoy ta ,kniht uoy oD

println(sock,".");   #  This will shut down the server
```

Named pipes

A named pipe uses a special file as a communication channel.

It is a first-in, first-out (FIFO) stream that is an extension to the traditional pipe mechanism on Unix / OS X and is also present on Windows, although the semantics differ substantially.

```
epipe = "/tmp/epipe";    # => Define a file as named pipe
server = listen(epipe)
```

Testing is possible using the echo server example. It clearly requires some changes to the argument parsing as we need to replace the port information with the named pipe.

From the command line, the process is exactly equivalent except for the `connect()` call.

```
np = connect("/tmp/epipe")
Pipe(open, 0 bytes waiting)

@async while true
    write(STDOUT,readline(np))
end
Task (waiting) @0x00007fe80df9c400

println(np,"You are old Father William");
mailliW rehtaF dlo era uoY
println(np,"."); # => Signal to shut down the server
```

Working with the Web

The World Wide Web (WWW) has become a popular medium to return information. Initially this was for web browsers as a result of CGI or server-side scripting, but recently it has been for more generalized services. We saw an example of the latter with the use of REST in conjunction with the CouchDB document database.

In addition to browsers being almost universally available, we noted that most firewalls are configured to permit the traffic of HTML data. Also, programs such as `wget` and `curl` can be used to query web servers in the absence of a browser.

In this section, we will consider Julia's approach and in particular to the facilities available under the group heading, JuliaWeb.

A TCP web service

Essentially, a web server is functionally little different from the echo server developed in the previous section. After some initial set up, it grabs a socket on which to `listen` and runs asynchronously, waiting for a connection that it then services.

What is different is that the web server needs to be able to return a variety of different file formats and the browser has to be able to distinguish between them. The simplest are textual data in plain form such as HTML markup, but also there are imagery (JPEG, PNG, GIFs, and so on) and attachments such as PDFs and Word documents.

To do this, the server knows about a series of formats termed MIME types, and sends metadata information as part of a response header using the `"Content-Type":` key.

The header precedes the data information, such as text or imagery, and in the case of the binary information it may be necessary to specify the exact length of the datastream using some additional metadata via the `"Content-Length:"` key.

In order to signal the end of the header information, a web server needs to output a blank line before sending the data.

The simplest form of header will just consist of the status code followed by the content type, and in the following example I will use the `quotes` file we looked at when considering string processing to return a random quote as plain text:

```
function qserver(sock::Integer)
  fin = open("/Users/malcolm/Work/quotes.txt");
  header = """HTTP/1.1 200 OK
Content-type: text/plain; charset=us-ascii

""" ;
  qa = readlines(fin);
  close(fin);
  qn = length(qa);
  @async begin
    server = listen(sock)
    while true
      qi = rand(1:qn)
      qs = chomp(qa[qi])
      sock = accept(server)
```

```
        println(header*qs)
      end
    end
end
```

 Note that the blank line in the response header indicates, a string is required.

The `200` status code sent is the expected `OK` value -- we will revisit status codes again in the next section.

The operation of the server program is very simple. As a prelude, this program opens the text file; ideally, the program should exit with an exception if this fails. Then it reads all the quotes, which are all one-liners, into an array and gets the number of entries (length) of the array.

The server action is just to generate an appropriate random number in range, look up the quote, append the response header, and return it.

Because the server is running asynchronously, it is simple to test it from the REPL:

```
qserver(8000); # Run it on port 8000 as port 80 may be in use
conn = connect(8000);
HTTP/1.1 200 OK
Content-Type: text/plain

Sailing is fun but scrubbing the decks is aardvark
```

The JuliaWeb group

Most web servers are constructed to respond to requests issued for a browser, rather than for a utility program such as `curl`.

Recall that a web server response may arise when a URL such as `google.com` is entered or as the result of submitting information, and clicking on a button or image. The former is termed a `GET` operation and the latter a `POST` operation. In fact, there is a set of other operations such as `PUT` and `DELETE` that are more common in RESTful services than in browsers.

We noted previously that the server is required to send back a response code and that the most common one is `200`, corresponding to `OK`. However, there are others that may occur, such as in case of redirection and error, one being the infamous **404, Page not found**.

So construction of an HTTP server requires considerable more effort than it may have appeared from the preceding example. Couple this with the fact that *POSTing* data may be denied and the GET operations may be expected to handle query strings, and the programmer may be pleased to have some assistance in constructing both web servers and web clients.

To this end, a series of routines grouped as JuliaWeb is available.

We used one of these HTTPClient previously while exploring RESTful services, which used the underlying LibCURL package to do much of the heavy lifting.

However, there is a separate subset of interrelated **Julia Webstack** packages and a separate web page is available at http://juliawebstack.org that provides some summary information and links to the individual GitHub repositories.

It is worth noting that the underlying request-response mechanism uses the GnuTLS package that is a wrapper around a shared library. The build process using the Pkg manager on, for example, Ubuntu Linux platform is not always straightforward and it requires additional development modules that the base distro does not provide. If you have built Julia from source, then these modules should be present. On the Red Hat/CentOS flavors of Linux, I have encountered no problems and also on the Windows operating system

The installation of GnuTLS under OS X uses Homebrew and I have had problems where brew becomes 'borked' and requires removing and reinstalling. If GnuTLS is not present then virtually the entire set of Julia Webstack routines is not available, but it is still possible to work with HTTPClient and the curl library as a method of generating HTTP requests.

In the rest of this section, I'll briefly give an overview of the Julia Webstack family of modules routines.

In the order of high-level to low-level functionality, these are:

- Morsel.jl: This is a Sinatra-like routable web framework
- Meddle.jl: This is arack-like request middleware stack
- WebSockets.jl: This is an implementation of the websockets protocol
- HttpServer.jl: This is a basic HTTP service over TCP
- HttpParser.jl: This is a wrapper for Joyent's http-parser lib
- HttpCommon.jl: This is a set of shared types and utilities

There is also an additional Requests.jl related package that can be used to deliver HTTP requests, similar to the HTTPClient request, but using the GnuTLS library as a means of transport.

I'l look at Morsel and WebSockets in the next two sections.

Using `Requests` is very simple; here is an example that gets the London Julia website's home page:

```
using Requests;
ljuug = "http://www.londonjulia.org";
resp = get(ljuug)
Response(200 OK, 10 Headers, 19289 Bytes in Body)
```

This returns a string that gives the status, number of response headers, and length of the HTTP body (in bytes). All these are available as fields in the response object.

```
names(resp)'
4-element Array{Symbol,2}:
 :status    :headers    :data      :finished
```

Here, of interest, is the response header that is returned as a dict hash:

```
julia> resp.headers
    "Date"                => "Thu, 19 Mar 2015 10:30:03 GMT"
    "http_minor"          => "1"
    "Keep-Alive"          => "1"
    "status_code"         => "200"
    "Server"              => "Apache"
    "X-Powered-By"        => "PHP/5.4.38"
    "Content-Length"      => "19289"
    "http_major"          => "1"
    "Content-Type"        => "text/html"
    "Content-Language"    => "en"
```

And also, the actual data that is returned by the web server as a XHTML document:

```
resp.data
"<?xml version=\"1.0\" encoding=\"utf-8\"?><!DOCTYPE html PUBLIC \"-//
W3C//DTD XHTML 1.0 Transitional//EN\" \"http://www.w3.org/TR/xhtml1/
DTD/xhtml1-transitional.dtd\">\r\n<html xmlns=\"http://www.w3.org/1999/
xhtml\" xml:lang=\"en\" lang=\"en\">\r\n<head>\r\n<title>London Julia
Users Group</title>\r\n<meta http-equiv=\"Content-Type\" content=\"text/
html; charset=utf-8\" />\n
</body>\r\n</html>\r\n"
```

As we saw with `HTTPClient`, the `Requests` package is capable of appending query strings to a `GET` request and emulating web forms when executing `POST` requests. This makes requests a viable alternative in working with RESTful systems.

For example, this executes a Google search for the London Julia (`ljuug`) group:

```
https://www.google.co.uk/?q=ljuug
```

The "quotes" server

In this section, I will look at the development of a more comprehensive "quotes" server using the Julia Webstack routines, similar to the simple one we saw earlier.

In order to add information, such as author and category, we will use the SQLiteDB quotes database created in the previous chapter and return the quote as formatted HTML text.

We will want to restrict the client requests to only those using GET, and not POST, PUT and so on. It is possible to deal with a query string such as `?cat=Politics` to select a quote from a particular group and I have included this within the code accompanying this book.

Deciding on how the server responses to client requests, and indeed with the validity of a request, is called routing. In our case all GET requests will be routed to the same routine and any others denied.

The server needs to do a little start up work in opening the quotes database and establishing the number of quotes available. This is similar to using the simple text file but a little more elaborate.

Random quotes are returned now with three fields: Author/Category/Text and these are marked up as HTML5, all inline, although a fully-fledged web server would probably refer to a separate CSS style sheet to decorate the text.

The function of the Morsel package is to provide a framework for complex routing. It is quite easy to do this using HttpServer directly, but Morsel will allow us to differentiate between GET and other requests:

```
using Morsel;
using SqliteDB
db = SQLiteDB("quotes.db");
try
  res = query(db,"select count(*) from quotes");
catch
  error("Can't find quotes table");
end
nq = res[1][1];
@assert nq > 0;
```

The first function of the server is to open the `quotes.db` database and get a count of total number of quotes. SQLite has the habit of creating empty databases when they do not exist, so we should check for their existence. However, we will get an exception error while querying the `quotes` table, if it does not exist, so effectively this confirms the database's existence.

Also, we need to check that there are some entries in the table, otherwise all the queries will give no result. Since we wish to output HTML markup to the browser, we define a `htmlH` header string and a `htmlF` footer string:

```
htmlH = """<!DOCTYPE html>
<html lang='en-US'>
<head>
<title>Julia Quotes Server<</title>
</head>
<body>""";
htmlF= "</body></html>";
```

In our case, creating the web server using `Morsel` is easy and we use the `route()` function to handle any requests other than `GET` requests:

```
app = Morsel.app();
route(app, POST | PUT, "/") do req, res
 htmlB = "<h2>Posting data to the server is not allowed</h2>";
 string(htmlH,htmlB,htmlF);
end
```

To handle acceptable queries we could use `route()` again, but there are convenient short forms for various request types, so in this case we can use `get()`:

```
get(app, "/") do req, res
  qid = rand(1:nq);
  sql = "select q.author,c.catname,q.quoname from quotes q ";
  sql *= "join categories c on q.cid = c.id and q.id = $qid";
  res = query(db,sql);
  author  = res[1][1];
  catname = res[2][1];
  quotext = res[3][1];
  htmlB = "<p>$quotext<br/><i>$author ($catname)</i></p>";
  string(htmlH,htmlB,htmlF);
end
```

The payload is exactly equivalent to that previously used. We generate a random number in range and extract the quote with that ID, together with the author and category.

Then we need to format the body text (as `htmlB`), append the header and footer, and return the result to the browser.

Finally, we start the server by specifying the port number:

```
start(app, 8000)
```

If we point a browser to `http://localhost:8000`, we should get a random quote from the such as:

```
To love oneself is the beginning of a lifelong romance.
Oscar Wilde (Books and Plays)
```

WebSockets

Probably all readers will be familiar with the process where when typing in the search box of Google, for example, the server returns a set of suggestions and they change as the search term is refined. The method used is called **Asynchronous JavaScript and XML (AJAX)**, although the mnemonic is largely anachronistic as far as the use of the XML term is concerned.

What is clear is that the overhead using HTTP protocols, in terms of client request and server response headers, is very large while providing such small payloads, perhaps hundreds of bytes of headers for just a few tens of bytes of information.

Web sockets were devised as a way of overcoming these problems.

The name "web socket" gives the impression that it's a traditional socket. In practice, it combines the parts of UDP and TCP; it is message-based such as UDP, but is reliable like TCP. WebSockets are upgraded from HTTP/1.1 through a system previously defined as part of the HTTP specification (which is, the upgrade header).

Through the HTTP handshake, it becomes feasible to proxy the connection without losing information. WebSockets send messages that can be ASCII or UTF-8 text, but also can comprise of binary.

Each message can also carry control information and is wrapped in a frame. Messages sent from the client to the server are obfuscated with a basic transmission mask of 4 bytes that is sent within each web socket package rather than the traditional AJAX overhead.

Conveniently, a WebSocket will use the normal HTTP/HTTPS ports, that is, 80 and 443 respectively. However, there are problems when operating over the Internet in that many firewalls will block the connection. This has lead to a slow uptake in their use on the Web as compared with conventional AJAX. In general, HTTPS connections are more successful than plain HTTP ones.

WebSockets are ideal for vehicles for chat services, as an alternative to the more usual ones using IRC and JABBER. A good example is provided in the package source of `Websockets.jl`.

Instead we will look at a version of the ELIZA program. ELIZA was a computer program written at MIT by Joseph Weizenbaum around 1965 and was considered at the time as an early example of primitive natural language processing. In essence, it was a simple chat program where the user types a question to ELIZA and the program acts as a therapist by replying to the query.

The concept was simple; ELIZA has a set of "keywords", and if the user query contains one of the words, a suitable ambiguous response is selected, otherwise an especially vague reply is given.

The following is the Julia version that uses WebSockets to keep the connection open. The user signals the end of the session by typing Bye of Goodbye.

Only a small set of keywords have been included and these are hardcoded into the source code, so that these plus the responses are a dictionary hash. In practice, these would be more extensive, probably contained in a text file that is read during startup.

To be a more convincing therapist, a large set of keywords should be used.

For greater flexibility, ease of maintainability, and better memory usage, a key-value store could be used and Redis makes a very good choice.

On startup, only the keys are read into an array using the KEYS * Redis command, and in case of a match the appropriate response string is retrieved from the server rather than being in memory:

```julia
using HttpServer
using WebSockets

const SDEF = "Tell me more ...";
const SBYE = "Goodbye, please let's talk again soon";

d = Dict();

d["hello"] = "Hi, my name is Eliza";
d["no"]    = "Tell me more about the detail.";
d["yes"]   = "Tell me more about the detail.";
d["you"]   = "Let's not talk about me.";
d["think"] = "Why do you think that?";
d["hate"]  = "So you hate something, tell me more.";
d["what"]  = "Why do you ask ?";
```

```
d["want"]    = "I'm here help you with what you want";
d["need"]    = "We all need many thing, is this is important?";
d["why"]     = "Remember therapy is good for you.";
d["know"]    = "How do you know that?";
d["can't"]   = "Don't be negative -- be positive!";
d["never"]   = "Don't be negative -- be positive!";
d["unhappy"] = "Why are you unhappy?";
d["like"]    = "Why do you like that?";
d["help"]    = "I'm here to help you.";


looping = true;
```

The SDEF and SBYE strings are used for default and closing responses.

The looping flag is used so that the bye keyword can be used to exit the chat loop. We have set up a few keyword primitives in a hash dictionary and these reference all other responses when a known word is used.

The main loop generates a WebSocket and pattern matching is very simplistic. It uses case-insensitive comparison but would not differentiate between words that are substrings of longer ones. For example, we use the "unhappy" word, so we can't have happy too. Also, if we had used happy then a sentence such as "I'm really unhappy" might result in an inappropriate reply:

```
wsh = WebSocketHandler() do req,clt
  while looping
    s0 = lowercase(read(client))
    s1 = SDEF
    for k in keys(d)
      s = lowercase(k)
      if s == "bye"
        looping = false
        s1 = SBYE
      elseif contains(s0, s)
        s1 = d[k]
        break
      end
    end
    write(clt, "ELIZA> $s1")
  end
end
```

Running ELIZA merely consists of creating a `server` object and running it on a convenient port:

```
server = Server(wsh)
run(server,8080)
```

Testing with WebSockets needs less involvement. It can be done using some JavaScript as part of a web browser. Most browsers now support WebSockets, although probably the best browser is Google Chrome, which provides an extension: `"Simple Websocket Client"`.

The following is a typical dialogue when chatting with ELIZA:

```
Hello
ELIZA> Hi, my name is Eliza
I need some help
ELIZA> I'm here to help you
I am so unhappy
ELIZA> Why are you unhappy?
I have problems coping with daily life
ELIZA> Tell me more ...
Bye, I'll call back tomorrow
ELIZA> Goodbye, please let's talk again soon
```

Messaging

Messaging is older than the web services and in some ways easier to provide. In this section, I'm first going to look at the elder statesman of messaging services: e-mail.

Nowadays, we also use systems that send SMS textual information and we will look at two of these: Twitter and Esendex.

E-mail

Sending e-mails conventionally happens on the well-known port 25, although other ports such as 465 and 587 are now more commonly used (http://www.esendex.co.uk).

This uses the **Simple Mail Transport Protocol (SMTP)**, which was first formulated in the early 1980s and consists of formulating a message the SMTP server can understand, with fields such as **To:**, **From:**, and **Subject:** together with the text of the message and then deposit in the mail service's outbound queue.

Receiving emails is a little different. This depends on one of the different protocols such as the **Post Office Protocol (POP)** or alternatively the **Internet Message Access Protocol (IMAP)**. Each has its own related set of ports, and in addition an e-mail client program may use a different server to receive e-mails from the SMTP server that it uses to send them.

In addition, we usually want the transmissions between e-mail client and server to be encrypted using SSH/TLS-type methods and this includes other well-known ports and some form of user/password authentication.

As part of JuliaWeb, Julia has a SMTPServer.jl package. This uses LibCURL.jl as its underlying method of sending e-mails and I've included an example in this book's source code.

Rather than discussing this, we will include some code that uses a common Python module, in a way similar to how we communicated with the MySQL database in the previous chapter:

```
using PyCall;
@pyimport smtplib;
fromaddr = "malcolm.sherrington@gmail.com";
toaddrs  = "malcolm@amisllp.com";

messy = """From: $fromaddr
To: $toaddrs
Subject: Test SMTP using PyCall

Testing - 1,2,3
""";

# Note that the blank line is necessary to distinguish
# the SMTP header from the message text.

username = fromaddr;
password = "ABCDEF7890";   # Not my real password

server = pycall(smtplib.SMTP,PyAny,"smtp.gmail.com:587");
server[:ehlo]();
server[:starttls]();
server[:login](username,password);
server[:sendmail](fromaddr,toaddrs,messy);
server[:quit]();
```

This code follows a fashion that is equivalent to the script in Python, the main difference being the nature of the function versus method calls between the two languages. For reference, the equivalent of a Python script is included with this book's code examples.

Returning briefly to the question of receiving e-mails via an e-mail "client" program, the POP-style of delivery is the much simpler to implement than IMAP. This can be done in Julia using the `LibCURL` package, although as yet there is no higher level package for POP to match that from SMTP.

Alternatively, the Python method can also be used by utilizing the `poplib` module, similar to the one in the preceding code that used `smtplib`. Again much of the coding in Julia can be deduced from first coding and testing in Python.

Twitter

`Twitter.jl` is a Julia package designed to work with the Twitter API v1.1. Currently, only the REST API methods are supported, although the author promises streaming methods, so please check. To understand the full functions, the reader is referred to Twitter API at https://dev.twitter.com/overview/documentation.

Twitter authentication used to be very simple, but now requires OAuth endpoints (see http://oauth.net) to provide connections, and to use this package you will need to pick up an API key from https://dev.twitter.com/. It is free, but you do need to set up an app on the dev site to have the key generated.

The `Twitter.jl` source on GitHub also has a pretty comprehensive `tests.jl` script that can be used to exercise the various function calls, once you have acquired a valid API key.

In the example I have chosen, I'm using the Twitter account for `@LondonJuliaUG`, the London Julia User Group, but the key has been changed from that used to run the code:

```
using Twitter;
twitterauth("12345678ABCDEFGH123456789",
"1234567890ABCDEFGHIJKLMNOPQRST1234567890abcdefgefh"
"1234567890ABCDEFGHIJKLMNOPQRST1234567890abcdefgefh"
"1234567890ABCDEFGHIJKLMNOPQRST1234567890abcde");
```

This constructs a structure of the `TWCRED` type that consists of 4 keys. Authentication occurs when a function is called, so it is only at this time we can determine that the authentication is correct.

In the case of an error, it returns a standard response structure via the `Requests.jl` package, with a status of `401 Unauthorised`.

We can confirm the name of the Twitter account from the `account_settings`:

```
settings = get_account_settings();
twit_name = settings["screen_name"]
println("This account is $twit_name");
This account is LondonJuliaUG
```

The following snippet gets the last set of tweets to the London Julia UG account using the `home_timeline()` function:

```
home_timeline = get_home_timeline();
typeof(home_timeline);   # => Array{TWEETS,1}
length(home_timeline);   # => 20
```

This is an `Any` array of the `TWEETS` type that has a large set of properties:

```
names(home_timeline[1])
29-element Array{Symbol,1}:
```

Some of the interesting ones are `:text`, `:user` and `:created_at`.

Many of the `TWEET` properties consist of arrays, which themselves may consist of hash dictionaries and these may point to other arrays as values. So navigation of the data returned is not straightforward. In particular, the `:user` structure is very complex. In order to explore this, one approach is to pick up the dataframe for `home_timeline[1]` and use `names()` to work the way down.

As an illustration, here is a dump of the last 20 tweets (today) to `@LondonJulia`:

```
for i in 1:length(home_timeline)
  df = DataFrame(home_timeline[i])
  user = df[:user][1]["name"]
  created = df[:created_at][1]
  text = df[:text]
  @printf "%2d %s : %s =>\n%s\n\n" i user created text
end
 1 The Julia Language : Sun Mar 03 04:28:59 +0000 2013 =>
("RT @dyjh: Free #OpenSource in #QuantFinance event 02.04. London filling
up quickly http://t.co/ujByhPEwcE #python #julialang #rstats #scala…")

 2 Data Science London : Sat Jan 28 11:55:07 +0000 2012 =>
{"Shelloid: open source IoT real-time big data platform w/ Node.js &amp;
Clojure https://t.co/HSyEXH9cwx cc @yoditstanton"}
```

```
Mango Solutions : Thu Mar 19 13:36:59 +0000 2015 =>
("RT @R_Programming: 60 Super Useful R Language Tips (and counting)..
Free PDF Download! \nhttp://t.co/TdzJtYUj1X #rstats #datascience
http://..."}
```

. . . .

. . . .

```
19 Jiahao Chen : Fri Mar 13 16:31:17 +0000 2015 =>
{"RT @HHMINEWS: Video: HHMI's Martin Burke talks about his lab's
new machine to automate synthesis of small molecules: https://t.co/
fJhA4I7PBr"}
```

```
20 Viral B. Shah : Tue Jan 18 17:03:36 +0000 2011 =>
{"RT @QuantixResearch: Quite impressed with how far #julialang
#deeplearning libraries have come.\n\nBegun using Mocha.jl &amp; KuNet.jl
for real w..."}
```

SMS and esendex

As a final example in this section, I will consider sending messages to mobile phones via a service called **esendex.com**. The REST API is lightweight and easy to use. Messages are sent and received as XML documents rather than in JSON format.

Using the APIs is possible to send, track, and receive SMS messages, although receiving requires additional setup. It is also possible to send voice as well as text messages, and if a message is routed to a phone that does not accept SMS, this is automatically converted from text to voice.

The service is not free but esendex does provide a 7-day free trial with up to 25 credits.

Registration is via an email address, which serves as the username. The system associates this with an account number and generates a password, both of which can be changed by logging on to the esendex website.

Then it is easy to test simple messaging by sending an SMS to your mobile with the ECHO service, which will confirm that it is set up correctly, but will cost you one credit!

For the developer, a number of APIs are available including SOAP and REST.

The first step is to try and send a text t directly from the shell using curl:

```
malcolm> MSG="<?xml version'1.0' encoding='UTF-8' ?>
<messages>
<accountreference>EX123456</accountreference>
```

```
<message>
<to>447777555666</to>
<body>Every message matters</body>
</message>
</messages>
```

```
curl -u Malcolm@amisllp.com:passwd -X POST -d $MSG \
    https://api.esendex.com/v1.0/messagedispatcher
```

The syntax of this message is very simple, it consists of a `<to>` field corresponding to the mobile phone number and a `<body>` tag for the message text, of up to 140 characters per credit.

The whole also needs to include the account reference name and it is possible to send a series of messages within a single API request. This is *POSTed* to RESTful message dispatcher service and authorization is provided using basic authentication.

The system returns a message ID that can be used for tracking purposes. The status of the message is also available by logging on the esendex website.

Also, there is a set of SDKs in many popular languages but not yet one in Julia.

However, the above procedure can be used in Julia by spawning a task or using either `HTTPClient` or `Request` to dispatch the message:

```julia
using URIParser, Requests

eacct = "EX123456"
uname = "malcolm@amisllp.com"
pword = "passwd"

dispatcher = "api.esendex.com/v1.0/messagedispatcher"
uri = URI(string(https://,uname,'@',pword,'/',dispatcher)

message = """"?xml version'1.0' encoding='UTF-8' ?>
<messages>
<accountreference>EX123456</accountreference>
<message>
<to>447777555666</to>
<body>Every message matters</body>
</message>
</messages>"""

post(uri; data = message)
```

Cloud services

The Julialang web home page states that *Julia is designed for parallelism and cloud computing*. We looked at running tasks in parallel and in this section, I'll close with a discussion of the cloud computing.

Using the Cloud is a relatively new computing business model, based on the concept of providing software as a utility service.

The idea is to call on resources as needed to meet demand and to pay for it as required in a way similar to utilities such as electricity and water, and therefore you do not have to provision your own resources to meet an estimated peak loading. This is often termed as **Software as a Service (SaaS)**.

Two of the early cloud providers were Amazon and Google. Both have slightly different emphasis of approach, but either can be used to run Julia, and we will consider each briefly in a Julia context later.

Among the other major cloud providers are Rackspace, Microsoft, and Oracle:

- Rackspace uses an open source system OpenStack, which uses Swift for parallelization processing and is becoming increasingly popular over Hadoop with the non-Java fraternity.

- Other providers, such as City Cloud and IBM Bluemix, are also using OpenStack and as an OS project you have the means to build your own corporate cloud. Currently it comes with machine instances for both Ubuntu and Red Hat Linux distributions.

- The Microsoft Cloud service is called Azure and is naturally very useful when running .NET and SQL Server applications. It does have some virtual machines based on Ubuntu Linux that run in a MS Windows server environment.

- Oracle Cloud is a relatively new entry to the marketplace. In addition to its flagship database, Oracle now has acquired Java and database products such as MySQL and Berkeley DB, now rebadged. As one might expect, the Oracle Cloud is extensively based on Java services.

If you have been working on JuliaBox, this works on Amazon Web Services by provisioning Docker "sandboxed" containers --so you have been using Julia in the cloud!

Introducing Amazon Web Services

Amazon is possibly the best known provider of cloud services for an individual or a small company. They are popular starting points.

To sign up only requires an Amazon account with an associated credit/debit card, which most users (of Amazon) may already have. Furthermore, Amazon offers a package for a year, which comprises of one small virtual machine. Amazon terms this as the *micro-instance*. Also, it offers a set of the most useful services termed as its "Free Tier". So it is possible to try Julia on AWS at no cost.

An instance (`http://aws.amazon.com/ec2/instance-types/`) is a type of virtual machine based on the processor type, number of cores, available memory, and runs from micro to extra-large. Naturally, bigger instances are priced at a higher rate.

Instances can be started by incorporating a choice of operating systems, including Debian/Ubuntu, Red Hat Enterprise, and CentOS, in addition to Amazon's own brand of Linux.

Once a running instance is started, additional software can be added, which does not come with the standard OS distro. Since at present this includes Julia, it is necessary to install it as a binary or build it from source, and then add in any required packages. This only needs to be done once, since the whole can be saved as an **Amazon Machine Instance (AMI)**, stored and the AMI used to spin up (create) new instances.

AWS comes with a very large set of services including SQL and NoSQL databases, data warehousing, application, and networking applications.

When using the free tier, the common services available are as follows:

- **S3**: Simple Storage Service
- **EC2**: Elastic Compute Cloud
- **DynamoDB**: Fast flexible NoSQL database

Among the non-free services, **Elastic Map Reduce (EMR)** is worth some further study.

Control of AWS, including procedures such as starting and stopping instances, copying files to and from S3, can be achieved via a web-based command program.

Also, there are various APIs and SDKs available, all fully discussed in the documentation (`http://aws.amazon.com/documentation/`) pages. Note that all of the previously mentioned services have RESTful interfaces and also there is a Python SDK, *boto*, with which it may be possible to communicate via *PyCall*.

In addition, Amazon provides a set of command-line tools that are useful for operations on files and instances, so in Julia the ability to execute CLI tasks directly offers another way to interact with AWS.

The AWS.jl package

At the time of writing the `AWS.jl` package is described as "work in progress", requesting more testing and users feedback.

It is worth noting that this package is concerned with running a virtual machine on AWS, not just running Julia, however, the two are not mutually exclusive.

The AWS package covers the S3 and EC2 services. The basis of the function calls is an AWS environment structure that is passed as the first argument:

```
type AWSEnv
    aws_id::String      # AWS Access Key id
    aws_seckey::String  # AWS Secret Key
    ep_host::String     # region endpoint (host)
    ep_path::String     # region endpoint (path)
    timeout::Float64    # request timeout (secs)
    dry_run::Bool       # dry run flag
    dbg::Bool           # print request and raw response
end
```

All these arguments are named parameters in the `AWSEnv` constructor, so need not be specified, in this case they revert to their default values.

A typical (full) call may be as follows:

```
AWSEnv(; id=AWS_ID, key=AWS_SECKEY, ep=EP_EU_IRELAND,
    timeout=0.0, dr=false, dbg=false)
```

The `AWS_ID` and the `AWS_SECKEY` are generated on signing up for AWS and need to be provided for (simple) authentication purposes. Clearing other forms of authentication is possible based on TLS public/private keys.

`EP_EU_IRELAND` is a constant defined in AWS as `ec2.eu-west-1.amazonaws.com` and is the AWS area where we keep our files.

The constructor will split is on / into host and path, so in the preceding call.

```
ep_host =  ec2.eu-west-1.amazonaws.com
ep_path = ""
```

The `AWS.S3` module uses the REST API and communication is via `HTTPClient` and not via requests; so it depends on `LibCURL` and not `GnuTLS`, although this may change in future releases of the package.

For storage associated with a specific account, S3 uses the concept of "buckets". A bucket is a collection of objects that we may think of as analogous to a folder, that is, as a collection of files.

An AWS account can create up to 100 buckets. When creating a bucket, we need to provide a bucket name and AWS region in which it is to be created.

The following code will create a private bucket and an object (file) in the bucket:

```
using AWS
using AWS.S3
env = AWSEnv(timeout = 90.0)
bkt = "amisllp_bucket_1"; # Name needs to be 'globally' unique
acl = S3.S3_ACL(); acl.acl="private"
resp = S3.create_bkt(env, bkt, acl=acl)
resp = S3.put_object(env, bkt, "first_file", "Hi there")
```

The return is of the package defined with the `S3Response` type:

```
type S3Response
    content_length::Int
    date::String              # The date and time S3 responded
    server::String            # Server that created the response
    eTag::String
    http_code::Int
    delete_marker::Bool       # Common Amazon fields
    id_2::String
    request_id::String
    version_id::String
    headers::Dict             # All header fields
    obj::Any
    pd::Union(ETree, Nothing)
end
```

The `http_code` field contains the status of the call and the `obj` payload.

If the `obj` response is XML representing a Julia S3 response type, then it is parsed and assigned by the package, otherwise it contains an `IOBuffer` object.

So the following will indicate the success of the call and the returned data:

```
println("$(resp.http_code), $(resp.obj)")
```

The following sequence will add a second file, list the bucket, then retrieve the first file, delete both files, and finally delete the bucket:

```
resp = S3.put_object(env, bkt, "second_file", "Blue Eyes ")
resp = S3.get_bkt(env, bkt)
resp = S3.get_object(env, bkt, "first_file")

myfiles = [S3.ObjectType("file1"), S3.ObjectType("file2")]
resp = S3.del_object_multi(env, bkt,
S3.DeleteObjectsType(myfiles))
resp = S3.del_bkt(env, bkt)
```

Now let's consider support for the EC2.

EC2 has two sets of APIs: a simple API that provides limited functionality and a low-level API that directly maps onto Amazon's **Web Services Description Language (WSDL)** for the service.

Here, we will just consider the simple API, although AWS.jl also has some support for WDSL.

Currently, the following are available and their purpose is reasonably clear from their function names:

- ec2_terminate
- ec2_launch
- ec2_start
- ec2_stop
- ec2_show_status
- ec2_get_hostnames
- ec2_instances_by_tag
- ec2_addprocs
- ec2_mount_snapshot

The general call to a ec2_basic() basic function has the following form:

```
ec2_basic(env::AWSEnv, action::String, params::Dict{Any, Any})
```

This bundles together the Dict params with an EC2 request. The keys in params must be those as listed in AWS EC2 documentation, values can be basic Julia types, dicts, or arrays.

Running a typical computational task on EC2 to use Julia may involve most or all of the following steps:

1. Set up the AWS configuration.
2. Create a config.jl file specifying EC2 related configuration.
3. Launch (or Start a previously stopped) a bunch of EC2 instances.
4. Optionally log in to one of the newly started hosts and perform computations from an EC2 headnode.
5. Or execute from a Julia session external to EC2.
6. Terminate (or stop) the cluster.

As mentioned, when looking at S3, AWSEnv() requires AWS_ID and AWS_SEC and also an AWS Region. Rather than hardcoding the keys, it is possible to include them as part of an .awssecret file in the home directory.

The configuration file will require the following entries:

```
ec2_ami = "ami-0abcdef";   # Specify the AMI to use.
ec2_install_julia = true;  # If true install from
ec2_sshkey = "xxxxx";  # SSH key pair to use
ec2_sshkey_file = "/home/malcolm/keys/keyfile.pem"   # Location of private
key
ec2_insttype = "m1.large";  # AWS type of instance
ec2_instnum = 21    # Number of instances
workers_per_instance = 8;  # Workers per instance
ec2_julia_dir = "/home/aalcolm/julia/usr/bin" # Julia installed path
ec2_clustername = "mycluster"   # An EC2 cluster name.
```

AMI.jl has a series of help scripts that interpret the config.jl file and encapsulate the desired EC2 operation.

These include launch.jl, start.jl, stop.jl, and terminate.jl.

Also, there is a setup_headnode.jl script that creates addprocs_headnode.jl to copy the scripts into /home/malcolm/run of one of the EC2 nodes, prints instructions to connect, and execute from the headnode.

Using these scripts from the localhost, that is machine external to EC2, would be similar to the following:

- Change and edit the config.jl script:
  - ```julia launch.jl```
  - ```julia setup_headnode.jl```

- ◦ `ssh into a headnode`
- Then working at the headnode:
  - ◦ `cd run`
  - ◦ `julia`
  - ◦ `julia include("compute_headnode.jl")`
  - ◦ `work ...`

After all work is done, exit from the host and from localhost, and it is important to run `julia terminate.jl`, otherwise the instances will continue to run and rack up charges.

The Google Cloud

Google Cloud services offer a realistic alternative to Amazon to run Julia in the cloud. Originally, it seemed to me that the two were quite different but now they seem to be converging in what they provide to the user, even if not how they provide it.

In fact when thinking of big data, Google were first on the scene with their academic paper on "big table" and the `BigTable` database is available in a fashion similar to Amazon's DynamoDB.

In a way similar to Amazon, if you have a Google account (Gmail/Google+) and provide billing details, then you have access to the Google Cloud.

Google uses the term "engine" to describe the services they provide and there are two distinct "flavours" of engine:

- App Engine
- Compute Engine

Google describes the App Engine as a PaaS. It is possible to develop applications in Java, Python, PHP, or Go without the need for operating system administration and servers management, nor to be concerned with load balance and elasticity.

Combined with the target development languages, there are existing frameworks such as Spring, Django, webapp2, and applications have access to Google core services such as mail, calendar, and groups.

The Google Compute Engine is based on a different paradigm much more akin to that of Amazon Web Services.

Virtual servers can be provisioned as Linux Virtual Machines based on either Ubuntu or Centos operating systems, and Google provides a "gallery" of well-known O/S databases including Cassandra, MongoDB, and Redis, plus popular web applications such as WordPress, Drupal, Moodle, and SugarCM. Both Apache and Tomcat web servers are also available.

Moreover, applications on the App Engine can communicate with the Compute Engine.

To control the Compute Engine, Google provides a web-based developer console. Using this is relatively straightforward, to create an instance specify the machine type and operating system plus the location (zone) of the Google Cloud.

Also, there is a command line set of utilities bundled as an SDK, and after installing and configuring it with the developer console, you can create the instance using the `gcutil` command.

In addition to the SDK, there is a `bdutil` package that includes Hadoop-specific configuration tools, such as the deployment tools, Datastore, and BigQuery connectors.

To use Julia on an instance requires some installation, either as a binary or building from source. Binaries are now available for both Ubuntu (using the `apt-get` command) and CentOS (using `yum`), and it is also possible to grab a distro from the Julia GIT repository and build it from source. Remember that the supplied operating systems do not come with all the prerequisite tools and libraries, so it is necessary to grab those first.

For example, on Ubuntu we may need to add gfortran, g++, ncurses, and so on, so it is a good idea to test the build procedure on a local machine before trying to execute the same on a Compute Engine instance.

```
sudo apt-get install g++ gfortran m4 make ncurses-dev
git clone git://github.com/JuliaLang/julia.git
make OPENBLAS_USE_THREAD=0 OPENBLAS_TARGET_ARCH=NEHALEM
```

Once Julia is built, without errors, it is possible to SSH to the instance and run it. Then access the package manager to download any required packages and copy across any code.

If you have created a multicore instance, the maximum is currently 32, it is possible to use the Julia parallel processing macros to test running tasks in a highly parallel fashion.

Parallel and distributed processing is one of the strengths of Julia and is being actively and rigorously pursued at the current time by the Julia Parallel community group. The reader is referred to their web pages at `https://github.com/JuliaParallel` for a full list of the workings of the group.

Recall that earlier we computed and displayed a Julia set.

Since each point is computed independently of its neighbors, it is possible to adapt the procedure to operate on separate sections of the image.

If we construct a distributed array, specify what function to use and what the array's dimensions are, it will split up the task automatically:

```
function para_jset(img)
    yrange = img[1]
    xrange = img[2]
    array_slice = (size(yrange, 1), size(xrange, 1))
    jset = Array(Uint8, array_slice)
    x0 = xrange[1]
    y0 = yrange[1]

    for x = xrange, y = yrange
      pix = 256
      z = complex(  (x-width/2)/(height/2),
        (y-height/2)/(height/2))
      for n = 1:256
        if abs(z) > 2
          pix = n-1
          break
        end
        z = z^2 + C
      end
      jset[y - y0 + 1, x - x0 + 1] = uint8(pix)
    end
    return jset
end
```

This function computes the pixel shading for the section of the imagery on which it is operating. Let's save it in a `para_jset.jl` file.

Assuming we have a 4-core CPU (such as an Intel x86), we can start Julia by using a command such as `julia -p 3` or use the `addprocs(3)` command later to utilize the additional cores.

We can then generate the complete image by using the following script:

```
using Images
require("para_jset.jl")

@everywhere width = 2000
@everywhere height = 1500
@everywhere C = -0.8 - 0.156im
dist_jset = DArray(para_jset, (height, width))
full_jset = convert(Array, dist_jset)
imwrite(full_jset, "jset.png")
```

The `DArray()` constructor will split the data depending on the number of processors in the image, so we just need to ensure that the height, width, and constant C are set on all the processors and run `para_jset()` on each slice.

The `convert()` function will reassemble the distributed array to give the full image:

Summary

In this chapter, we outlined the means by which Julia can be used to develop and interact with networked systems.

First, we looked at services that use the UDP and TCP protocols, and then we looked at how to implement a simple echo server. Also, we investigated the emerging subject of WebSockets and continued by considering messaging systems involving e-mail, SMS, and Twitter.

Finally, we concluded with an overview of running Julia on distributed systems in the cloud and ended with an example of asynchronous execution to speed up (appropriately) the generation of a Julia set.

In the next chapter, we will be returning to explore some more advanced features of the Julia language by going under the hood, examining code generation and the low-level API, testing, and profiling. We will finish with a discussion of community groups and highlight the work of a couple of these groups that match some of my personal and professional interests.

10
Working with Julia

If you have reached this point in the book, probably you will have worked through some of the examples, looked at the Julia modules that are useful to you, and written some of your own code.

Possibly you will want to package your code in a module and share it with the Julia community. Alternatively, you may want to work within a community group that develops and maintains existing packages and adds new ones.

When sharing your code and working with others, it is important to bear in mind that the source will be looked at and possibly mentored, so certain questions of style, efficiency, and testing come more into play.

This final chapter addresses some of these topics and will hopefully start you a long and fruitful romance with Julia.

Under the hood

This section looks at some topics outside conventional Julia coding, so you may want to omit it for the first reading. However, you may also find it interesting!

Working with Julia is about enabling the analyst/programmer to develop enterprise grade code without the need to develop in a second (compiled) language due to a necessity to improve the performance.

It is true Julia that is fast, but this is not what makes it special. However, it is quite nice that it is fast and I'll first look at some of the reasons why.

Stephen Hawking in *A Brief History of Time* quotes a well-known anecdote concerning a lecture Bertrand Russell was giving in the 1920s on cosmology, when the known universe was considered to be comprised of just our Milky Way galaxy.

Russell described how the Earth orbits around the sun and how the sun, in turn, orbits around the center of a vast collection of stars called the galaxy.

At the end of the lecture, a little old lady at the back of the room got up and said, "What you have told us is rubbish. The world is really a flat disc supported on the back of a giant tortoise."

Russell replied, "But what is the tortoise standing on?"

"You're very clever, young man," said the old lady. "It's turtles all the way down!"

Julia is turtles all the way down, almost.

First, we will consider what the bottom turtle is standing on.

Femtolisp

Julia was preceded by an earlier project by one of the three main Julia developers, Jeff Bezanson, who developed a lightweight Lisp parser, which would be quick, require only a small amount of memory, and remain flexible. At that time this space was occupied by **PicoLisp**. The name, presumably, was chosen since **femto** is the next order of 1000 down from **pico**.

The Julia system encompasses **femtolisp** at its heart. It is responsible for parsing the code before passing it down to the LLVM compiler to produce machine code.

It is not always known that Julia can be started in Lisp mode using the `-lisp` switch:

```
julia --lisp
;  _
; |_ _ _ |_ _ |  . _ _
; | (-|||_()|_|_)|_)
;-------------------|------------------------
>
```

While this book is about Julia and not Lisp, the following example of a recursive definition for the factorial function should be clear enough:

```
(define (fac n)
(if (<= n 0) 1
            (* n (fac (- n 1)))))
> (fac 10); # => 3628800
> (fac 20); # => #int64(2432902008176640000)
> (fac 30); # => #uint64(9682165104862298112)
> (fac 40); # => -70609262346240000
```

Clearly, some of the results for higher factorials look distinctly odd—why this is so we will discuss later.

Here is a second (recursive) example of the Fibonacci sequence:

```
(define (fib n)
   (if (< n 2) n
                 (+ (fib (- n 1))
                    (fib (- n 2))))))
> (fib 10); # => 55
> (fib 20); # => 6765
> (fib 30); # => 832040
> (fib 40); # => 102334155    ( very slow )
```

Here recursion is not a great choice, since each call generates two additional calls and the process proceeds exponentially.

Tail recursion or just plain loopy coding, which essentially is the same thing, is a better option, and I've included the alternates in the code accompanying this book.

The Julia API

Building Julia from source generates a set of shared libraries, whereas a binary package comes with these libraries prebuilt. Most are coded in C but some of the dependencies, such as `lapack`, contain Fortran code, which is why a `gfortran` compiler is needed to be installed from source.

Central to the system is `libjulia`, which comprises the `femtolisp` compiler and a `libsupport` support library. The latter may be considered as the CORE and is written (mainly) in C, in contrast to the BASE written in Julia.

The CORE corresponds to the glue between Julia runtime and the underlying operating system, and the routines by which Julia communicates with the CORE is the Julia API.

Looking at source listing in BASE will show calls to functions with the `ji_.` prefix. The first argument does not specify a shared library, which is equivalent to using `libjulia`.

For example, in `utils.jl` the `time_ns()` function makes a call to `jl_hrtime` as:

```
time_ns() = ccall(:jl_hrtime, Uint64, ())
```

This returns the system time as an unsigned 64-bit integer in nanoseconds.

This is used by `@elapsed` and other macros to give more accurate execution timings.

To review the API, pull a copy of the `Julia.jl` distribution from GitHub and look at the `C` listings in the `src` subdirectory.

Real applications will not just need to execute expressions, but also return their values to the host program. `jl_eval_string` returns a `jl_value_t*`, which is a pointer to a heap-allocated Julia object.

Storing simple data types such as `Float64` in this way is called boxing, and extracting the stored primitive data is called unboxing.

The following C program uses the API routines to output the value π^2

First, we need to point to the location of the Julia core library by calling the `jl_init()` routine and also execute the `JL_SET_STACK_BASE` C-macro, which is defined in the `julia.h` file:

```
#include <stdio.h>
#include <math.h>
#include <julia.h>
#define LIBEXEC "/usr/lib64/julia"

int main() {
    jl_init(LIBEXEC);
    JL_SET_STACK_BASE;
    jl_function_t *func = jl_get_function(jl_base_module, "^");
    jl_value_t *arg1 = jl_box_float64(M_PI);
    jl_value_t *arg2 = jl_box_float64(2.0);
    jl_value_t *ret = jl_call2(func, arg1, arg2);
    if (jl_is_float64(ret)) {
        double pi2 = jl_unbox_float64(ret);
        printf("PI (squared) is %f\n", pi2);
    }
    return 0;
}
```

The power function is implemented in the CORE and retrieved by `jl_get_function_t()` that returns a pointer. We need to box-up both the arguments, π and 2, in order to pass them to the routine using `jl_box_float64()`.

The power function (`^`) has 2 arguments, so we call `jl_call2()` to run it. It returns a pointer to a `float64`, which we can confirm via `jl_is_float64()`.

If `true` than we can unbox the function value and print it in C.

When building the program (`pisqd.c`), we need to pass the location of the Julia header file and the Julia library to `gcc`:

```
export JINC=/usr/include/julia
export JLIB=/usr/lib64/julia
gcc -o pisqd -I$JINC -L$JLIB -ljulia pisqd.c
```

Code generation

Julia generates code right down to the machine assembly level, which is the reason that its performance is close to that of C and Fortran code. Other languages such as JavaScript and Go, both using the Google V8 engine and LuaJIT, use similar approaches and provide equivalent performance.

Python has numerous ways of speeding up performance. This also includes Numba, which uses an LLVM approach but (at present) comes with some limitations.

It is difficult to envisage R and MATLAB/Octave embracing LLVM without major rewrites.

In Julia, code is generated (conceptually) in various stages and the generated source can be inspected via a set of `code_*()` routines.

These can get complex quite quickly, so I'm going to illustrate the process with a simple function that increments its argument:

```
inc(x) = x + 1
```

The first two stages (lowered, typed) create a functional representation in the form of a lambda expression, and then create a specific instance for a specific set of argument(s):

```
julia> code_lowered(inc,(Int64,))
1-element Array{Any,1}:
 :($(Expr(:lambda, {:x}, {{},{{:x,:Any,0}},{}}, :(begin
        return x + 1
    end))))
julia> code_typed(inc,(Int64,))
1-element Array{Any,1}:
 :($(Expr(:lambda, {:x}, {{},{{:x,Int64,0}},{}}, :(begin
        return (top(box))(Int64,(top(add_int))(x::Int64,1))::Int64
    end::Int64))))
```

The third stage is to create the LLVM code, which would run on the virtual machine. This could be thought of as equivalent to Java/JVM or .NET/CLR code/:

```
julia> code_llvm(inc,(Int64,))
define i64 @julia_inc_20105(i64) {
top:
  %1 = add i64 %0, 1, !dbg !1248
  ret i64 %1, !dbg !1248
}
```

This code is pretty obvious: %0 and %1 are pseudo-registers.

1 is added to %0 and the result written to %1, which is returned as the function value.

Unlike Java or .NET that require runtime environments to execute their code, this is passed to the LLVM compiler for the host machine and then turned into native code.

For Windows, recent Macs, and Linux, this will be in Intel x86 assembly language:

```
julia> code_native(inc,(Int64,))
   .section     __TEXT,__text,regular,pure_instructions
Filename: none
Source line: 1
  push   RBP
  mov    RBP, RSP
Source line: 1
  lea    RAX, QWORD PTR [RDI + 1]
  pop    RBP
  ret
```

push/mov at the beginning and pop at the end of the code are for housekeeping that will occur for any function call to preserve the stack base pointer (RBP).

The actual statement that does the addition and loads the return register (RAX) is:

```
  lea    RAX, QWORD PTR [RDI + 1]
```

If we call inc() with a real argument rather than an integer, we can look at the code by specifying a Float64; skipping the first two stages, we get:

```
julia> code_llvm(inc,(Float64,))
define double @julia_inc_20106(double) {
top:
  %1 = fadd double %0, 1.000000e+00, !dbg !1251
  ret double %1, !dbg !1251
}
julia> code_native(inc,(Float64,))
```

```
      .section    __TEXT,__text,regular,pure_instructions
Filename: none
Source line: 1
    push   RBP
    mov   RBP, RSP
    movabs   RAX, 4540233472
Source line: 1
    addsd  XMM0, QWORD PTR [RAX]
    pop   RBP
    ret
```

Here the add instruction in the LLVM is replaced with a fadd and now the constant is 1.0

The x86 code reflects this. The curious 454 0233472 value is actually 1.0E+00 when written out as bits, and the value is now returned in the XMM0 first extended register rather than in RAX.

Whereas this code is relatively short, you may wish to see what code is generated when the argument type is Rational and work through the LLVM and x86 assembly listings.

For a more complex example, we will look at Julia version of the Fibonacci function seen earlier in femtolisp.

A simple Julia (recursive) definition of the Fibonacci function would be as follows:

```
function fib(n::Integer)
    @assert n > 0
    return (n < 3 ? 1 : fib(n-1) + fib(n-2))
end
```

Here, I am restricting the argument of the type integer and asserting that it is positive.

Just look at the first stage (lowered code):

```
code_lowered(fib,(Integer,))
1-element Array{Any,1}:
 :($(Expr(:lambda, {:n}, {{},{{:n,:Any,0}},{}}, :(begin
    unless n > 0 goto 0
    goto 1
    0:
    ((top(getfield))(Base,:error))("assertion failed: n > 0")
    1:
    unless n < 3 goto 2
    return 1
```

```
    2:
    return fib(n - 1) + fib(n - 2)
 end))))
```

I'll leave it as an exercise to generate the remaining stages of the coding.

Performance tips

Julia is quick, but poor coding can slow it down markedly. If you are developing enterprise software and/or distributing on GitHub, you need to pay more attention to some of the features and nuances of the language.

The online manual has a long section on performance tips, including a useful style guide and a section of frequently asked questions, which will prove to be illuminating. I've cherry-picked a few that I found of interest.

Best practice

First, a few points about variables, arrays, and types:

- **Global variables**: These may change at different points, so it is hard for the compiler to optimize the code. Wherever possible, variables should be locally defined or passed to functions as arguments. If a variable is actually being used to store a value that does not change, this should be declared as `const`.

- **Changing a variable type**: If you are accumulating a sum of floating point numbers, be careful to initialize the starting point for total as `0.0` and not `0`, as the latter will generate an implicit integer or specify the type explicitly as `total::Float64 = 0`. Similarly, for example, when allocating an array for a list comprehension use a construct such as `zeros(N)` or `Array(Float64,N)`.

- **Accessing arrays**: Julia stores matrices and higher dimensional arrays in column/last index order. This is similar to Fortran, R, and MATLAB but differs from C and Python that use row-ordering. So looping over a matrix, for example, `A[M,N]` is significantly quicker when done as follows:

```
for j = 1:N, i = 1:M
    A[i,j] = randn()
end
```

- **Explicitly type fields**: When creating composite types, ensure that the fields are given a specific type as shown in the following code, otherwise the compiler will generate them as {Any}:

```
type OrderPair
    x: :Float64
```

```
        y::Float64
    end
```

The next few points refer to functions and their arguments:

- **Allocating function outputs**: If a function returns an array or a composite type, it is better to pre-allocate the output rather than have it allocated within the function body.

- **Measure performance**: The `@time` macro is very useful as it returns both the elapsed time and memory allocation. If memory location is unusually high, it is probably an indication of type instability, that is, a variable is defined as one type but is being converted to a different one.

- **Type-stability**: When possible, ensure that a function returns the same 'type' of variable. As an example, suppose we have a function that returns its argument for positive values but zero when the argument is negative. This should be written as: `pos(x) = (sign(x) < 0) ? zero(x) : x --` using `zero(x)` rather than just 0, which would return an integer regardless of the type of x.

- **Multiple function definitions**: Because different versions of the code are generated for differing argument types, it is better to break a function down to its elemental constituent code as many small definitions allows the compiler to directly call the most applicable code.

- **Kernel functions**: A common functional paradigm is to perform some initial setups, execute the main core (kernel) code, and then do some post-processing to return the function value. It can be beneficial to encapsulate the kernel as a subroutine.

Here are a few miscellaneous tips that seem worthy of note.

You should attend to deprecation warnings, which can arise from changes in the next version of Julia. In addition to being a source of annoyance, a deprecation warning by its nature is only reported one time but the fact that it has been issued needs to be checked each time it is called. This check imposes a real overhead to the execution times.

Here are some annotation macros that can be used as pragmas to the compiler to speed up the execution times:

- `@inbounds` can be used to eliminate array bounds checking within expressions. Out of bounds accesses may cause a crash or corruption of the data, so we need to be sure that the references are appropriate.

- @fastmath allows the floating point optimizations that are correct for real numbers but leads to differences for IEEE numbers.

- @simd can be placed in front of the for loops that are amenable to vectorization, but the documentation for this is may be depreciated at a future date.

Profiling

Profiling is a procedure to determine the time spent in various parts of the code.

In Julia prior to version v0.4, the profiler package used was IProfile.jl and profiling was done by means of the @iprofile macro.

From v0.4, profiling has been moved in to the Julia base and the macro is now @profile, but the operation in both is similar, and here I'm describing the IProfile package.

As an example, recall the calculation of the price of an Asian option by the Monte Carlo simulation, which we saw in the first chapter of this book.

All that is needed is to wrap the function code in a @íprofile begin . . . . end block and then it will be profiled each time it is called:

```
@iprofile begin
  function asianOpt(N=10000,T=100;
      S0=100.0,K= 100.0,r=0.05,v=0.2,tma=0.25)
    dt = tma/T;
    S = zeros(Float64,T);
    A = zeros(Float64,N);
    for n = 1:N
      S[1] = S0
      dW = randn(T)*sqrt(dt);
      for t = 2:T
        z0 = (r - 0.5*v*v)*S[t-1]*dt;
        z1 = v*S[t-1]*dW[t];
        z2 = 0.5*v*v*S[t-1]*dW[t]*dW[t];
        S[t] = S[t-1] + z0 + z1 + z2;
      end
      A[n] = mean(S);
    end
    P = zeros(Float64,N);
    [ P[n] = max(A[n] - K, 0) for n = 1:N ];
    price = exp(-r*tma)*mean(P);
  end
end
```

The `asianOpt()` function must be in a file (`asian-profile.jl`), which is included in the REPL. This is necessary so that the source code is available to the profiling system.

Now we execute the function once to force its compilation, clear the profile stack, and run the function again:

```
using IProfile
include("asian-profile.jl")
asianOpt(1);
@iprofile clear
asianOpt(100000); # => 2.585150431830136
```

The profile report is output by using `@iprofile report`, as shown in the following:

```
@iprofile report
  count   time(%)   time(s)  bytes(%) bytes(k)
      1     0.00   0.000000    0.00        0  # line 3, dt = tma / T
      1     0.00   0.000001    0.00        1  # line 4, S = zeros(Float64,T)
      1     0.11   0.000650    0.44      800  # line 5, A = zeros(Float64,N)
 100000     0.17   0.000965    0.00        0  # line 7, S[1] = S0
 100000    34.34   0.196964   98.68   179200  # line 8, dW = randn(T)*sqrt(dt)
9900000    16.29   0.093405    0.00        0  # line 10,
    z0 = (r -0.5*v*v)*S[t-1]*dt
9900000    14.95   0.085731    0.00        0  # line 11,
    z1 = v*S[t-1]*dW[t]
9900000    12.55   0.071965    0.00        0  # line 12,
    z2 = 0.5*v*v*S[t-1]*dW[t]* dW[t]
9900000    20.04   0.114914    0.00        0  # line 13,
    S[t] = S[t-1] + z0 + z1 + z2
 100000     1.31   0.007534    0.00        0  # line 15, A[n] = mean(S)
      1     0.06   0.000317    0.44      800  # line 17, P = zeros(Float64,N)
      1     0.18   0.001019    0.44      800  # line 18,
    $(Expr(:comprehension,:(P[n] = max(A[n]-K,0)),:(n = 1:N)))
      1     0.01   0.000042    0.00        0  # line 19,
    price = exp(-r * tma) * mean(P)
```

We can see that over 34.34 percent of the time is spent in the generation of the `dW` stochastic array and almost all the remainder time in calculating the `S[]` array.

Profiling can be disabled by using `@iprofile off` and re-enabled by `@profile on`.

Lint

Lint("fluff") was the name of a program that flagged some suspicious and non-portable constructs in C language source code. The term is now applied to suspicious usage in software written in any computer language and can also refer more broadly to syntactic discrepancies in general.

For example, modern lint checkers are often used to find code that doesn't correspond to certain style guidelines.

In Julia, linting is implemented via the Lint.jl package.

It checks for over 50 warnings/errors. For a full list please, look at the online documentation at https://github.com/tonyhffong/Lint.jl.

Running this is as easy as follows:

```
using Lint
lintfile( "your_.jl_file" )
```

This becomes recursive in any 'included' source, so there's no need to be checked separately.

The output is in the file.jl [function name] Line# CODE Explanation format.

Here, the code is INFO, WARN, ERROR, or FATAL.

I ran the code provided with this book through Lint, and came up with a warning on etl.jl (which I've left in!):

```
lintfile("etl.jl")
etl.jl:37 [          ] WARN
  "cat" as a local variable might cause confusion
  with a synonymous export from Base
etl.jl:54 [          ] WARN
  "cat" as a local variable might cause confusion
  with a synonymous export from Base
```

 There is no function name as these warnings are in the main part of the code.

If lintfile() finds no errors it generates no output, so it is possible to apply an @isempty() check on the linting to keep the source(s) 'clean'.

Lint understands about Julia versioning, so it will not complain, for example, about missing Base.Dates in 0.3 or missing Dates in 0.4:

```
if VERSION < v"0.4-"
    using Dates
else
    using Base.Dates
end
```

Review the documentation to look at the use of the @lintpragma macro to suppress unwanted checks, print out values, and add information messages.

Lint can be used with installed packages and it finds them from .Julia, in the usual way. As a convenience, a lintpkg() separate function is provided:

```
lintpkg("Lint")
```

This unsurprisingly shows no errors!

I'll leave it to you to look at some of the packages you have installed.

To generate more output from file, I've altered in a couple of places the file comprising the Asian option calculation:

```
function asianOpt( N::Int=10000.0,T::Int=100;
    S0=100.0,K= 100.0,v=0.05,v=0.2,tma=0.25)
```

And the following:

```
S[t] = S[t-1] + z0 + z1 + z2 + z3;
```

Also, I added a two lint pragmas near end of code:

```
  . . .
  P = zeros(Float64,N);
  @lintpragma "Print type P"
  [ P[n] = max(A[n] - K, 0) for n = 1:N ];
  price = exp(-r*tma)*mean(P);
end
@lintpragma "Info me I've deliberately hacked this"
```

Running this through Lint gives the following:

```
lintfile("asian-lint.jl")
typeof( P ) == Array{Float64,1}
asian-lint.jl:1 [asianOpt        ]
  ERROR  Duplicate argument: v
```

```
asian-lint.jl:1 [asianOpt        ]
   ERROR  N type assertion and default inconsistent
asian-lint.jl:9 [asianOpt        ]
   ERROR  Use of undeclared symbol r
asian-lint.jl:12 [asianOpt        ]
   ERROR  Use of undeclared symbol z3
asian-lint.jl:19 [asianOpt        ]
   ERROR  Use of undeclared symbol r
asian-lint.jl:21 [                ]
   INFO   I've deliberately hacked this
```

The print type pragma comes first and the messages follow in the next pass.

Debugging

A debugging facility had been recognized as a requirement right back in the days of, now defunct, the JuliaStudio program.

Since Julia compiles to bit code using LLVM, there is ongoing work to utilize its debugging facilities via LLDB.

At present, there is a Debug.jl good package that proffers the usual facilities, such as setting breakpoints, printing out values, and much more, and is convenient to use rather than peppering code with a series of the println() statements.

To illustrate this, I've taken the asian-profile.jl listing, replaced the @iprofile begin ... end with @debug, and inserted two breakpoints (@bp).

As with profiling, the file needs to be included in the REPL, so that Debug has access to the source code:

```
julia> using Debug
julia> include("asian-debug.jl")
asianOpt (generic function with 3 methods)
```

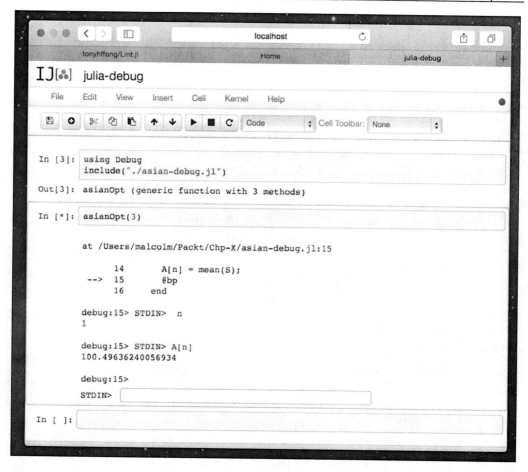

One breakpoint is in the main loop following the calculation of the mean value of the stock for a single run.

Execute the loop 5 times as follows:

```
julia> asianOpt(5)
at /Users/malcolm/Packt/Chp-X/asian-debug.jl:15
      14          A[n] = mean(S);
--> 15          @bp
      16      end
```

Notice that this works quite well with Jupyter /IPython, see the preceding figure as the notebook opens up a STDIN box for interactive usage.

The debugger has a set of single character commands:

```
h: display help text
s: step into
n: step over any enclosed scope
o: step out from the current scope
c: continue to next breakpoint
l [n]: list n source lines above and below current line
p cmd: print cmd evaluated in current scope
q: quit debug session -- forces an error("interrupted")
```

Any other input is interpreted as a request to display the value of a variable.

This poses a problem in our source if we wish to examine the current value of n, and it conflicts with the step over command. To work around this, it is possible to type <space>n, which will display the value as required:

```
debug:15>  n   # => 1
debug:15> A[n]  # => 105.60875364467921

debug:15> c
debug:15>  n    # => 2
debug:15> A[n]  # => 97.41505241555782
```

Some of the debugger's internal state is available to use through the following session variables:

- $n: The current node
- $s: The current scope
- $bp: Set{Node} of enabled breakpoints
- $nobp: Set{Node} of disabled @bp breakpoints
- $pre: Dict{Node} of grafts

For example, in addition to setting a breakpoint with the @bp macro, it is possible to set one "on-the-fly" by setting to the current line and using $push!($bp, $n)).

Also, existing breakpoints can be removed by using $delete!($bp, $n)) or ignored/disabled with $push!($nobp, $n)).

So, we can skip out of the loop and pick up a breakpoint after evaluating the Payoff matrix:

```
debug:15> $push!($nobp, $n)
debug:15> c
at /Users/malcolm/Packt/Chp-X/asian-debug.jl:19
        18      [ P[n] = max(A[n] - K, 0) for n = 1:N ];
```

```
--> 19      @bp
    20      price = exp(-r*tma)*mean(P);
debug:19> P # => [5.6087536446792,0.0,3.64496052229,0.0,2.415052415557]
debug:19> s (twice)
debug:21> price # => 2.3047629672105345
debug: 21> q
```

Developing a package

In this section, I'm going to look at some aspects of package development.

These comprise the various approaches you may adopt to write a package, the procedures to adopt when you want to upload and maintain it via Git as part of a registered Julia module.

I'll conclude by looking at how this strategy might be applied to the case of handling NetPBM images and sketch out the embryonic package, the full source is available in the code downloads accompanying this book.

Anatomy

A minimal package, to be saved to GitHub, should consist of a README.md markdown file and the src and test folders. The src folder contains all the code and the test folder has one or more test scripts that can be used to check the functionality of the package.

In Julia, the package name is normally chosen in the form of MyMod.jl (for example) and there should be a file in the src folder also called MyMod.jl. This is the main module and may reference other modules (that is, use these modules) or include other Julia files. In fact in many larger packages, the main module basically comprises a set of file inclusions.

Suppose we wish to bundle the code for the hi(), inc(), fac(), and fib() functions in MyMod, then layout of MyMod may be similar to:

```
module MyMod
export hi, inc, fac, fib;
hi() = "Hello"
hi(who::String) = "Hello, $who"
inc(x::Number) = x + 1
function fac(n::Integer)
  @assert n > 0
  (n == 1) ? 1 : n*fac(n-1);
end
```

```
function fib_helper(a ::Integer, b::Integer, n::Integer)
    (n > 0) ? fib_helper(b, a+b, n-1) : a
end
function fib(n::Integer)
    @assert n > 0
    fib_helper(0, 1, n)
end
function pisq(n::Integer)
    (n <= 0) ? error("zero or negative argument") : begin
      s = 1.0
      for k = 1:n
          s += (-1.0)^k/(1.0 + k)^2
      end
      return 12*s
    end
end
end
```

Conventionally, code is not indented between the `module` .. `end`, as this would result in the entire code source being indented except in the first and last lines.

Our simple module consists of a series of functions. The export statement contains the names of functions that we want to make visible when the package is referenced by `using MyMod`.

In our package, all functions except `fib_helper()` are exported. This function, as the name suggests, is used by the `fib()` function to provide a tail-recursive procedure to calculate the Fibonacci function, which does not experience the exponential growth in execution times when using a purely recursive algorithm.

To add these to a Julia package, we need to have a few extra files.

First, there should be a `LICENSE.md` markdown file, stating that the package is licensed under the MIT license and contains a copyright notice listing the package authors. The file is mainly boilerplate and any example from the package you have installed will suffice as a template.

Next, there can be a `REQUIREMENTS` file. This file lists the packages and Julia version ranges required by this package, and is intended as input to a (future) meta-generator to determine the requirements for the Julia registry. The file is optional and if not present, suggests that there are no dependences.

Finally, there may be a `.travis.yml` YAML file, which is used by the Julia automatic testing system. Later, we will see how this is constructed.

In addition, you may wish to provide a few additional files or folders. For example, you may add an examples folder to contain code that illustrates the use of the package.

You may have a docs folder, often with **restructured (RST)** files to create only documentation. Also, you may need to supply datasets for the tests and examples in a data folder.

The test folder will comprise one (or more) scripts to be used in verifying the correct behavior of the module.

The Base class contains a Test module that is not loaded when Julia starts up and needs to be imported. It defines and exports a set of macros:

@test, @test_fails, @test_throws, @test_approx_eq

Also, there are a set of handlers for the various test outcomes: success, failure, and error, which can be imported and modified.

The package tests are driven by a runtests.jl script, for large packages this often includes other scripts. The script has to have the using clauses referring to both itself and Base.Test.

So, for our simple MyMod package, the runtests.jl might comprise the following:

```
using MyMod
using Base.Test
@test hi("Blue Eyes") == "Hello, Blue Eyes "
@test inc(11//7) == 18//7
@test fac(7) == 5040
@test fib(10 == 55
@test_approx_eq inc(2.3 ) 3.3
```

This should provide no output, as all the tests will succeed. When testing floating point arithmetic, it is possible to use @test but it is better to use @test_approx_eq( ), which compares ~ 1.0e-16.

Notice this macro takes two arguments, so the == is not required.

With the pisq() function, we need to be more specific:

```
julia> @test_approx_eq pisq(100000)  pi*pi
ERROR: assertion failed: |pisq(100000) - pi * pi| <= 1.77635683e-11
  pisq(100000) = 9.869604401689116
  pi * pi = 9.869604401089358
  difference = 5.997584651140642e-10 > 1.7763568394002505e-11

@test_approx_eq_eps  pisq(100000)  pi*pi  1.0e-6; # Test is OK
```

You may also wish to look at FactCheck.jl, which is a Julia testing framework.

This adds more functionality than that of Base.Test. and consists of a series of blocks of assertions such as:

```
facts ("Fact message") do …
    @fact 'expr' => 'value'
end
```

Related facts can also be grouped as a context inside a facts block.

For MyMod, I've deliberately added a couple of erroneous facts:

```
facts("MyMod Arithmetic Tests") do
    @fact inc(2.3)  # => 3.4
    @fact fac(5)  # => 120
    @fact fib(10)  # => 54
    @fact pisq(100000)  # => roughly(pi*pi, 1.0E-6)
end
```

```
MyMod Arithmetic Tests
   Failure    :: (line:366) :: got 3.3
     inc(2.3)  => 3.4
   Failure    :: (line:366) :: got 55
     fib(10)  => 54
Out of 4 total facts:
   Verified: 2
   Failed:   2
```

Taxonomy

> *"All generalizations are dangerous, including this one."*
>
> — *Alexander Dumas*

I've divided the type of packages under four headings, in order to identify the different strategies that you may adopt when developing a module:

- **Native**: This type of package will rely on Julia coding except that there may be calls to routines in Base and API.

- **Dependent**: Here, a package is dependent on one of the existing ancillary packages, building on prior work. For example, some of the modules in JuliaWeb using libcurl or GnuTLS.

- **Wrapper**: This package does core calling mainly to routines that target a specific shared (C/Fortran) library. It may be necessary to install the library where possible -- either as a binary distro or building from source. In some cases, such as database wrappers, we can assume the library exists otherwise there is no point of this package.

- **Tasking**: Base functionality comes from a separate task. A couple of examples might make this clear, those being PyCall and Gaston. These will impose platform specificity. For example, Gaston works well with Linux, it is possible for it to work on OS X using Quartz, but is difficult on Windows.

Clearly, there may be some cases where a package adopts a mixed strategy spanning more than one class. Under such circumstances, it may be useful to create a submodule as part of the main package.

While interfacing with a specific system, you may be able to write native Julia code or make calls to an existing shared library. These may be identified as high-level and low-level interfaces and the following are the steps you may consider:

- Before deciding on implementation strategy for your package, you should briefly list the functionality intended as a first draft. This will include a set of "must have" routines to make the module practicable, together with some other functionality you consider as desirable but which you are able to consign to a TODO list.

- Next define on any types which will be useful in encapsulating the module's data structures.

- Following on this define constants and construct macros which will be of use by the package functions.

- Finally write the functions and construct the tests which form the basis for the runtests.jl script.

In developing the package, you will normally have developed some extensive Julia snippets. This will be of great benefit to users of your package, and should be included as part of an examples subdirectory, without forgetting to include any required data files, such as CSV datasets and images.

Finally, provide reasonably thorough documentation, either in terms of a comprehensive README.md markdown file or, what is becoming increasingly popular, by means of the Sphinx framework and RST files as part of the https://readthedocs.org/ online system.

Using Git

While constructing a package that is to be loaded by Julia and ultimately published to the web, a number of different files are required.

Before creating these, it is necessary to create a .gitconfig file in your home directory by entering:

```
git config --global user.name " Malcolm Sherrington"
git config --global user.email "malcolm@amisllp.com"
git config --global github.user "sherrinm"
```

Skeleton versions of the package files can be created within the Julia environment using the package manager:

```
julia> Pkg.generate("MyMod","MIT")
INFO: Initializing MyMod repo: /Users/malcolm/.julia/v0.3/MyMod
INFO: Origin: git://github.com/sherrinm/MyMod.jl.git
INFO: Generating LICENSE.md
INFO: Generating README.md
INFO: Generating src/MyMod.jl
INFO: Generating test/runtests.jl
INFO: Generating .travis.yml
INFO: Generating .gitignore
INFO: Committing MyMod generated files
```

This adds the embryonic package to the current repository corresponding to the version of Julia being executed (that is, v0.3, v0.4) It can be loaded, but has no functionality until your versions of MyMod.jl and runtests.jl are uploaded to replace the stubs.

The license file (LICENSE.md) will pick your name from the .gitconf file and probably can be left as it is. On the other hand, the README.md file contains only a main title line consisting of the package name and should be given more attention.

The Pkg.generate() also creates the Travis YaML file (.travis.yml) and a .git subdirectory that contains sufficient information for use with the GitHub system:

This can be listed using git show:

```
$ cd /Users/malcolm/.julia/v0.3/MyMod
$ git show
commit e901cc6a3d1fbad5b1ec6dfa03d0cde324aa4b1c
Author: Malcolm Sherrington <malcolm@amisllp.com>
Date:   Fri Apr 10 13:53:44 2015 +0100
   license:   MIT
   authors:    Malcolm Sherrington
   years:     2015
   user:      sherrinm
```

Although optional, and hence not generated, you will probably need to create a REQUIRE file that comprises the version(s) of Julia under which the module should work correctly, together with a list of other packages to be included when the package is added.

It is possible to use the @osx and @windows constructs to indicate modules required for specific operating systems.

For example, the REQUIRE file for Cairo.jl (currently) is:

```
Compat 0.3.5
Color
BinDeps
Graphics 0.1
@osx Homebrew
@windows WinRPM
```

Publishing

At present your package is only available locally on your own computer. To make it available to more developers, you will need an account on GitHub account; if you have filled in the github.user config entry in the preceding code, you will already have one, if not then register for one, it's free.

First, you need to create the remote repository by pushing your code into GitHub. The Julia package manager does not do this automatically, so you need to use git itself. There is also a command line tool *hub* (https://github.com/github/hub) that simplifies the syntax markedly.

This can be used to create in the package repository and have it automatically uploaded via GitHub's API. Once done, it is possible to use the published repo using Pkg.clone():

```
julia> Pkg.clone("git://github.com/sherrinm/MyMod.jl")
```

At this stage, it is a good idea to have a few people look at the package and provide some feedback. Later, you can decide to have it registered as an official Julia package.

For this, you need to add it to your "local" copy of METADATA using Pkg.register():

```
julia> Pkg.register("MyMod")
INFO: Registering MyMod at
  git://github.com/sherrinm/MyMod.jl.git
INFO: Committing METADATA for MyMod
```

This creates a commit in the `~/.julia/v0.3/METADATA`. This is still locally visible and in order to make it visible globally, you need to merge your local METADATA upstream to the official repository.

The `Pkg.publish()` command will fork the METADATA repository on GitHub, push your changes to your fork, and open a pull request. If this fails with an error, it is possible to publish manually by "forking" the main METADATA repository and pushing your local changes using `git`; the procedure for this is discussed in detail in the Julia documentation.

If you are making an official version of your package or releasing a new version, you should give it a version number using `Pkg.tag()`:

```
julia> Pkg.tag("MyMod")
INFO: Tagging MyMod v0.0.1
INFO: Committing METADATA for MyMod
```

You can confirm the tag number using `cd /Users/malcolm/.julia/v0.3/MyMod && git tag`.

If there is a REQUIRE file in your package, it will be copied to the appropriate place in METADATA when tagging the (new) version.

Note that it is possible to specify a specific version number using the `Pkg.tag()` command by supplying a second argument such as `v"1.0.0"`.

Alternatively, you can make use one of the `:patch`, `:minor`, or `:major` symbols to increment the patch, with minor or major version number of your package accordingly.

As with `Pkg.register()`, these changes to METADATA are only locally available until they've been uploaded to GitHub. Again this is done using `Pkg.publish()`, which ensures the package(s) repos have been tagged and opens a pull request to METADATA.

Community groups

The number of packages written in Julia continues to grow at a superlinear rate. At the time of writing, there are more than 600 registered packages and many more available from programmers on GitHub but as yet unregistered with the Julialang group.

As usual, developers tended to make use of their own packages when writing new ones than those of colleagues and eventually those from the community at large.

This has led to the formation of groups of developers with shared interests, these are termed community groups and are referenced on the Julia website as part of the community section (http://julialang.org/community/).

Some of the larger groups such as JuliaStats and JuliaOpt maintain their own websites separate from GitHub and individual package documentation sources may also be found at http://readthedocs.org.

For example, the JuliaStats web pages are on http://statsbasejl.readthedocs.org/ and the documentation for the StatsBase package is to be found on http://statsbasejl.readthedocs.org/.

Thus, you should not only look at community group packages but are encouraged to use the web search engines, in order to pick up recent work that has not been registered with Julia.

Classifications

As I commented earlier when discussing the types of packages, applying any specific taxonomy to software is not always easy and many exceptions occur to test the rule. Nevertheless, I feel there is enough to be gained in an overview of community groups to attempt the process again.

Therefore, I'm going to classify the types of groups under three main headings:

- **General purpose**: These correspond to topics that may be of use to the analyst working in his/her own field. Obvious examples of these are statistics, optimization, and database.

- **Topic specific**: These are more applicable to persons working in that particular area. At present there are embryonic groups for BioJulia and JuliaQuantum. Also, in the financial sector we have previously met one or two packages from JuliaQuant, such as TimeSeries, MarketData, and Quandl.

- **Niche**: This is harder to define, but I am looking at topics that cover the use of specific hardware or a less conventional computing paradigm such as the use of GPUs (JuliGPU) or parallel computing (JuliaParallel).

In the next couple of sections, I'm going to provide a few examples of groups for the latter two categories that appeal to me, not necessarily in my professional career, but in my wider interests as a whole. I will avoid statistics, optimization, and finance, as you will have encountered many examples of these earlier in this book.

JuliaAstro

As a member of the Baker Street Irregulars Astros, a curious set of enthusiasts who meet regularly in Regent's Park to prove that it is possible to see something in the London skies other than the moon and also as a software consultant who has worked for the European Space Agency and German Aerospace (DLR), my attention was grabbed by the JuliaAstro group and I'm going to give a couple of examples chosen from there.

JuliaAstro has its own web pages at `http://juliaastro.github.io/`, and this contains links to documentation for individual packages, plus a reference to the julia-astro mailing list.

This can be thought of as the equivalent of the Python astropy modules (`http://www.astropy.org/`) that are distributed as part of the Anaconda sources.

Cosmology models

Firstly, I'll look at `Cosmology.jl` that defines various models of the universe depending on the amount of real matter, dark matter, dark energy, and so on. This is reasonably compact, native code package that defines a set of abstract cosmologies and then goes on to establish specific instances depending on the parameterization. An instance can then be used to establish distance and time estimates for this particular model.

Cosmological models had their origin in the work of Friedmann in the 1920s, in solving Einstein's equations for general relativity. This established the principle that a "static" universe would be unstable and led to Einstein inserting a repulsion term, the cosmological constant (Λ) in his equations, which following the work of Hubble on the expanding universe, Einstein came to regret.

However, current thoughts that the universe is not only expanding, but doing so at an increasing rate, has led to the introduction of cosmic repulsion again, in terms of the postulation of dark energy.

The original Friedmann solution does not account for any repulsion term, that is, only assumes mass and gravitational attraction. It defines a critical density above which the universe is closed (elliptic) and will eventually contract, or density below which it is open (hyperbolic) and will continue to expand. A density parameter, Ω, is defined as the ratio of the matter's actual density to the critical density.

So if $\Omega = 1$, the universe is termed as flat, that is, Euclidian. For all the other cases, the curvature is non-Euclidian.

The principle function in the `Cosmology.jl` is `cosmology()` that consists only of named parameters as follows:

```
function cosmology(;
  h = 0.69,   # Dimensionless Hubble paramater
  Neff = 3.04,   # Effective number of neutrino species
  OmegaK = 0,   # Curvature density
  OmegaM = 0.29,   # Matter density
  OmegaR = nothing, # Radiation density
  Tcmb = 2.7255,   # Cosmic Microwave Background Temperature
  w0 = -1,   # Dark energy equation of state ...
  wa = 0 )   # ... w0 + wa*(1 - a)
```

If we just run the function with the default values:

```
c = cosmology()
FlatLCDM(0.69,0.7099122024007928,0.29,8.77975992071536e-5)
```

This returns a *Flat* universe and looking at its values as follows:

```
 julia> names(c)'
1x4 Array{Symbol,2}:
 :h   :Ω_☒   :Ω_m   :Ω_r
```

The Omegas are the densities for dark energy, total matter (dark + baryonic), and radiation:

```
So:   julia> c.Ω_☒ + c.Ω_m + c.Ω_r; # => 0.99999...... ~ 1.0
```

OmegaL (Ω_☒) is computed from the OmegaK curvature density, which is the Friedmann constant ($\rho/\rho crit$) minus 1, that is, it is zero-based.

If OmegaR (Ω_R) is set to `nothing`, then it is calculated from effective number of neutron species (Neff) and the background cosmic radiation temperature (Tcmb).

By forcing OmegaL to be computed, we can ensure the Open (OmegaK > 0) or Closed (OmegaK < 0) cosmological models.

This package is similar to some online calculators such as Ned Wright's at UCLA (http://www.astro.ucla.edu/~wright/CosmoCalc.html). In this package, we input the Hubble factor as a dimensionless quantity, whereas the UCLA calculator uses the actual value.

Other routines are available to compute distances, volumes, and times for various models.

Not all are exported, but are still available by fully qualifying the function call:

```
Cosmology.hubble_dist_mpc0(c); # => 4344.8182, Hubble distance
Cosmology.hubble_time_gyr0(c); # => 14.1712,   Hubble time
```

It is possible to apply a redshift factor to these calculations as follows:

```
z = 1.7;  Cosmology.Z(c,z); # => 1.
Cosmology.hubble_dist_mpc(c,z); # => 1714.4094
Cosmology.hubble_time_gyr(c,z); # => 5.5918
```

Also, as with the results of the UCLA calculator, we can obtain estimates of the universe metrics, such as diameter, volume, and age. This is done as shown in the following commands:

```
comoving_transverse_dist_mpc(c, z); # => 4821.0198 Mpc
angular_diameter_dist_mpc(c,z);     # => 1785.5628 Mpc
luminosity_dist_mpc(c,z);           # => 13016.753 Mpc
comoving_volume_gpc3(c,z);          # => 469.3592  Gpc3
age_gyr(c,z);                   # => 3.872 GYr
where
1 Gyr = 1,000,000,000 years.
1 Mpc = 1,000,000 parsecs = 3,261,566 light years.
```

The Flexible Image Transport System

Now, I'll discuss the use of the **Flexible Image Transport System** (FITS) that was standardized in the early 1980s and is most commonly used in digital astronomy.

A FITS file consists of one (primary) or more **header and data units** (HDUs). It is entirely possible that an HDU may consist entirely of a header with no data blocks.

Usually a FITS file may consist of a primary header followed by a single primary data array. This is also known as Basic FITS or Single Image FITS (SIF).

Alternatively, a multiextension FITS (MEF) file contains one or more extensions following the primary HDU.

Header information may be in two formats: fixed (80 bytes) or free.

These consist of a keyword, followed by a value, and additionally a comment describing the field; = and / are used to delimit the keyword, value, and comment. There are some mandatory keywords that must be provided in fixed format.

The last field in the HDU just comprises the END word.

A basic FITS HDU for the Cygnus X-ray source (Cygnus X1) would be similar to:

```
SIMPLE  =                       T / Conforms to the FITS standard
BITPIX  =                      16 / number of bits per data pixel
NAXIS   =                       2 / number of data axes
NAXIS1  =                     250 / length of data axis 1
NAXIS2  =                     300 / length of data axis 2
OBJECT  = 'Cygnus X-1'
DATE    = '2006-10-22'
END
```

This is a two-dimensional dataset (250x300), taken on October 22, 2006.

It is usual to provide more information in the header, for example, where the image was acquired.

FITS files can be viewed by a variety of software packages; on Linux/OS X, we can use GIMP and on Windows, we can use IfranView.

Also, there is a specialist program *Aladin*, which is written in Java, and runs on all platforms. Aladin is developed by the *Centre de Données astronomiques de Strasbourg* and described as a *Sky Atlas*. It provides the combination of various FITS images, enabling the possibility to combine and view object imagery acquired from IR, visible, UV, and X-ray telescopes.

I'm going to look at an image of our big sister, the Andromeda Galaxy (M31), sourced from the NASA/ESA Hubble Space Telescope, and catalogued as f001a066 using the FITSIO.jl.

A view of the file as seen via Aladin is given in the following figure:

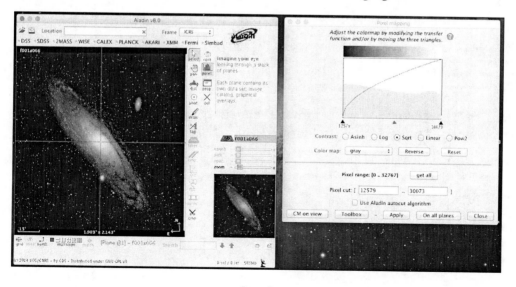

`FITSIO.jl` has provided methods of working with FITS files, which it terms as high-level and a low-level APIs.

The low-level API is a wrapper around NASA's C-library and has a great deal of flexibility; the high-level API is a native Julia package.

Both are excellently documented at https://julia-fitsio.readthedocs.org.

The high-level API

The high-level API uses a FITS constructor to read a FITS dataset:

```
julia> f001a = FITS("f001a066.fits")
file: f001a066.fits
mode: r
extnum exttype          extname
image_hdu

julia> names(f001a)'
1x4 Array{Symbol,2}:
 :fitsfile  :filename  :mode  :hdus
```

The file `f001a0066.fits` has a single HDU, referenced as the first element in the array:

```
julia> f001a[1]
file: f001a066.fits
extension: 1
type: IMAGE
image info:
  bitpix: 16
  size: (7055,7055)
```

We can get the number of dimensions of the imagery and its size as follows:

```
ndims(f001a[1]); # => 2
size(f001a[1]); # => (7055,7055)
```

Also, the `read()` function will return the entire image and the `readheader()` will create a parsed representation of the HDU's metadata:

```
data   = read(f001a[1]);
header = readheader(f001a[1]); # =>
length(header); # => 128

header["BITPIX"]; # => 16
header["SCANIMG"]; # => "XJ295_A066_01_00.PIM"
header["TELESCOP"]; # => "Palomar 48-in Schm"
```

Our image was taken by the Mount Palomar Samuel Orchin 48 inch telescope.

Along with the header values, it is possible to get the comment fields as shown in the following code:

```
getcomment(header,"TELESCOP")
"Telescope where plate taken"
```

The header also contains the latitude and longitude of the Mount Palomar site and the date and time when the image was acquired.

```
header["SITELAT"]; # => "+33:24:24.00       "
header["SITELONG"]; # => "-116:51:48.00       "
```

The FITS constructor can take a second argument termed as the mode that can be `"r"` (read-only), `"r+"` (read-write), or `"w"` (write). The default is `"r"` but it is possible to create a new file using a mode of `"w"`. In this mode, any existing file with the same name will be overwritten:

```
julia> f = FITS("newfile.fits", "w");
```

When created, we write the image data and optionally the header to the file using the `write()` function:

```
data = reshape([1:120000], 300, 400);
write(f, data)   # Write a new image extension with the data
write(f, data; header=my_header)   # Also write a header
```

The low-level API

The low-level API is an interface to the `CFITSIO` library and has much more functionality. If we consider just reading meta-information, this is returned unparsed as a series of triple string (`"key"`,`"value"`,`"comment"`), one per line:

```
using FITSIO
f001 = fits_open_file("f001a066.fits")
FITSFile(Ptr{Void} @0x00007faf9c4de6d0)

n = fits_get_hdrspace(f001)[1]; # => 128
128 entries in the header

for i = 1:n
   println(fits_read_keyn(f001,i))
end
("SIMPLE","T","FITS header")
```

```
("BITPIX","16","No.Bits per pixel")
("NAXIS","2","No.dimensions")
("NAXIS1","7055","Length X axis")
("NAXIS2","7055","Length Y axis")
("EXTEND","T","")
("DATE","'09/07/04            '","Date of FITS file creation")
("ORIGIN","'CASB -- STScI      '","Origin of FITS image")
("PLTLABEL","'SJ01467           '","Observatory plate label")
("PLATEID","'A066             '","GSSS Plate ID")
("REGION","'XJ295            '","GSSS Region Name")
("DATE-OBS","'1987/09/20        '","UT date of Observation")
```

This is a series of tuples that will need to be split in to the separate consistent fields programmatically.

Alternatively, it is possible to call the `fits_hdr2str()` routine to obtain the entire header information as a single string. This consists of fixed length records of size 80 bytes with the = and / delimiters in the ninth and thirty-second positions respectively:

```
DATE-OBS=           1987/09/20     / UT date of Observation
```

JuliaGPU

One of the main themes of my professional career has been working with hardware to speed up the computing process. In my work on satellite data, I worked with the STAR-100 array processor and once back in the UK, used Silicon Graphics for 3D rendering of medical data. Currently, I am interested in using NVIDIA GPUs in financial scenarios and risk calculations.

Much of this work has been coded in C, with domain-specific languages to program the ancillary hardware. It is possible to do much of this in Julia with packages in the JuliaGPU group.

This has routines for both CUDA and OpenCL, at present covering:

- **Basic runtime**: CUDA.jl, CUDArt.jl, and OpenCL.jl
- **BLAS integration**: CUBLAS.jl, CLBLAS
- **FFT operations**: CUFFT.jl, CLFFT.jl

The CU* style routines only applies to NVIDIA cards and requires the CUDA SDK to be installed, whereas the CL* functions can be used with variety of GPUs. CLFFT and CLBLAS do require some additional libraries to be present, but we can use OpenCL as it is. The following is output from a Lenovo Z50 laptop with an i7 processor and both Intel and NVidia graphics chips:

```
julia> using OpenCL
julia> OpenCL.devices()
OpenCL.Platform(Intel(R) HDGraphics 4400)
OpenCL.Platform(Intel(R) Core(TM) i7-4510U CPU)
OpenCL.Platform(GeForce 840M on NVIDIA CUDA)
```

Here is a script that will list the platforms (GPUs) present on your computer:

```
using OpenCL
function cl_platform(pname)
  @printf "\n%s\n\n" pf
  for pf in OpenCL.platforms()
    if contains(pf[:name],pname)
      @printf "\n%s\n\n" pf
      @printf "Platform name:\t\t%s\n"  pf[:name]
      if pf[:name] == "Portable Computing Language"
        warn("PCL platform is not yet supported")
        continue
      else
        @printf "Platform profile\t\t:%s\n"  pf[:profile]
        @printf "Platform vendor:\t\t%s\n"  pf[:vendor]
        @printf "Platform version:\t\t%s\n\n" pf[:version]

        for dv in OpenCL.available_devices(pf)
          @printf "Device name:\t\t%s\n" dv[:name]
          @printf "Device type:\t\t%s\n" dv[:device_type]
          gms = dv[:global_mem_size] / (1024*1024)
          @printf "Device memory:\t%i MB\n"  gms
          mma = dv[:max_mem_alloc_size] / (1024*1024)
          @printf "Device max memory alloc:\t%i MB\n" mma
          mcf = device[:max_clock_frequency]
          @printf "Device max clock freq:\t%i MHZ\n"  mcf
          mcu = device[:max_compute_units]
          @printf "Device max compute units:\t%i\n"  mcu
          mwgs = device[:max_work_group_size]
          @printf "Device max work group size:\t%i\n"mwgs
          mwis = device[:max_work_item_size]
          @printf "Device max work item size:\t%s\n"  mwis
        end
```

```
      end
    end
  end
```

I ran this routine on a laptop with both Intel HD and NVIDIA GeForce chips that gave the following results and selected the NVIDIA GeForce device for a specific platform profile:

```
julia> cl_platform("NVIDIA")
OpenCL.Platform('Intel(R) OpenCL' @x000000012996290)
OpenCL.Platform('NVIDIA CUDA' @x000000000519ef60)
Platform name:                NVIDIA CUDA
Platform profile:             FULL PROFILE
Platform vendor:              NVIDIA Corporation
Platform version:             OpenCL 1.1 CUDA 6.0.1
Device name:                  GeForce 840M
Device type:                  gpu
Device memory:                4096 MB
Device max memory alloc:      1024 MB
Device max clock freq:        1124
Device max compute units:     3
Device max work group size:   1024
Device max work item size:    (1024,1024,64)
```

To do some calculations, we need to define a `kernel` to be loaded on the GPU. The following multiplies two 1024x1024 matrices of Gaussian random numbers:

```
import OpenCL
const cl = OpenCL
const kernel_source = """
  __kernel void mmul(
  const int Mdim, const int Ndim, const int Pdim,
  __global float* A, __global float* B, __global float* C) {
    int k;
    int i = get_global_id(0);
    int j = get_global_id(1);
    float tmp;
    if ((i < Ndim) && (j < Mdim)) {
      tmp = 0.0f;
      for (k = 0; k < Pdim; k++)
        tmp += A[i*Ndim + k] * B[k*Pdim + j];
        C[i*Ndim+j] = tmp;
    }
  }
"""
```

The kernel is expressed as a string and the OpenCL DSL has a C-like syntax:

```
const ORDER = 1024;   # Order of the square matrices A, B and C
const TOL   = 0.001;  # Tolerance used in floating point comps
const COUNT = 3;      # Number of runs

sizeN = ORDER * ORDER;
h_A = float32(randn(ORDER)); # Fill array with random numbers
h_B = float32(randn(ORDER)); # --- ditto --
h_C = Array(Float32, ORDER); # Array to hold the results

ctx   = cl.Context(cl.devices()[3]);
queue = cl.CmdQueue(ctx, :profile);

d_a = cl.Buffer(Float32, ctx, (:r,:copy), hostbuf = h_A);
d_b = cl.Buffer(Float32, ctx, (:r,:copy), hostbuf = h_B);
d_c = cl.Buffer(Float32, ctx, :w, length(h_C));
```

Now, we create the Open CL context and some data space on the GPU for the d_A, d_B, and D_C. arrays

Then we copy the data in the h_A and h_B host arrays to the device and then load the kernel onto the GPU:

```
prg = cl.Program(ctx, source=kernel_source) |> cl.build!
mmul = cl.Kernel(prg, "mmul");
```

The following loop runs the kernel for COUNT times to give an accurate estimate of the elapsed time for the operation.

This includes the cl-copy!() operation that copies the results back from the device to the host (Julia) program:

```
for i in 1:COUNT
  fill!(h_C, 0.0);
  global_range = (ORDER. ORDER);
  mmul_ocl = mmul[queue, global_range];
  evt = mmul_ocl(int32(ORDER), int32(ORDER),
              int32(ORDER), d_a, d_b, d_c);
  run_time = evt[:profile_duration] / 1e9;
  cl.copy!(queue, h_C, d_c);
  mflops = 2.0 * Ndims^3 / (1000000.0 * run_time);
  @printf "%10.8f seconds at %9.5f MFLOPS\n" run_time mflops
end
0.59426405 seconds at 3613.686 MFLOPS
0.59078856 seconds at 3634.957 MFLOPS
0.57401651 seconds at 3741.153 MFLOPS
```

This compares with the figures to run this natively without the GPU processor:

```
7.060888678 seconds at 304.133 MFLOPS
```

That is, using the GPU gives a 12-fold increase in the performance of matrix calculation.

What's missing?

We have covered lot of ground in this book. The aim, as I stated at the outset, was to provide sufficient material for you to be able to use Julia in your work now. Out of necessity, this has been broad rather than deep; there are so many topics to cover, each of which could merit a book on its own.

I was told when starting this book that it would be harder to decide what to leave out rather than what to put in and this has been proven to be true. So I've listed some of the other facets of Julia that I researched but eventually omitted:

- OpenGL graphics
- Parallel processing
- Functional programming
- Symbolic computation
- Econometrics
- Neural nets and Bayesian statistics
- Natural language processing

There is significant work by the Julia community in all these fields and many more.

Julia is a rapidly changing language, it has not yet reached the v1.0 status. It is probably better to get over the 'pain' quickly rather than go through the machinations that Perl and Python have undergone of late and the consequences that may follow.

Doubtless, things will have changed, new packages added, and others decaying through lack of attention. However, Julia is a very useable language, even as I write this and more so when you are reading this.

The Julia website is your friend. It is well maintained and gives links to all important resources. Also, you need to be aware and participate in the various mail lists and Google groups.

If you are an academic, use it in research, or if a data scientist use it in your analysis. Superficially, it is a very easy language to learn but like the proverbial onion peel away one layer and another will appear.

Julia is strongly typed, but you can work without types. Julia uses multiple dispatch but you need not be aware of it. Above all, you can free yourself from being a user of a language to being a developer in one.

Julia gives you all that at no extra cost.

As I said at the beginning of this chapter, "it turtles all the way down", almost.

Summary

This concludes our whirlwind review of Julia. It is worth re-emphazing to the reader that Julia is not yet v1.0, so some of the features described may be deprecated or permanently changed as you read this book. The Julia documentation and its code listings provide all the answers and hopefully you will be able to find your way around these by now.

In this chapter, we addressed a variety of topics that should be of use to you in moving from a analyst/programmer to a contributor and developer.

We began with a peek "under the hood" to find out why Julia does what it does and quickly. At present, most computer languages utilizing LLVM do it via a separate compilation stage. The magic of Julia is that it takes a conventional-style procedural code and takes this way down to the machine level in a single process.

Then we continued with thoughts on some tips and techniques that will be of help in creating enterprise-quality Julia code and covered topics such as testing, profiling, and debugging. This led to the discussion of a taxonomy of Julia modules and the considerations and steps involved in developing your own package.

Finally, we highlighted the work done by Julia Community groups, identifying (imperfectly) three types: general purpose, topic-based, and specialist. Since most of the examples in this book have been from the first type, we closed by looking at the work of a couple of examples in the second and third categories: JuliaAstro and JuliaGPU.

I believe that Julia stands out as a scripting language at present, as it is both very simple to use and extremely powerful. It allows the analyst to transcribe his/her pseudocode almost directly to Julia, and also empowers the developer to achieve some amazing things while remaining within the language.

If you have got to this point, I hope you share my opinions and that this book will have helped you in some small way in becoming a Julian.

Index

A

abscissa 256
ACID (atomicity, consistency,
     isolation and durability) 269
Active Directory (AD) services 291
Amazon Machine Instance (AMI) 328
Amazon Simple Storage System (S3) 28
Amazon Web Services 328
annotation macros
  @fastmath 348
  @inbounds 347
  @simd 348
aqua 251
arguments
  default arguments 72-74
  optional arguments 72,-74
  passing 71
arithmetic operator 36
arrays
  about 37, 38
  accessing 346
  elemental operations 40
  operations, on matrices 39
  simple Markov chain 41
Asynchronous JavaScript and XML
     (AJAX) 318
AWS.jl package 329-332
Azure 327

B

basic graphics, Julia
  about 232
  Cairo 234, 235
  text plotting 232, 233
  Winston 236-239
Basic I/O
  about 143
  binary files 150-152
  disk files 145-147
  Terminal I/O 143-145
  text processing 148-150
basic linear algebra system (BLAS) 109
Bayesian inference Using Gibbs
     Sampling (BUGS) 226
Bayesian methods 225
benchmarks 24
BigFloats 49
BigTable 268
binary files 150-152
bits 36
Bokeh 255, 256
Booleans 36
Bool type 36
boxing 115
Bulls and Cows computer implementation
  example 46, 47
byte array literals
  about 45
  rules 45

C

C
  about 106, 107
  Julia API, calling from 114-116
Cairo 234-260
CAP rule (Consistency, Availability,
     and Partition Tolerance) 269

ccall
  syntax 106
CentOS
  Julia, installing on 8-11
  URL, for downloading 8
Character Large Objects (CLOBS) 271
Char type 42
Chinook database
  URL 279
Cloud services
  about 327
  Amazon Web Services 328
  AWS.jl package 329-332
  Azure 327
  Google Cloud 333-336
  Oracle Cloud 327
  Rackspace 327
Clustering.jl 177
commands
  executing 132, 133
  running 134, 135
Comma-Separated-Value files.
    See **CSV files**
community groups
  about 362
  classifying 363
  general purpose 363
  niche 363
  topic specific 363
complex numbers
  about 48-50
  Juliasets 51-53
Compose
  about 244
  example 244-246
  URL 245
composite types 54
conversion
  about 99
  defining 99
CouchDB
  about 299
  URL 299
cross product 102
CSV files 153-157

C types
  array conversions 108
  mapping 108
  type correspondences 108, 109
CUDA
  routines 370
curl
  used, for retrieving web page 110, 111
CVODES 207
Cypher 302
Cython 5

D

DArray 130
data arrays 60, 61
Database Interface (DBI) 270
database management system (DBMS) 269
databases
  about 29, 267
  considerations 270
  interfacing to 269, 270
DataFrames package 163
DataStructures package
  about 64
  Deque type 64
  Queue type 64
  Stack type 64
data visualization
  about 240
  Compose 244-246
  Gadfly 240-243
DBDSQLite.jl package
  URL 283
DBI.jl package
  URL 283
DBI method
  about 283
  MySQL 283, 284
  PostgreSQL 285, 286
  SQLite 283
debugging 352-354
decompositions 192, 193
default arguments 72-74
delimited files. *See* **DLM files**
devectorized code 55, 56

dictionaries 61-63
differential equations
  about 203
  non-linear ordinary differential
      equations 206-208
  partial differential equations 209-211
  solution of ordinary differential
      equations 204-206
digital signal filters 200, 201
discrete Fourier transform (DFT) 197
disk files 145-147
distributions
  about 180
  kernel density 181
Distributions.jl 180
DLM files 153-157
document databases 290
document datastores 294-296
dot product 102

E

eigenvalues 193-195
eigenvectors 193-195
Elastic Compute Cloud (EC2) 28
Elastic Map Reduce (EMR) 328
e-mail 321-323
enumerations 94, 95
enum macro 124-126
esendex.com 325
estimation 175
explicitly type fields 346

F

Fast Fourier Transform (FFT) 6
femto 340
femtolisp 340, 341
filesystem
  working with 136, 137
filtering 198, 199
first-class objects, functions 68-71
fixed vector module 101, 102
Flexible Image Transport System (FITS)
  about 366, 367
  high-level API 368, 369
  low-level API 369, 370

Fortran 106, 107
Fortran routine
  calling 109, 110
frequency analysis 197
functions
  about 67
  arguments, passing 71
  first-class objects 68-71
  kernel functions 347
  multiple function definitions 347
  outputs, allocating 347
  performance, measuring 347
  scope 76-79
  type-stability 347

G

Gadfly
  about 240-243
  plot elements 244
Gaston
  about 250
  example 251, 252
generalized linear model (GLM)
  about 185-187
  methods 186
Git
  used, for developing package 360
global variables 346
gnuplot 28
Go
  versus Julia 5
Google Cloud 333-336
graphic engines
  about 247
  Gaston 250-252
  PGF plots 253, 254
  PyPlot 247-250
graphics support, Julia 27
graphic systems 302-304
graph stores 290
greatest common divisor (GCD) 83

H

HDF5 157-159
header and data units (HDUs) 366

Hiredis.jl 291
Homebrew 25
hypothesis testing 183, 184
HypothesisTests.jl
  reference link 183

I

IDAS 207
IJulia 6, 14, 113
image processing 202
Images.jl package 262
Images package 262-264
ImageView package 262-264
instances
  about 328
  reference link 328
integers 34-36
interfacing techniques 283
Internet Message Access Protocol
      (IMAP) 322
ISAM (index sequential access method) 291

J

Java Database Connectivity (JDBC) 270
Java (JavaCall.jl) 113
Java Native Interface (JNI) 113
JavaScript
  versus Julia 5
Java Virtual Machine (JVM) 113
JDBC 288
JSON
  about 297, 298
  URL 297
Julia
  about 1, 2, 15, 16
  basic graphics 232
  building, from source 8
  comparing, with other languages 4, 5
  features 5, 6, 30
  homoiconic macros feature 31
  installing, on CentOS 8-11
  installing, on Mac OS X 11
  installing, on Windows 11
  interlanguage cooperation feature 31

multiple dispatch feature 31
packages, installing 20-22
parallel processing feature 30
philosophy 2, 3
role, in big data 3
role, in data science 3
sources 7
uninstalling 29
unregistered package, adding 30
URL 2
URL, for checking performance 4
URL, for documentation 7
URL, for running 1
versus Go 5
versus JavaScript 5
versus Mathematica 5
versus MATLAB/Octave 5
versus Python 4
versus R 5
via console 16-20
Julia API
  about 114-342
  calling, from C 114-116
JuliaAstro
  about 364
  cosmology models 364, 365
  URL 364
Julia coding, concepts
  about 339
  code generation 343-345
  femtolisp 340, 341
  Julia API 341, 342
Julia Data format (JLD) 158
JuliaGPU 29, 370-374
Julia package
  references 267
Julia Parallel community group
  URL 335
JuliaQuant 29
Juliasets 51-53
JuliaStats
  about 189
  reference link 172, 363
JuliaWeb group 313-315
Julia Webstack
  about 314
  URL 314

JuMP 212, 213
Juno
  about 13
  functionalities 13
Just Another Gibbs Sampler (JAGS) 226
just-in-time (JIT) 6

K

kernel density estimation (KDE) 181
key-values (KV) systems 291-294
KINSOL 207
knapsack problem 213

L

libhdfs 28
Lightweight Directory Access
        Protocol (LDAP) 268
linear algebra
  about 190
  decompositions 192, 193
  eigenvalues 193-195
  eigenvectors 194, 195
  simultaneous equations 190, 191
  special matrices 196
Linear Algebra PACKage (LAPACK) 190
Lint 350, 351
Lint.jl package
  reference link 350
Linux distributions
  reference link 8
Linux Mint Debian Edition (LMDE) 8
logical operator 36
Looking-Glass World echo server 307-310
Low-Level Virtual Machine (LLVM) 2

M

Mac OS X
  Julia, installing on 11
macros 118-120
MariaDB driver
  URL 280
Markov processes 225
Match.jl package 79

Mathematica
  about 27
  Mathematica.jl 113
  versus Julia 5
Mathematical Operations
  URL, for manual 49
mathematics 27
MathProgBase interface
  NLopt, using with 220
MATLAB (Matlab.jl) 113
matrices
  about 55
  devectorized code 55, 56
  multidimensional arrays 56-58
  vectorized code 55, 56
Maximum-a-Posteriori (MAP)
        estimation 180
MCMC frameworks 226-229
MCMC.jl 177
message passing interface (MPI) 30
messaging 321
messaging services
  e-mail 321-323
  esendex 325, 326
  SMS 325, 326
  Twitter 323, 324
metaprogramming
  about 116
  macros 118-120
  symbols 117
  testing 121, 122
methods, generalized linear model (GLM)
  coef 186
  deviance 186
  df_residual 186
  glm 186
  lm 186
  predict 186
  stderr 186
  vcov 186
Microsoft Cloud service 327
Minimalist GNU for Windows (MinGW) 12
Monte Carlo Markov Chain (MCMC) 226
multidimensional arrays
  about 56-58
  broadcasting 58

multiple dispatch
  about 95, 96
  conversion 99
  fixed vector module 101, 102
  parametric types 97, 98
  promotion 99
MultivariateAnalysis.jl 177
MySQL
  about 283, 284
  URL 280

N

named parameters 76
named pipes 311
native interfaces 275-278
Neo4j
  about 299, 302
  URL 299
NLopt
  about 217-219
  references 217
  using, with MathProgBase interface 220
non-linear ordinary differential
          equations 206-208
normal matrices 59
NoSQL databases
  graph stores 290
  wide-column stores 290
NoSQL datastores
  about 290
  document datastores 290, 294-296
  key-value systems 290-294

O

OAuth
  URL 323
ODBC 278-282
OpenCL
  routines 370
Open Database Connectivity (ODBC) 270
Optim 214-217
optimization problems 211
optional arguments 72-74
Oracle Cloud 327
osutils.jl file 107

P

package development
  anatomy 355-358
  aspects 355
  Git used 360
  taxonomy 358, 359
package management 24
packages
  adding 24-26
  exploring 26, 27
  Java (JavaCall.jl) 113
  listing 24-26
  Mathematica (Mathematica.jl) 113
  MATLAB (Matlab.jl) 113
  publishing 361, 362
  removing 24-26
  R (Rif.jl) 113
  selecting 26, 27
pandas Python module 175
partial differential equations 209-211
performance tips
  about 346
  best practice 346, 347
  debugging 352-354
  Lint 350, 351
  profiling 348, 349
Perl
  about 139
  one-liners 139, 140
Personal Package Archive (PPA) 7
PGF plots
  example 253, 254
pico 340
PicoLisp 340
pipe operator 138
pipes 137, 138
plot elements, Gadfly
  geometries 244
  guides 244
  scales 244
  statistics 244
Plot.ly
  about 256-259
  URL 256
PostgreSQL 285, 286
Post Office Protocol (POP) 322

process intrinsics, SimJulia
  get 222
  hold 221
  observe 222
  put 222
  queue 221
  release 222
  request 222
  sleep 221
  wait 221
  waituntil 221
profiling 348, 349
programming environments
  interfacing with 105
promotion
  about 99
  defining 100
PyCall 6, 111, 286-288
pyMPI 30
PyPlot
  about 247
  example 247-250
Python
  about 111, 112
  versus Julia 4

Q

Queen's problem 79-81
quotes server 316, 317

R

R
  versus Julia 5
Rackspace 327
raster graphics
  about 259
  Cairo 260, 261
  Winston 261, 262
rationals 48
rational type 81-83
Rcpp 5
RDatasets.jl
  reference link 168
RDatasets package
  about 167
  data, joining 168-171

data, sorting 168-171
data, subsetting 168-171
reference link 167
RdBu (from Red to Blue) 262
realistic graphics
  creating, with Winston 22, 23
reals
  about 48, 49
  BigFloats 49
  built-in functions 49
  operators 49
  special values 49
redirection 137, 138
Redis.jl 291
registered packages
  reference link 26
regular expressions 44, 45
relational databases
  about 268, 271
  building 272-275
  DBI method 283
  JDBC 288-290
  loading 272-275
  native interfaces 275-277
  ODBC 278-282
  PyCall 286-288
Representational State Transfer
    (RESTful) 270
RESTful interfacing
  about 296, 297
  graphic systems 302-304
  JSON 297, 298
  web-based databases 299-301
restructured (RST) 357
Riak 299
Rmpi 30
R (Rif.jl) 113

S

samples 175
selected topics 177
semantic versioning
  reference link 46
servers 305
sets 63, 64
shebang convention 272

Sierpinski gasket 246
signal 197
signal processing
  about 197
  digital signal filters 200, 201
  filtering 198-200
  frequency analysis 197
  smoothing 198, 199
Sim.jl
  about 207
  URL 207
SimJulia package
  about 221
  process intrinsics 221, 222
Simple Mail Transport Protocol
    (SMTP) 321
simple MapReduce 132
simple Markov chain 41
simple statistics 173, 174
simultaneous equations 190, 191
smoothing 198, 199
SMS 325
sockets
  about 305
  TCP 306
  UDP 306
Software as a Service (SaaS) 327
solution of ordinary differential
    equations 204-206
source
  Julia, building from 8
source stack
  exploring 12, 13
sparse matrices 59, 60
specialist packages 29
special matrices
  about 196
  symmetric eigenproblem 196
SQLite
  about 275, 283
  URL 275
Stan 226
statistics
  about 27, 172
  estimation 175
  pandas Python module 175
  reference links 27

samples 175
simple statistics 173, 174
StatsBase.jl
  reference link 172
stochastic problems 220
stochastic simulations
  about 221
  bank teller example 222-225
  SimJulia 221
strings
  about 42, 43
  byte literal arrays 45
  regular expressions 44, 45
  unicode support 44
  version literals 46
structured datasets
  about 152
  CSV files 153-157
  DLM files 153-157
  HDF5 157-159
  XML files 162
Sundials 207
symbols 117
symmetric eigenproblem 196

T

tab-separated file (TSV) 153
tasks
  about 126
  distributed arrays 130, 131
  parallel operations 128-130
  simple MapReduce 132
taxonomy, packages
  dependent 358
  native 358
  tasking 359
  wrapper 359
TCP socket 306
TCP web service 312, 313
Terminal I/O 143-145
testing
  about 121, 122
  error handling 123, 124
TextPlots package 232
text plotting 232, 233
text processing 148-150

time series 177-179
Twitter
  about 323, 324
  URL 323
Twitter.jl 323
typealias keyword 92, 93
type system
  about 81
  rational type 81-83

U

UCLA
  reference link 365
UDP socket 306
unions 92, 93
unixODBC
  URL 280

V

variable 33
variable argument list 74, 75
variable type
  determining 34
  modifying 346
vectorized code 55, 56
vehicle datatype 84-92
version literals 46

W

Web
  using 255
  working with 311
web and networking support, Julia 28
web-based databases
  about 299-301
  CouchDB 299
  Neo4j 299
  Riak 299
web page
  retrieving, curl used 110, 111
WebSockets 318-321
well-known ports 305, 306
wide-column stores 290
Windows
  Julia, installing on 11

WinRPM 25
Winston
  about 236, 261, 262
  example 236-239
  realistic graphics, creating with 22, 23
wxt 251

X

X11 251
XML files 160-162

Y

Yellowdog Updater and Modified (YUM) 8

Thank you for buying
Mastering Julia

About Packt Publishing

Packt, pronounced 'packed', published its first book, *Mastering phpMyAdmin for Effective MySQL Management*, in April 2004, and subsequently continued to specialize in publishing highly focused books on specific technologies and solutions.

Our books and publications share the experiences of your fellow IT professionals in adapting and customizing today's systems, applications, and frameworks. Our solution-based books give you the knowledge and power to customize the software and technologies you're using to get the job done. Packt books are more specific and less general than the IT books you have seen in the past. Our unique business model allows us to bring you more focused information, giving you more of what you need to know, and less of what you don't.

Packt is a modern yet unique publishing company that focuses on producing quality, cutting-edge books for communities of developers, administrators, and newbies alike. For more information, please visit our website at www.packtpub.com.

About Packt Open Source

In 2010, Packt launched two new brands, Packt Open Source and Packt Enterprise, in order to continue its focus on specialization. This book is part of the Packt Open Source brand, home to books published on software built around open source licenses, and offering information to anybody from advanced developers to budding web designers. The Open Source brand also runs Packt's Open Source Royalty Scheme, by which Packt gives a royalty to each open source project about whose software a book is sold.

Writing for Packt

We welcome all inquiries from people who are interested in authoring. Book proposals should be sent to author@packtpub.com. If your book idea is still at an early stage and you would like to discuss it first before writing a formal book proposal, then please contact us; one of our commissioning editors will get in touch with you.

We're not just looking for published authors; if you have strong technical skills but no writing experience, our experienced editors can help you develop a writing career, or simply get some additional reward for your expertise.

R Object-oriented Programming

ISBN: 978-1-78398-668-2   Paperback: 190 pages

A practical guide to help you learn and understand the programming techniques necessary to exploit the full power of R

1. Learn and understand the programming techniques necessary to solve specific problems and speed up development processes for statistical models and applications.

2. Explore the fundamentals of building objects and how they program individual aspects of larger data designs.

3. Step-by-step guide to understand how OOP can be applied to application and data models within R.

IPython Interactive Computing and Visualization Cookbook

ISBN: 978-1-78328-481-8   Paperback: 512 pages

Over 100 hands-on recipes to sharpen your skills in high-performance numerical computing and data science with Python

1. Leverage the new features of the IPython notebook for interactive web-based big data analysis and visualization.

2. Become an expert in high-performance computing and visualization for data analysis and scientific modeling.

3. A comprehensive coverage of scientific computing through many hands-on, example-driven recipes with detailed, step-by-step explanations.

Please check **www.PacktPub.com** for information on our titles

CPSIA information can be obtained
at www.ICGtesting.com
Printed in the USA
FFOW02n1550280316
22733FF

9 781783 553310